Advanced Praise for

'Gosh! Powerful stuff. In a world of abundance ...g is laid out before us, the difficulty is not choosing where to start but knowing when to stop. Angela's frankness will resonate with so many people, as will her strategies that took her from caterpillar to butterfly.'

Andy Cope, Best-selling Author – The Art of Being Brilliant & Shine

'When I first met Angela in 2014, she hadn't set her sights on changing her lifestyle. When we met again a few years later, she explained that she was on a mission to improve her health, fitness and wellbeing. Since then, I've watched her focus on this goal, taking the consistent steps to achieve it and inspiring a host of others as she goes.

The honest way she shares her story and the method she used to create a mindset shift, will undoubtedly help and inspire countless women and men to believe they can do the same.'

Greg Searle MBE, Olympic Gold Medallist and Leadership Development Coach

'The fastest way to be successful is to find someone who has achieved what you want to achieve and do what they did. In short, read this book and do what Angela did. She is a role model and her success is astonishing.'

David Taylor, Best-selling Author – The Naked Leader

Congratulations to Angela Cox on saying ENOUGH. Congratulations for making those mammoth realisations and life-enhancing changes.

Angela's story is raw, relatable and very, very readable. And Angela Cox, you are most definitely enough and more.

Lucy Donoughue – Happiful Magazine

Enough

Angela Cox

Cover Image © KT O'Shaughnessy

Web– www.abiggirlsjourneytolean.co.uk

Instagram/Twitter – @coxange78

Facebook Public Page BGJTL - A Big Girl's Journey to Lean

Facebook Group – A Big Girl's Journey to Lean

You Tube Channel – A Big Girl's Journey to Lean

Blog – Self-Love-Ninja.Blog

For my three Heroes...

Grandad. Always by my side, you taught me how to be kind.

Joe Wicks, The Body Coach. For illuminating the way.

And last but most special, my husband, Mr. Cox. For loving all of me, always, and without exception.

The Little Girl Inside

Everyone you meet is fighting a battle you know nothing about.
Be kind. Always.
Ian McClaren

Contents

Prologue

I am standing in front of a full-length mirror, taking a selfie. Today I have chosen a crisp white fitted blouse tucked in to a vintage leather skirt, knee high boots and woollen patterned tights. I run the palm of my hand across my stomach. I beam. I feel fantastic, strong. It is still somewhat of a novelty, this new me. The outfit I am wearing is a world away from the clothes that have hidden me for most of my adult life. This Me, hiding behind a suit of self-conscious lethargy and pain, kept there by a cruel voice in my head reminding me not to have ideas above my station, battling with a Me that wants to be determined, fierce, confident and beautiful.

I look at the photograph I have taken on my phone ready to post it to Instagram, where I will be celebrated by friends and supporters and no doubt condemned by others. Then, just as I am about to hit the 'post' button, I see her. Nine years of age and struggling.

I am never without her, this nine-year-old me. She is with me wherever I go. She is there when I am vulnerable. She is there when I am being targeted by Trolls. This nine-year-old, frozen in animation. In pain. In confusion and despair. Back when life first showed me its teeth. When I would first realise that everything I knew, everything that was safe and good and loving, was not so. The direction of your life and who you are and might become, can change forever in a single unspeakable, confusing, violating, sexual act against you. Because you are nine and you do not understand it. It will hang above you like a shadow and you will become so accustomed to the pain and shame of it, that it becomes you. You will even learn to protect those who should be blamed from the pain of this shadow, such is the devastating nature of this act of war.

You will grow up, finding ways to cope with this pain and you will become the greatest actress that ever lived. People will meet you and think that you are the life and soul of the party. Angela Cox - enthusiastic, driven, always smiling. It is an exhausting charade but perfect to throw people off the scent to protect the little nine-year-old within who is struggling still.

But here's the thing.

You realise one day, that there's a way out. There's a way out from under the shadow, from behind the charade and you decide to jump off the vicious merry-go-round hand in hand with her, your nine-year-old self.

It is then you decide to become all that she and you can be.

This is the story of that nine-year-old girl who stepped out of the shadow and into the sun.

Part One

Becoming the Big Girl

These mountains that you are carrying, you were only supposed to climb.
Najwa Zebian

1

Chapter One

My eyes are glued to the plate of biscuits nestling on the coffee table. I've already had two, yet desperately want more. The living room is noisy, full of the familiar sounds of family members chatting and laughing, but I am so absorbed in my inherent need for the biscuits that everything around me becomes white noise, as if I am underwater. The voices in the sea around me are muffled, the sights blurred, and my hands are becoming sweaty as I fight the frantic urge to eat.

'Help yourself love,' my aunt says, caringly.

'No, I'm fine.' I answer, distracted.

My inner voice is scolding me not to take another. 'People will think you are greedy, you can't let anyone see you'.

My inner voice has been very busy lately.

Later, when the table has been cleared, I delve into the bin, find the remaining biscuits, take them into the bathroom and eat them. Momentary relief is followed by instant regret and then the inevitable new feeling that has begun peppering my days of late, shame.

This has become a new normal in my little world that is now anything but.

It is 1987. I am nine years of age and the middle sibling of three. I am the bridge between them. My favourite book is Matilda by Roald Dahl and my favourite film is Grease. I think Sandy is the most beautiful girl I've ever seen. I love to dance and sing into a hairbrush.

I am loved by my Mother who keeps our home like a pin in paper and a charismatic Dad with an entrepreneurial spirit that could give Dragon's Den a run for their money. My favourite person in all the world is my Grandad, my Mum's Dad. This has and never will change. Even now. He is my constant and my Hero. I never feel safer than when he is there, even if it is just the thought of him. Despite being left by my Grandmother for a millionaire named Bill with his big house and gravel drive to bring up my mother alone, life has not soured him. We sing 'The Sun Has Got His Hat On' even when it hasn't, and we go on trips, just me, without my other siblings, to restaurants and to the theatre.

I like school. I am a good, conscientious student with a glint in my eye and a love of mischief but I never ever get caught. I wear my Goody Two Shoes badge with a sense of pride and tongue placed firmly in my butter-wouldn't-melt cheek.

I am nine years of age and Happy-Go-Lucky. Singing with all my heart as an Angel in the Christmas Concert. Giggling with my friend Emily. Running on the gravel drive of 'Rich Nan's' house. Playing 'Kirby' in the back street. Popping the tar that bubbles up between the cobbles with lolly sticks. Running down to piles of presents on Christmas morning. Trying on my Nan's diamond rings while I snuggle in bed with her.

These are the snapshots of my family album, a family which I think is like any other in its ordinary extraordinariness.

But all this is before.

A permanent line has been drawn in the foundations of who I am and means that with just nine years of being, life is suddenly divided into a 'before' and an 'after'.

Things that cannot ever be undone, unfelt, unseen, unlived have separated the then from the now.

I am nine years of age and I am eating a chocolate Easter egg. I catch sight of myself in a mirror at the other end of the room. I am shovelling the chocolate in. Huge shards of broken chocolate. I barely finish a piece before pushing the next in. I am focused completely on the task.

I am nine years of age and a line has been drawn. A permanent line.

I continue to devour the Easter egg, watching myself as I do so.

I am nine years of age and a man I have trusted all my little life has just taken me to a room that has watched me be nine and happy and has pushed his penis into my mouth.

I am nine years of age and I am paralysed by fear.

I continue to stuff the chocolate into my mouth to rid myself of the taste of his violation within me.

3

His words 'Say nothing' still stinging my ears, I finish the egg and frantically open my sister's to carry on eating. Hearing her approach, I hurriedly place the uneaten half back into the container. It looks untouched, unchanged and seemingly perfect. But I know that only half of it is there now and I cannot change that. When she eventually discovers the crime, I indeed, say nothing.

I am nine years of age and my life has changed forever in ways that I, at nine years of age, can't yet begin to comprehend.

This was the first time. It was not the last.

The little nine-year-old me who has embraced life in happy-go-lucky fashion, is no more. She is replaced by a very different little girl who learns very quickly that not even her Hero can save her from her fate. I know what has happened, what is happenING, isn't normal but the story of shame I start to tell myself repeatedly is just one of the many ways in which I remain at the mercy of my Abuser. My young mind tells me that this doesn't happen to good girls. That people would think of me badly if I were to tell them. They would disapprove and judge and so, not wanting to disappoint anyone, I say nothing. I spare them. I keep the terrible, dark secret to myself and discover that Secrecy is Shame's greatest ally.

My Abuser is perfectly positioned in my world to take advantage of each opportunity that arises to plunge me deeper into turmoil and darkness, as it gets as bad as it could get. While it is happening, I take myself off into my own little world and remain completely unresponsive, just waiting patiently for it to be over. Even now, at such a young age, I have worked out that it is easier to blank out what is happening as it is happening. My face is always covered during the abuse and further compounds my confused belief that I am ugly.

Turning to food has become a constant in my young life. Within the space of a few months I've become utterly obsessed with it. I spend an unhealthy amount of time thinking about sneaky ways of obtaining it to fulfil my desire to numb. Binge eating in secret has become my medicine, my way of blocking out what is happening. I get food from anywhere I can. I rifle through cupboards and create a stash. A slice of bread, a piece of cheese, some ham, a packet of

4

crisps, a biscuit, cream crackers and other bizarre combinations – it really doesn't matter. It must go undetected. I do not want my parents to suspect anything and a little bit of everything won't be noticed. I take one item at a time, hiding it under my t-shirt until I get to my room where I put it under my bed. Once I've gathered enough throughout the day I eat, and in the meantime, I think of nothing else. The binge could even take place straight after dinner, but it won't stop me. The desire to eat, creates an odd sensation of emptiness that overrides any feelings of fullness or sickness. It is never about the taste of the food - I rarely taste it because I eat it so quickly. It is about the quantity and the fact I can eat it in secret and nobody will know. It is the numbing effect, like a drug, that momentarily takes away the shame, before turning in on itself and multiplying the shame tenfold.

And while I am drowning, life around me carries on in that way that it always does. Bound by my shameful secrets, I try my hardest to be the Angela everyone thought they knew but no longer exists. Some of the changes are impossible to conceal however and before too long, school also becomes a place of turmoil when the name calling starts. The adage about sticks and stones has never washed with me. With each 'Fatty' and worse, 'Tank', I am sent further down a bottomless pit of self-loathing.

To further my misery and confusion, I find myself dealing with an increasing number of girls picking fights with me. With an already looming shadow of injustice above me, coupled with my constant helplessness at the hands of an Abuser I cannot stop, I fight back. I am never really fighting the girl in front of me of course, not really. I am fighting my situation and it often comes as a release. It feels good. With each punch, my anger, my fear, has somewhere to go. Soon, I lose count of the fist fights in which I am involved. The altercations happen in the playground and are rarely seen by the teaching staff. There is only one teacher supervising the whole playground, so a lot of things go unnoticed which is welcome from my perspective. Though I never start the fights, I would be horrified if the teachers knew I'd partaken. I am living a double life and I am barely coping in either. I sometimes have to tell my mother about these events due to the markings, scratches and bruises, but I make it

5

explicitly clear it wasn't my fault. In response, she always says 'these girls are jealous of your brains and your beauty'. This puzzles me because I do not and cannot see my beauty. I know I have brains because I am generally regarded as 'top of the class' but I also know the real truth - I am being attacked again and again because I am fat and ugly.

Time passes and my little world is becoming more and more difficult. There isn't a single person with whom I can share my shameful secrets. Not even my Hero still, even though I spend most weekends on day trips with him or staying at the big house with the gravel drive where my 'Rich Nan' lives with her Millionaire, Bill.

Memories of this time remain fragmented and bittersweet, as if someone has ploughed a field and uncovered pieces here and there that have taken decades to decipher and put back together. My Grandfather always remains an island of calm but it is the memories of my Nan, who had become poorly, and the big house with its gravel drive, and its Millionaire named Bill which are most jumbled up in my adult mind, looking back. It is a jigsaw that I continue to try and finish some thirty years later. To try and find how each piece fits. Even now. As I get to truly know who I am, the jigsaw becomes more complete. The picture that has been jumbled and blurred at the edges for so long slowly takes shape.

And I have come to realise that some of the missing pieces were missing for a very good reason.

My weekends at the big house with the gravel drive and the Millionaire called Bill were packed full of memories, placed very carefully away at the back of my mind somewhere, when they were replaced by more pressing dangers introduced by the hands of my Abuser. It's amazing how the mind can work. How it can edit the bad bits. Maybe for your own protection, who knows? The truth is that as the pieces of that particular part of my young life have begun to weave themselves back together, I have realised that there were fleeting occurrences that would prepare me for that very first violation at 9. Situations that would give me a sense of foreboding whenever I would have to go to visit my Nan. At only six years of age, when Bill with the big house and the gravel drive would insist on taking me to the pink shower room and wash me between my legs with his fingers, while his wife, my grandmother, was dying in the other room. And try as I might, although the veil has been lifted on these occasions and I know them to be true, I cannot remember his face at all. Just his boots, the sour smell of pipe smoke which hung over him, the stinging memory of Dettol roughly placed on my young cut knee, and his dreadful, dreadful secret. And while my little head was packing all these horrors away, I continued to perfect my new normal of secret bingeing.

Soon, even the basic practicalities of my days start to pinch, quite literally. Finding clothes to fit became an increasing challenge and what fitted one month would be bursting at the seams the next. I recall wearing a dress for my birthday party which I was supposed to wear again for my cousin's christening a few months later. The event was in Yorkshire and I travelled there with my paternal grandparents with the dress packed in my case. On the morning of the christening, I tried on the dress, but the buttons adorning the front wouldn't fasten. I had nothing else to wear and felt dreadful showing my Grandma the gaping dress. She had brought two outfits with her and I was forced to wear her flowery elasticated waist calf length skirt and matching blouse. Deeply humiliated, there was only one drug to numb it. I spent a lot of the afternoon taking food from the buffet and eating it under the table.

The opportunities for humiliation started to come thick and fast. I had been invited to my friend's birthday party that was to be held, rather excitingly, at a nightclub her stepfather had hired. I couldn't believe we were going to be allowed into a club! The whole class were talking about their outfits during the weeks that preceded. They would be shopping at Tammy Girl and Chelsea Girl, neither of which made clothes for girls like me. I longed to shop there like everybody else but instead suffered yet another embarrassment by having to wear an outfit from the ladies' section of C&A, a shop which had clothing better matched to my mother's generation. I went to the party dressed like a 30-year-old. Behind my well-rehearsed fixed smile, my fragile heart was breaking.

Secondary school was looming and with a new school came a new uniform. I recall taking a trip to the uniform shop to buy the specific print school skirt. They were made from a brown and yellow thick checked material - a most hideous combination in my opinion - worsened by the fact that skirts meant for my age wouldn't fit. I was forced to buy an age 15 skirt which fell so far below the knee, I looked ridiculous. Needless to say, I spent most mornings rolling it up at the waist, giving it a somewhat wonky hem to match a wonky self-image, creating even more bulk around my middle. The uniform which was specifically designed to make everyone look the same, to blend in, just made me stand out like a sore, ill-fitting thumb.

In the background, the white noise of abuse continued, plunging me further and unknowingly into patterns of self-destructive coping behaviours. While I stood in the eye of a chaotic storm around me, food was my constant.

But the storm raged on. Life decided to double-down on the chaos by introducing a new chapter and characters to my story. There were lots of children and teenagers residing in the streets surrounding my house. This meant it was relatively easy to find a friend to hang out with and for some reason, I was drawn to spend time with teenagers who were much older than me. I was often to be found listening to music in the houses of teenagers who were at least 16 years old. One of the girls always had carrier bags full of chocolate bars and she would let me eat as many as I wanted. I was grateful for her apparent generosity and didn't mind when she told me how she'd perfected the way to steal them from the local shop. She explained that it was easy and she did it a few times each week.

Knowing they were stolen didn't stop me eating them - I needed them, and their provenance didn't matter at all until the rules of our engagement suddenly changed one day when out of the blue, she started to push her fingers inside me and insisted I do the same to her. She carefully explained that if I didn't tell anybody, I could have as much chocolate as I wanted, and anyway, she explained, she was just teaching me what I would need to know when I was older. These ordeals would take place in her bedroom and continued until she moved to a new house a year or so later. It always felt weird, but I wondered if this was what girls did together and – as with the other 'life lessons' that were being thrown at me against my will– I decided to keep it to myself. What was another secret to add to the burden of shame I carried around on my young shoulders?

Some welcome distractions appeared in my life when I started working at the Market on Saturdays. It was my first taste of financial liberation. I was paid twenty pounds per shift which was a small fortune to me and of course, provided me with the funds to buy sweets and chocolate. My lifeblood. Breakfast and lunch was paid for as part of the shift and it was my job to order and collect it for all the ladies who worked on the stall. If there is one thing that is crucial to a secret binge eater, it is that nobody, under any circumstance, should find out or suspect anything. Ordering a dozen sausage and egg sandwiches was the perfect disguise for my bingeing because the café worker wouldn't possibly think they were all for me. I would purchase the sandwiches for the ladies and instead of buying one for myself, I would order three more, adding my own money to cover the cost. There was always a strategy. I would break the sandwiches into halves and put them into my rucksack before returning to the stall so that if anybody would see me eating a sandwich and caught me with a full one again, they would know I'd had more than one. In halves, it would look like I was still finishing the first one. The lengths I would go to in order to disguise my habit was startling and would be repeated over again at lunchtime. Life had become a matter of navigation and strategy. Of ducking and diving. Of hiding and trying to run from something that would always catch up with me. Every. Time.

My new workplace was the perfect environment to perfect my self- destructive skills too. There were several sweet stalls on the market and I would purchase items from each of them, ending up with a large stash of chocolate and sweets, finally supplemented by a quick stop at the bus station shop. If I bought one packet of sweets from several places, the stall owners wouldn't think I was greedy. I would then visit the bakery next to the bus station and purchase multiple cream cakes which I would make a point of saying were for my family. Beestings were my favourite cakes which were made from sweet bread filled with creamy custard. With my bag full of sugar laden treats, I'd take the bus home and would not think about anything else but the binge I would have later. It was all consuming and as soon as I got to the comfort of my bedroom I would eat every last thing, always at lightning speed and never pausing to appreciate the taste but embracing the numbing sensation which would hit me like a wave of freedom and relief from the pain of the storm raging around me. The debris - the wrappers, bags and cake boxes would be cleared carefully into my rucksack to be disposed of in an outdoor bin at a later stage. I couldn't possibly use the house bin for fear I'd be caught out. Exposed. My secret revealed.

I was so worried about what people would think of me. What would they think if they knew? Frankly, had I ordered the three breakfast sandwiches I intended eating from the café rather than the dozen for the stall staff, would the café worker really have thought less of me? Would the lady in the cake shop immediately think the four cream cakes were for me had I not insisted on my well-rehearsed decoy of 'treating my family'? Would either of them even care or give it a second thought? The shame I felt about the binge eating inspired increasingly creative and eccentric methods in my plight to hide my habit. There was one giveaway however, that all the planning and navigating could not conceal: my ever-increasing weight. It sought to burden my battle against my situation even further. The storm of abuse raged on and I was running out of places to hide from it.

With a school performance on the horizon, I was asked by the dance teacher to audition for a part. I was amazed but thrilled to be given the lead role of Medusa. I felt a flash of approval and acceptance. Not only had I got the starring role but I had beaten the slim girls to it! My elation would soon turn to dismay however, when I was handed a slip of paper with the costume requirements written upon it. The black and white text blurred as the tears welled in my eyes.

'Please provide your child with a green leotard and green tights.' I read.

I looked down at my tummy, its size distorted by the rolls school skirt material folded at my waist and I cried. There was no way on earth I could wear a skin-tight leotard in front of an audience. What would people think? All they would see would be my rolls of fat. They would think I was disgusting.

I informed the teacher that I did not want to play the part and removed myself from the potential humiliation. It would not be the last time that I sat on the side lines, looking on and wanting desperately for things to be different. For me to be different.

Soon, life would remind me of its fragility, when my lovely Nan who ran off to marry a Millionaire, who would cuddle me up gently to her when I seemed inexplicably distressed while I stayed at the big house with the gravel drive, who would let me wear her diamonds and eat Vienetta in bed, had lost her cruel fight with Cancer. In a disturbing dream I had at that time, which is still as vivid to my adult mind as if I had dreamt it last night, I am standing at my Nan's funeral, watching her rise from Death at the front of the Church. I stand and watch as fireworks explode gloriously, beautifully from her coffin, lighting up everyone in the church. Music is playing and everyone is dancing and melting into a deathly black puddle like the witch in the Wizard of Oz, is Bill.

Chapter Two

I am 12 now and life has moved on in the way that life does. Some things have changed and others have not. Confusion still reigns large in my young life and I find myself at the centre of situations which appear without my invitation to cause more confusion and disarray.

Standing at a bus stop one evening, I am approached by a girl from school who suddenly and unexpectedly, drags me to the ground by my hair. My head is smashed into a wall and I am kicked mercilessly as I lie on the floor in shock. I manage to clamber to my 12-year-old feet and fuelled by anger at the injustice of another violation against me, I viciously fight back before we are interrupted by a group of boys. I make my way home, shaking and utterly confused as to the reason for her attack against me. My mother takes one look at me and my injuries and panics. I spend the evening at A and E where they see to the huge lump on my head. If only they could all see what was going on inside, but nobody could. If only I could tell my Mother that her little girl was accustomed to pain now, but I couldn't. The following day, my mother demands answers and repercussions from the Head Teacher but to no avail, and so the direction of my life changes once more, totally unexpectedly but gladly this time, and I am moved to a small private Secondary School in the town.

I settle quickly, and soon become known as 'Teacher's Pet', working hard to maintain this position. Despite this, I am a complete rule breaker and often instigate water fights, am a fan of passing notes around the class and with my best friend Leigh by my side, would always be up to no good. I never once get caught, but it becomes more and more evident that I detest rules and regulations and kicking against them provides a release from the constant pressure of being the best and needing approval.

And He was still there of course. My Abuser. Making sure that my life was less than it should be. Less safe and joyful and twelve-year-old-like. And to accompany the abuse, was the bingeing. The ritual of food collection and hiding and momentary relief continued.

Soon I would turn 13 years of age and my newfound Teenager status also brings with it a gift from Mother Nature herself, when I start my periods. My Abuser is privy to this fact one day when I am at his mercy once more. Realising what is happening, he rubs himself against me rather than pushing himself into me and, not understanding what semen is, I think that his ejaculation is urine. Horrified that my Mother would think that I'd wet myself, I tell him that I am going to tell her that he has urinated on me. Panicking, he begs me not to say anything. I don't, and while the familiar feeling of fear which has thrived in the pit of my stomach from the age of nine remains for a while, it proves to be the last time he violates me.

I would learn very quickly however, that the true damage of the abuse has set up home in my life and while the physical violation has stopped, the inner torment and bingeing has not. Rather than being a numbing agent to alleviate my shame, it has become my way of working, my way of living. I have done it now for four years and it has become my new normal. I am, however, becoming increasingly self-conscious about my size and wish I could find a way to stop overeating.

By age fourteen, I am easily the largest girl in the class and while I am popular and well liked and still try to do my best to impress the teachers, I do not impress myself. Not at all. Most days I order a salad sandwich for lunch in a vain attempt to 'diet' and then undo the good intentions by eating three Mars bars bought at the train station on the way home. The binges are well and truly part of my life and I feel powerless to resist the ever-increasing temptation.

One day, I read a problem page letter in a teenage magazine and my eyes widen with anticipation. A girl had written in to ask if using salt water to make herself sick could damage her health. I'd never heard of this and it was music to my ears. I was aware of eating disorders and knew that some girls would make themselves sick after eating by sticking fingers down their throats but that's not what this was. This was an answer. A fix to my problem. I'd attempted many times after a bingeing session to make myself sick and it never worked – I couldn't bring myself to vomit. But drinking salt water could be my saviour and help me to dispel the food after I'd

13

devoured it and allow me to lose weight and wear clothes meant for my age.

I have developed an overwhelming urge to be slim like the other girls at school. I wanted to buy clothes from Topshop and River Island and look trendy. I was spending some of the market job money on a new pair of jeans every week. I had half a dozen pairs in several colours, but sadly they were men's 32-inch waist. These were recommended by the market stall holder as the only jeans that would fit my waist and they needed to be turned-up several times at the ankle. I'd wear jeans on the hottest of hot days, believing my legs to be too fat for shorts. American baseball jackets were also at the height of fashion, but I couldn't fit into the teenage sizes, so had to buy men's sizes, too.

It took me a few days to pluck up the courage to give salt water a try, but when I did and it worked I was over the moon. I'd found a formula and I would use it for the next few years. I gave absolutely no regard to the health risks associated with this method even though I felt poorly a lot of the time. The weight started to fall off and in the final year of school I was a 'normal' size and that was the most important thing, wasn't it?

I was in the Air Training Corps (ATC) during that time, with a new circle of friends. Within a week of joining I'd been made the Lead probationer which meant I would be asked to take charge of the probation group when a Non-Commissioned Officer left the room. When I look back on the routines of the ATC, I am surprised I enjoyed it as much as I did. It was so hierarchical, full of rules and at the time it could be quite degrading. I recall an incident during a cadet camp where we were sent on exercise into a forest. I was captured by the 'enemy' (a group of RAF personnel) who tied me to a chair. One of the men noticed my French manicured nails and gestured to the other men to show them. He told me that nail polish was not suitable and proceeded to bite off each one my nails as I remained tied in the chair. I sat, livid, humiliated, as the others laughed at his actions. It seemed that life continued to throw its challenges my way, often to my utter consternation.

Despite elements of the Training Corps' ethos not being in line with my values, I was still proud to chosen as the Lead. Not

14

everyone was happy however. There were only handful of girls in the group and unfortunately, one of them took umbrage to the fact that I had been chosen ahead of her and shockingly pulled a knife from her pocket one day, threatening to stab me with it as soon as we were outside the gates. With hindsight I can see that she was consumed with jealousy, but at the time I remember wondering what on earth was wrong with me to be attracting such violence, and I was genuinely scared. I reported her and she was dismissed. I continue to this day to be taken aback when I garner such negativity, even if the knives have now become words from faceless Trolls. They are equally as shocking to me and sadly, harder to dismiss.

Suddenly, a new phase starts in my life when I begin to attract boyfriends. It feels new and exciting, because one of the outcomes of the abuse is a fear that I am not lovable. This has been instilled in me by the things that my abuser has repeatedly told me. He'd tell me I'd never get a boyfriend because I was 'fat and thick' and so I make the most of any attention I get from the opposite sex, in case another one didn't come along. It made me clingy and eager for approval, which was the exact opposite of everything we were told in the girly magazines about playing it cool. I didn't know the meaning of playing hard to get. I would write letters and buy presents to try and please the boys, and when they felt stifled and ultimately ran a mile, I would implode, feeling rejected and believing that, as my abuser had said so many times, I wouldn't be loved. This would take me back to my place of solace and safety – bingeing - and I would eat away the hurt and rejection.

I continue to be eager to please my parents, and so I decide, to their delight, to apply for a RAF Sixth Form Scholarship. This was the ultimate prize if you were in the Air Training Corps, and having already bagged First Class Cadet of the Year, I was encouraged to go for it. Only a handful of females were awarded this scholarship each year and I was determined to get one. I needed to travel to Manchester for the interview which would be with three RAF officers at the Military Careers Office. I had to dress smartly and ended up wearing a black skirt which belonged to my mother and my aunt's Jaeger blazer. I was 16 years old and wearing the blazer of a 60-year-old because once again, I didn't have anything that fitted me.

15

The interview went well. The panel of RAF officers were impressed with my GCSE grades, the fact I had been Head Girl at school and my work ethic, having worked on the market stall for several years. I made it through the first stage which led to an invite to RAF Cranwell for the official assessment. Thankfully, I didn't need to share a room with anybody which was such a relief. Even more of a relief was the fact that my bedroom had a sink in it. I was so conscious about my body - even though at this stage I was reasonably slim - that I didn't want to take a shower in front of anyone. I spent the weekend washing in the sink instead.

I mixed well with the other applicants and tried to create a steady balance between leadership and follower-ship in all the group exercises. This was always a challenge, because there were some candidates who were constantly trying to hog the limelight. I worried that I might be fading into the background, but remained true to myself and only took the lead when I deemed it appropriate. I was put through aptitude tests and assessments and this was followed by another interview. One thing I have always been complimented on is my personality and one of the instructors made a point of stating that my personality was 'unique'. I wasn't sure whether this was good or bad for the RAF, but I was delighted when I was written to several weeks later to say I had been awarded the scholarship. Wow, it was real - one day I was to become a RAF Officer.

I commenced my A levels and at the same time I started working in a hotel as a waitress. With it came multiple opportunities to indulge and I would often stockpile the desserts that went uneaten from buffets or wedding receptions and devour them later. This would be followed by purging to dispel the food and then would come the inevitable period of guilt and disgust which would almost certainly lead to another binge.

I was still attracting men both at college and at work. It was always a huge shock to me that anybody would find me attractive - a limiting belief that was deeply rooted. I became desperate not to let anybody go and on several occasions, I slept with men who clearly saw me as an easy target. This included a businessman staying at the hotel, a fellow student at the college and even a famous footballer. They would drop me as easily as they'd picked me up and this did little to improve my self-esteem and led to yet another toxic cycle of trying to demonstrate I could attract a man and keep a man. I wish so much that I could go back and speak to that Me. To reassure her. To tell her that life wouldn't always be so confusing.

Hindsight, however, is a stickler for timing and it refuses to be rushed.

I was in a mess and sex was very confusing for me. I didn't understand it, having been introduced to it at such a young age and in such awful circumstances. It was not a great example of what sex represented. In my experience, sex meant lying still and waiting for it to be over, hardly the most thrilling experience for anybody taking me to bed. Considering all I'd been through, I was not afraid of sex or of men for that matter. I was intriguingly maybe, quite the opposite. Maybe I was searching for an understanding? For something about Men and Sex to make sense. I knew that it was a way to get attention and it fed my need for approval. My rejection by them all however, would only serve to exacerbate my confusion.

One evening, I walked into the hotel kitchen and a new chef was standing behind the hot plate. He'd arrived from another hotel in the chain to cover sick leave and he was funny, always charming the waitresses with lots of banter. He was short with blond cropped hair and a golden tan and while I didn't fancy him, I thought he had a good body. When he flirted with me, I told myself there was no way I'd ever date him. A few nights later however, when a crew of hotel staff went to a nightclub after work I would see another side to him. I was getting attention from a hotel resident who had been staying at the hotel for a few weeks. He was there too and in his drunkenness, was pestering me. When Paul saw my attempts to push him away, he stepped in, held my hand and told the man that I was with him. That night we kissed.

Paul lived at the hotel and we began seeing each other a lot. This distracted me from my studies, but I didn't care. He would cook for me after a shift and we would laugh and stay up late together with the rest of the team. Sometimes we'd only go to bed an hour before the breakfast shift started so I would often report for duty still full of alcohol, but given everybody else on the team did the same, it didn't seem to matter. I still wasn't physically attracted to Paul, but he was

17

kind and we had fun and he didn't reject me. He was a safe bet, which surely meant I couldn't get hurt.

At this stage, I was experimenting with starving my body. I was trying to go without food for several days to see if it would help me lose weight. It would almost always end in a huge binge followed immediately by another period of starvation. This was my vain attempt to stop being sick using the salt water. My dentist told me my teeth were in a poor state and I needed a filling or two each time I visited. This was undoubtedly linked to the purging and overload of sugar, although I didn't share that information with the dentist. I'd been on a starvation mission for two days but then something unusual happened: I collapsed at work.

I'd been working for twelve hours and had had little sleep the night before. It was a hot, sunny day and my body hadn't had any food, fuelled only by only a few sips of water. I was feeling odd, like I was two seconds behind everyone else. I went into the changing room which was near the hotel kitchen and tried to make sense of the dizzy feeling that was overwhelming me. Shortly afterwards my legs gave way and I fell to the floor. I tried to stand up, but couldn't and I dragged myself to the door and into the kitchen. One of the chefs caught sight of me on the floor and ran over to help. My breathing was quickening and I felt weak and disorientated. The hotel manager called out for somebody to phone for an ambulance whilst Paul held me in his arms. I don't remember getting into the ambulance. I was taken to hospital where I was met by my parents.

'Who is Paul?!' was their first line of enquiry.

'He's my boyfriend,' I replied wearily.

'Oh no, that's not happening Angela, no way!' my Dad responded, fervently.

But I was a teenager and so this simply made me even more determined to see Paul.

While I don't blame my parents for what happened to me at all, I truly don't, there was a period in my late teens when I wanted to punish them for not seeing it. I no longer wanted their approval, in fact I seemed to be hell bent on seeking their disapproval and had even found myself lashing out physically at my Dad through utter frustration at my inner turmoil. It was never about the apparent source of the argument of course. I was lashing out at the confusion and shame I carried with me always.

I spent several days in hospital on various drips, but a diagnosis was never fully established, or at least I cannot recall it. Paul visited me every day. He would bring me chocolate bars and baguette sandwiches filled with cheese because despite my situation, my appetite was still intact. Whilst in hospital, I decided that I was going to stop the starving/bingeing cycle and instead try to lose weight by dieting sensibly.

I was a size fourteen at this stage and was feeling fat and frumpy. There were lots of girls working at the hotel and they were super slim and wore lovely clothes from Top Shop and River Island and I felt inadequate in comparison. I would still shop in shops meant for more mature women which meant I was always dressed much older than my years. When I got home from hospital, I pulled out a piece of paper that I had been given by a friend a few months before. It detailed a five-day medical diet which would see me eating strange food combinations like beetroot, egg and green beans in the same meal. My friend had said it was a miracle diet and she had lost lots of weight following it before her holiday. It sounded horrible, but it promised ten pounds of weight loss and it also included a scoop of vanilla ice cream on one of the days which made it more appealing.

Paul would prepare the weird meals at the hotel making it easier for me and I managed to stick to the diet for the entire duration. I weighed myself every day, sometimes twice daily and the pounds were dropping off. At the end of the five days I'd lost eight pounds, but was starving. So, I celebrated with fish, chips and a barm cake (bread roll) from the local chip shop. The next morning, I had gained three pounds and was devastated. To ease my misery, I went to the shop and bought four bars of chocolate and a family sized Victoria sponge cake. My shopping basket also included a magazine which had a 'Lose 7lbs in 7 days' promise on the front page. Whilst ingesting the cake and chocolate, I studied the diet plan which this time involved mostly eating soup made from vegetables and lots of spices alongside poached chicken breasts. I decided to start the next day. And so, my relationship with Miracle Cures and Quick Win diets began. I treated myself to a takeaway pizza and garlic bread the evening before I started the 'Lose 7lbs in 7 days plan'.

I was still heavily involved with the RAF as part of the scholarship and they arranged for me to go on a training expedition. I really didn't want to go. By now, my indifference to Paul had blossomed into infatuation and I wanted to spend all my spare time with him. Fuelled by my crippling low self-worth, I believed that if I went away, he might meet somebody else and leave me.

I hated the RAF hierarchy. The rules and routines of the training approach convinced me that it wasn't the career for me but I reluctantly took the long train journey to Aviemore and arrived at the camp nevertheless. We were asked to prepare a presentation to deliver to other members of the group that evening and I chose to speak about Altruism, an ironic choice considering I was doing little to care for myself. Back then, presentations were done using acetate and overhead projectors – tools rather archaic in comparison to today's technology. I painstakingly prepared colourful visuals and thought about the key messages I would put across. I realised I was good at this, I could deliver a compelling presentation and sure enough that is what I did. I had the group eating out of my hand and the presentation concluded with a rapturous applause.

The next day was a somewhat different story however. We were to set out early in the morning to climb the Cairngorms and I had been worrying about this for most of the previous night, consoling myself hidden in the bathroom by eating the chocolate bars I'd bought at the train station. My mind was closed to the possibility I might enjoy it and I spent the night and morning convincing myself I couldn't do it. The minibus dropped us at the location, we dismounted and found our backpacks. It was cold and the fog was hanging low over the mountain; yet the group were in high spirits as we set off on the climb. We were half an hour into the hike when I realised I couldn't continue. The pace was relatively fast and being desperately unfit I was struggling to keep up. My quads were burning with pure fire and I was out of breath - the noise of my heavy breathing was making me feel embarrassed. I am almost certain nobody had given this a second thought, but my ears were hearing a breathing not dissimilar to that of Darth Vader. I had told myself repeatedly that I couldn't do it and I was giving in to that voice. I lied to the instructor, saying I had pains in my chest and the shortness of breath hadn't happened before, so there must be something wrong. He looked concerned and asked one of his crew to take me slowly back to camp. I spent the day hanging out at the barracks instead of climbing the mountain and the mysterious fake chest pains obviously subsided, although I kept up the pretence to a certain extent. I felt bad that I had lied, but I couldn't face admitting that I was unfit due to lack of exercise.

Day three was all about rock climbing and abseiling. Once again, I shut my mind to the possibility of being able to do this. I was convinced that because I was fat and unfit I wouldn't be able to scale the rock and that I'd be too heavy for the abseiling rope.

'What will people think when they see your bum strapped into a harness?' I repeated to myself.

I once again informed the instructor that I felt unwell and would need to sit it out. By the end of the day, I was back on a train home, much to my father's dismay. I was standing in my own way, creating mental barriers that prevented me from taking part, and embracing wonderful opportunities, as a result.

Not long after this, I decided that the RAF was not for me. I knew I was turning my back on an opportunity many would relish, but I saw the rules as something to bend and break, as something that was limiting me. I couldn't see that my greatest limitations were self-imposed. I asked the Hotel's General Manager to give me a decent job and I bravely informed my parents I was taking a job as a Banqueting Manager. My parents were not excited about it, but I was adamant and so, with that chapter of my life over, I threw myself into my work at the hotel and quickly became a trusted and reliable member of the team.

Soon, I was given more responsibility. I was offered the role of Christmas Co-ordinator, a role I enjoyed immensely. I was good at talking to people and found it easy to listen to people's needs and then offer solutions that would fulfil these. I was a natural sales person. I also continued to diet and by now was encouraging other people in the office to get involved. We experimented with many diets from Slim Fast through Cabbage Soup and 1000 calories per day. The diets would last for a few days, maybe a week, and then I'd give in to a binge before starting another one.

Paul and I were now living together in staff quarters at the hotel. It was pretty shoddy - just a room and a shared bathroom - but we decorated it and bought some furniture. We didn't have to pay for the room, so we had our wages at our disposal, to spend as we liked. We worked long hours and after work we would stay up drinking and eating pizza or raiding the hotel fridges with other members of the team. We would buy bottles of vodka to put into the hotel stock and in return the Bar Manager allowed us to drink what we wanted. We were working hard and playing hard.

Every time Paul got drunk, he became very possessive. Even a glance at another man would result in my being accused of having an affair with him. This could be exhausting, because he would be completely unreasonable and would often turn nasty calling me a slag or worse. There were two outcomes to these evenings. One would be a huge row followed by him sleeping somewhere else; the other would be a huge row followed by us making up in the bedroom and on one of the latter occasions we even managed to set the hotel staff quarters on fire by knocking over a candle. This saw the whole hotel evacuated and we were not at all popular with the General Manager. Chaos surrounded us but I was too near it to see clearly.

We moved around to different hotels for a few years and I was very well paid for my age, always managing to get leadership roles with lots of responsibility. Despite my youth, I was ambitious and had the drive to improve and I certainly wasn't a pushover. Paul and I secured great jobs in a Lake District hotel. We hired a van and moved all our furniture and possessions to the staff quarters there and the next morning we reported for duty. I was to be the Restaurant Manager and Paul was the Sous Chef. The General Manager greeted us, handed me some keys, showed me how to use the till and then gave me a card with his number on it. He told me he was going away for two nights and I was in charge. Every bedroom of the hotel was occupied that weekend and I soon established that there were barely any staff employed to run it. After five hours of running around like a headless chicken trying to cover reception, bar and restaurant in an unfamiliar setting, I was struggling to cope. I couldn't believe the Manager had left me in this situation and after dealing with another disgruntled customer complaining about the slow service, I rang him. I asked him to come back because Paul and I would be leaving the next morning. As the chaos continued around me, I got on the phone to several hotels in the area and secured an interview the next day. Within 24 hours we had secured new jobs and had moved again to a large hotel in Windermere.

Professionally, I could be proactive, bold and courageous. Personally, my life continued to be fractious.

The new job held a lot of responsibility for a girl under twenty, but I made it work. I was Conference and Banqueting Manager and would often manage events for more than 500 people, leading a team of 20. It was hard work but we had such a giggle and given the long hours we worked, we got to know each other very well. Paul's controlling behaviour became difficult to cope with during this time and so I decided to end the relationship. I felt a new-found sense of freedom and the binges that continued to curse my life, became less frequent. I was mostly existing on soup during this time and lost weight again, getting down to a size 16.

I started to see one of the Senior Managers at the hotel for a while. The fact that Paul continued to be a constant in my life as he lived in the staff quarters, didn't stop me. I was well accustomed to living in confusion. It might even have been part of the appeal. The manager had no intention of having a relationship, but this arrangement seemed to suit me at the time. I felt constant pressure from Paul however who, knowing about the situation, was hell bent on stopping it, and after a few months I gave into his relentless attempts and we decided to get back together.

It was an invitation for the stifling behaviour to be reintroduced into my life, as if I hadn't had enough of it the first time.

Paul and I made a decision to buy our first house and we moved back to my hometown. I knew it was high time to decide on a career. Hotel life was fun, but I couldn't envisage myself in this lifestyle in the long-term and so I applied for a job in a bank. I was offered a position as a cashier and decided to take it, taking a pay-cut to secure it. On my second day I was asked to work through a list of prospects, call the customers and attempt to make appointments to discuss banking products and services. It turned out I was effective at this and within a few weeks I'd been promoted by the bank into a sales role as a Customer Advisor; this was followed by the task of running a branch just a few months later. My selling skills and leadership potential had once again come to the fore and I was given responsibility beyond my experience. I worked hard and was determined to succeed, despite feeling like a swan swimming most days.

Paul and I moved into our new home and I noticed that I was spending less time with him. He'd work evenings and weekends and I worked daytimes, Monday to Friday, so would spend a lot of time alone and would fill that time with eating. I'd drive to the supermarket and buy boxes of cream cakes; family sized chocolate bars and large packets of crisps and I'd sit and eat them watching TV. I was bored, lonely and craving excitement. The weight was creeping on and over the space of a year I had gone from being a size fourteen to a size eighteen. My uniform jacket was so small that there was a six-inch gap between the edges and I could barely move my arms because the sleeves were so tight.

Mitchell, a rescue dog, arrived on the scene and provided an opportunity to get out and walk. I didn't really want a dog but was convinced it was a good idea by Paul. Mitchell had been mistreated previously and was not well trained but he was loving. I suppose that he really was the perfect dog for me! One day after my Saturday morning shift at the bank, I took him for a walk on the field. A man approached me and started to ask me questions about the dog which was not unusual, many people did. The next thing I knew this man had pulled a hunting knife from his pocket. I saw the flash of the silver blade shimmer as the sunshine made contact with it and immediately felt my heart rate quicken as my eyes darted around the cricket pitch assessing the situation. The man grabbed my arm and started trying to drag me towards the bushes. I was utterly determined he was not going to hurt me and I used all my weight to pull away from him. Mitchell was going crazy, barking at the man who eventually let go and ran away. Shaking, I called the police from my mobile and then much to my confusion heard the siren of the police car before the call had even connected. I wondered how they had got to me so without me filing a report and it later transpired that the knife wielding man had exposed himself to a little girl and she had run home and told her parents who had called the police. They captured the man and found the knife in his possession and I was interviewed later that day. Traumatised, there was only one place to turn to deal with the terrifying episode, and it wouldn't be towards the man I was sharing my life with. I had a well rehearsed coping mechanism now. This latest trigger would inevitably lead me further down the negative path of searching for another solution to solve my increasing weight gain.

There was a sun-bed shop across the road from the bank in which I worked and I would pop in at lunchtime for a session in a time before the horrors associated with them were known. One day, the owner showed me a new range of pills she had bought. They were appetite suppressants and she claimed they had helped her to lose weight. They cost £19 for a month's supply and whilst this seemed a lot of money, I felt compelled to purchase them. They were my new hope. My quick fix. The answer that had eluded me so far. This time, was different. I didn't eat during the day for a few weeks so they seemed to be doing exactly as they promised- to suppress my appetite – a positive in my book. The downside, however, was that I felt dreadful most of the time. I had severe headaches and felt dizzy whenever I went from sitting to standing. The pills contained a substance called *hoodia*, a plant based product derived from Africa which is known for its appetite suppressing qualities. Whilst I wasn't consuming my usual intake of food throughout the day, by the evening time I felt so unwell that I would binge to make myself feel better, undoing the effects of the day. I ceased taking the pills after a few weeks, but this wouldn't be the last time I would waste money on 'wonder pills' in a bid to lose weight.

I was stuck. Lost in a Maze which seemed to have no exit and I really didn't know where to turn.

Chapter Three

It is now March 2003, and Paul and I have moved into our second home. I am working as an Account Manager for a loan company which is part of a large bank. We'd made a decent return on our first house and used the funds to purchase a lovely 1930s semi-detached house with a large garden. Despite having good jobs, we didn't have a lot of money due to spending everything we had on the property and so it wasn't the brightest idea to book our wedding for 30th May 2004, something we couldn't really afford.

I continued to sleep walk through my personal life. I'd settled into a routine of eating takeaways and carb-laden meals as part of my normal eating plan. I was at a point where I didn't care what I was eating in front of people and so would eat junk food all the time. It wasn't even kept as part of my secret binges anymore. And because it too was a well-rehearsed part of the rhythm of my life, I continued to make attempts to lose weight. I joined a local health club and would go along with my friend, Siobhan. We'd join in the step and aerobic classes and I'd wear men's polo shirts and three-quarter length shorts to cover the bulges. I enjoyed the exercise, despite having a beetroot red face throughout the session but I didn't lose weight because I wasn't controlling the calorie intake and I'd often stop at McDonald's on the way home from class to reward myself. I deserved a big mac, fries and milkshake, surely. This new attempt at an exit from the Maze was again short-lived and I ceased my membership before it was due to expire, lying to the health club that I was moving to a new house. It seemed an easy lie compared to the lies I was telling myself.

By now, I was wearing size twenty-two clothing and was feeling miserable. I was never able to dress appropriately for summer because I was embarrassed about my size. Picture this: a desperately hot day, thick black tights, a long black skirt and a black fleece.

'Are you not hot?' asked Siobhan, clearly concerned.

'No, I'm absolutely fine,' I lied, trying to convince an unconvinced Siobhan.

The truth was far too painful and even more uncomfortable to deal with than the layers of clothes I tried to hide behind.

I was withdrawing from the world and spending more time alone at home dwelling on the past and not being able to make sense of it. How could I? I'd even started to take time off work, a day here, two days there because I couldn't face people. I was working with such lovely colleagues at the time and felt guilty for passing on my workload to them but there were days when I could do nothing other than stay in bed and eat.

I was headed towards a collision. Something was going to give and on a routine visit to my Mum's one afternoon, something snapped inside me. I had to tell her and Dad about the abuse. My relationship with my parents has always been a strong one, particularly with Mum. She was always there for me as a stay at home mother and did a wonderful job. I didn't want to hurt them but I simply couldn't hold it in any longer. Slowly, through uncontrollable tears, I explained what had happened. That I had been abused. That their little girl had been abused at the hands of a Man they trusted completely and that it happened week after week for several years. They sat stunned but listened carefully, as I revealed the details, and I could see they had absolutely no idea how to react. How could they? How can any parent prepare themselves for that? It breaks my heart, as a mother myself to know the devastation they must have felt by my painful admission that day. Ever the Empath, I was almost more concerned about their pain than I was of my own.

Mum suggested I go to the doctor to ascertain if I should start seeing a counsellor, and so, the next morning I visited my GP. I broke down in his office and at the end of the appointment was handed a sick note for anxiety and a prescription for anti-depressants. The prescription landed at the back of a drawer, I couldn't accept that I needed this sort of medication. Diet pills, yes, but not mood enhancers. That was going too far! A few days later, I received a letter with an urgent referral to see a psychologist.

It would be many years later until my Parents would discuss this situation again.

The Psychologist was called Ian. He had a warm and friendly demeanour and was very handsome. I felt embarrassed on first meeting him; firstly because of my size and secondly because I had made absolutely no effort with my appearance. My hair was lank, I didn't wear any makeup and I covered my huge stomach in a red hooded top belonging to Paul. I sat opposite him and his amazing posture, wanting the ground to swallow me up. I tried to address my appearance, clumsily offering some futile excuse. How on earth could I let him in? How could I tell him the awful details of my abuse? The therapy room was set up awkwardly - his chair on one side and mine on the other. There was at least a three metre gap between the chairs and this made me feel rather odd. Alone. Exposed. I didn't like this at all. I wondered why on earth there needed to be such a distance and moved my chair forward a little. There was nothing to hide behind. I sat uncomfortably in the chair trying to shield my tummy with my arms, and he did his best to make me feel at ease by asking a series of non-intrusive questions. I saw Ian every Friday for twelve months and while he was lovely to chat to and we got along well, I often did my best to discuss anything but the abuse and he seemed happy for me to carry on.

And carry on I did. When I would open up about the abuse, I suddenly found myself worried that Ian would disapprove of me and would edit my truth. I'd miss out crucial parts of the jigsaw. I couldn't bear for him to know it all - I failed to tell him how my coping mechanism for the shame was secret eating and bingeing. I never brought up the use of salt water, or the fact that I would starve myself. I also omitted the information that the abuser would cover up my face during episodes, and I didn't ever mention the frequent sessions when the girl would touch me inappropriately or the trauma I'd feel around Bill. Had I felt able to uncover the whole story in front of him, he might have been able to understand the compelling need for approval, my low self-esteem and the dangerous relationship I had created with food. Instead he thought I had depression and we simply focussed on the abuse itself and a myriad of other non-relevant subjects other than the real issues which by now were habitual and continued to have a strangle-hold on me.

While it would be nearly a decade later that I would truly begin to understand my demons and fully piece the jigsaw of my life together, there was one clear benefit from the therapy - it helped me to understand that I had the power to remove the abuser from my life. I am grateful for that at least. While the sexual side of the abuse had ceased on the day he'd thought he'd been caught out, I had continued to carry the huge burden of the emotional hangover with me. Because this man was still very much part of everyday life. His existence continued to torment me and sullied my life with an undercurrent of control fuelled by the injustice of him getting away with it.

I suddenly realised that only I could do something about it. For her. For little 9-year-old Angela who was full of hopes and dreams and innocence. I could do it for her. For us.

I could say, 'Enough'.

I could report him to the authorities. I could tell more people what had happened and remove him from the picture through social exclusion. Expose him for the truth of what he was. What he is.

I could say 'Enough'.

Knowing I could do it was one thing. Making it happen was another.

It would take several more years for me to take that step. To utter 'Enough' to the suffering.

Around the same time as I started therapy, my friend Siobhan announced that she was joining a local 'Slimming World' class and I decided to go along with her. I had a year to lose weight ahead of my wedding and I was determined that 'big bride' was not the look I was going for. I went along to the first class and the format immediately appealed to my competitive nature and the need for approval. The fact that there was a 'Slimmer of the Week' award and you could eat what appeared to be mountains of food was just the arrangement I needed. I indulged in the obligatory 'start of diet' binge the night before, whilst reading the booklet which outlined the difference between red and green days and which foods were 'unlimited'. A red day meant I could eat as much meat, chicken and fish as I wanted and a green day allowed unlimited amounts of pasta, rice and potatoes.

I vowed, once again, to give this diet my very best and for the first week I did exactly that. I always found the first week of a new diet easy due to the sheer novelty. Sure enough, the weekly weigh-in showed I had lost eight pounds! I was dancing inside as Donna, the Slimming World consultant, presented me with a half stone award. It provided the motivational boost and Slimming World became a part of my routine.

Siobhan and I worked together, so we took it in turns to cook lunches for work which omitted the need to purchase calorie-laden baguette sandwiches from the deli. However, despite being able to eat large quantities of food on the diet, I still felt the urge to binge in secret and after a few weeks I started to give in to this craving. It would overwhelm me. An inner voice would take over my body and I was powerless to resist the force of it. It must sound ridiculous to those who have never experienced it, but like an alcoholic needs vodka or whiskey, I needed to binge on sugar & fat. Little did I realise at the time the extent of what these feelings were. That I had no power, no choice in what was happening.

Having to get weighed at Slimming World meant I was desperate not to gain weight. I started to cut out meals and was surviving on two crisp breads and low-fat cheese triangles for the day after a binge. It was a miserable existence, but it meant that each week I – and importantly, the others - would see a weight loss on the scales.

In my infinite wisdom, I also started to smoke cigarettes. I didn't understand why - I hadn't recognised smoking as an appetite suppressant, I was just surrounded by people who did it and therefore joined in. It's a habit that made its place in my life for two years, not that I would admit this to my parents, blaming Paul when questioned about the remnants of ash strewn across the back seat of my car when questioned by my Father. Smoking had proved to help me reduce my food intake and so, when I managed to give up with the help of Alan Carr's book, the results were devastating on my weight loss journey.

I needed to find another helping hand with my mission to lose the pounds, one which allowed me to binge and still lose weight without having to starve the day after. My Devastating Saviour would come in the form of laxatives. Just like the salt water solution had appealed to me in my teens, the laxatives shone like a beacon of hope in my hour of need. Much like a moth who flies too close to the flame however, it was inevitable that I would be burnt.

The side effects of the laxatives were dreadful. I would often wake at 4 AM with severe griping pains in my stomach before its contents would empty from me with such a violent rush, I'd be left sweating from the shock. Cramps and frantic rushing to the loo would continue until mid-morning and despite this I would repeat the process each time I had a binge. I gained a strong sense of satisfaction from being in control and it helped to block the feeling of shame. Or so I thought. Talk about a ridiculously flawed mind-set. I was in fact spiralling out of control, not knowing how my destructive behaviour would end.

Laxatives became the norm and using them ensured that each week when I got on the scales every Tuesday at Slimming World, I would be applauded for my weight loss. I would weigh myself at home each day, too; if by Sunday it appeared I had gained a few pounds during the week, I would increase the laxatives and reduce the food intake on the Monday. On Tuesdays I didn't eat at all until after the evening weigh-in and hardly drank any water to ensure I weighed the minimum possible. This would be further assisted by the removal of shoes, watch, jacket, necklace and earrings before stepping on the scales. Thank goodness it couldn't measure the weight of my burdensome shame. My wedding was drawing closer and I had managed to lose over five stones. I felt great in a size fourteen skirt and sixteen top, even though I wasn't toned at all due to lack of exercise.

Four weeks before the wedding, Paul and I went to a hotel by the Coast for the night. I decided to take the weekend off Slimming World, as a treat. We had a late lunch in the bar, which included a burger and chips and several fizzy drinks. Just a few hours later we went to Pizza Hut and treated ourselves to a huge pizza with garlic bread and an ice cream from the self-serve machine, not to mention the litres of Coca Cola. I was totally stuffed, the carbs laying heavy in my tummy. That feeling didn't pass, which was odd, because my body was accustomed to eating large quantities of food.

I don't remember going to sleep that night. I do recall waking in the very early hours, and feeling an excruciating pain from the most intense indigestion, as if there was a vice squeezing the middle part of my inner torso. The only relief came from crawling on all fours.

Desperate for it to stop, I was crying in agony and calling out to Paul to wake up. Thankfully he hadn't been drinking that night, and through tears of pain I explained I required urgent medical care. We decided to drive back to home from the hotel and on the way had to stop the car to allow me to be sick several times.

When I arrived at the hospital the nurse looked shocked and ushered me to a cubicle straight away. She told me my skin was yellow - a sign of jaundice - and a later scan revealed that I had gall stones. I had no idea what this meant, but the doctor insisted I was admitted. An ERCP procedure was carried out the next day under sedation. This was meant to release the stones from the tube attached to the gall bladder, but it appeared to do nothing to ease the pain. 'It's usually the large ladies who have problems with gall stones,' explained the surgeon carrying out the procedure.

Nice bedside manner Mr.

'But I've lost five stones!' I told him proudly.

He looked suitably impressed, and I was placated, of course.

The pain continued. The next day a different Consultant came to see me and said that as the ERCP hadn't improved the situation, my gall bladder would need removing, but due to it being Easter weekend they would send me home and I would be added to the waiting list. He added that the operation would initially be conducted via key hole, but may progress to open surgery if the gall bladder was too infected. The difference in recovery between these two procedures was three weeks. By now the pain was so acute I was taking morphine though a PCA machine which delivered a dose of the pain killer into my blood stream each time I pressed a, button. The thought of going home was not filling me with delight and added to this was the ticking clock of the impending wedding. What if the pain didn't stop and I needed to come back to hospital again next week or the week after?

I lost the plot, not helped by the narcotics, and insisted the operation take place that day. The consultant was arrogant in his response, something that despite my youth, I truly despised and only served to make me more persistent which eventually paid off. I was taken down to the theatre the next day.

I was told I'd been lucky that the operation had remained a keyhole procedure. The gall bladder was severely infected and had been a challenge to remove. I was thankful that the operation had not escalated to the open surgery method, because this would have meant a longer period of recovery and major scarring.

I hadn't eaten any food for four days and for once in my life, had no desire to eat. It was as if my body had gone into shut down and didn't require any fuel. I felt so exhausted I wasn't even getting the urge to binge. The day after my operation, I lay on the hospital bed with zero energy and little enthusiasm. A nurse took my blood pressure and looked puzzled.

'Have you looked in the mirror this morning?' she asked, handing me a small compact mirror.

I was shocked by the face staring back at me.

The whites of my eyes were now a very vibrant yellow, a sure sign of a liver infection that would see me having to remain in hospital 'for some time'. The 'some time' turned into over two weeks and when I emerged from hospital I had lost over a stone in weight.

It was little consolation in the grand scheme of things however, because there was another dreadful situation playing out in the background of my life. My new-found confidence brought on by my recent image change, also brought with it attention from a colleague at work. My relationship with Paul had been rocky for many of the nine years we had been together. We didn't spend a lot of time together, and the time we did would often be spoilt by drink-induced arguments and Paul's constant belief that I was seeing somebody else. This would drive me to distraction, particularly when his accusation began to have some substance when I started a relationship with a Senior Manager at the bank. I knew this was wrong - I was in a relationship, and yet the attention was too much to resist. We would chat for hours on the phone each day and meet up whenever work allowed. It was dangerous and wrong but, great fun. He was so refreshingly different to Paul and the last thing I expected was to have this man tell me that he loved me. I was, once again, at the centre of a storm of chaos, not really knowing how to get myself out until fate stepped in.

While I was in hospital, Paul took my work phone home to put it on charge. The next day he returned to the hospital I could see something was wrong. I had other visitors at the time and Paul sat quietly with a face like thunder. He looked furious and I couldn't understand why. When the visitors left, he threw the phone on to the bed and asked me why I had a very familiar text message from a 'David' who called me 'Gorgeous'. I had messaged David earlier to say I missed him, but had deleted the text immediately after sending it. David had replied a few hours later and Paul happened to stumble upon the response. I lied and said the text must have been meant for somebody else and then I went into rebel mode stating that if he didn't trust me, we should call off the wedding. He said that wasn't what he wanted, but the next few days were frosty.

I messaged David to say we couldn't speak for a few days.

My life was still an unbelievable mess. I was marrying a man I knew I didn't want to spend my life with. I was having an affair with another man, who although was lovely, was again not the person I would want to be committed to in the long-term. I called a halt to the affair. I was still battling the demons of my youth and needed to think seriously about my future. I was shackled to the destructive relationship with food, despite successfully losing weight week after week for the whole year. On the face of it I was successful, scratch the surface and I was crumbling.

Chapter Four

The wedding day came and went.

I felt like I was in a bubble from the first moment until the last, going through the motions with a fixed smile and a heavy heart. I was disconnected, elsewhere, watching on. Numb.

I knew that I shouldn't be marrying Paul. On the morning of the wedding there was a huge buzz of excitement amidst the bridesmaids and I was aware I was painting on a smile. My Mum sensed that something was wrong and asked me if I still wanted to go through with it whilst I was getting into my dress. Despite my overpowering doubt, I went ahead. The dread of what people might think, was stronger than my unhappiness. My doubts were further confirmed when, during the evening reception, Paul accused me of having an affair with one the guests who was actually attending with his wife. I wasn't. We spent an hour arguing and then went back to our room, ate room service burgers and feel asleep without consummating the marriage.

This was the new natural of our relationship now. The trust had eroded. Respect had vanished. We were at an impasse and we pretended it didn't exist. It was an exhausting charade.

We went to Jamaica on our honeymoon. It was an 'all inclusive' holiday which meant that food was available constantly. On the day of the wedding I was wearing a size fourteen dress and had lost a total of six stone. I felt absolutely amazing. On our honeymoon, however, all thoughts of losing weight left my head and I indulged in sugar-laden cocktails and multi-course meals for breakfast, lunch and dinner. Whenever food was readily available I was unable to control my intake and as the days ticked by, my clothes were becoming tighter and tighter. I was in a permanent state of 'carb bloat'. I seemed to think about nothing else, and as soon as one meal was over I'd be focused on when I could have the next one. I wasn't hungry. I just needed to fill an overwhelming sense of emptiness.

On the return journey back to reality, the jeans I was wearing on the outbound flight wouldn't fasten. When we got home and I stepped on the scales, the realisation hit me - during a nine-day holiday, I had gained a full stone in weight.

The feeling of shame smashed into me like a truck.

Not only I was now married to a man I didn't really love. I had also returned to the slippery slope of weight gain.

I dragged myself through eight married months until my miserable reality was impossible to ignore. I couldn't do it anymore and in a single moment of clarity one day, I realised that if I wanted to be truly happy, only I could make it happen, nobody else could make me happy. That included the man I was married to. My decision making can often seem impetuous, yet I rarely regret a choice I make and I have come to trust my instinct and follow my gut. The situation I was in was rendering me miserable as I felt stifled by the constraints imposed by Paul. I acknowledged that his inherent insecurity and jealousy weren't helped by my having an affair. He had continued to accuse me constantly seeing other men and when I found myself one day agreeing to meet a guy I'd met through work, I knew that it was the final signal that I needed to exit the marriage. For both our sakes.

As I pulled onto the driveway, I knew what had to be done. I opened the front door and stepped into the hallway, hearing the sound of the television coming from the lounge. I took a deep breath to compose myself and calmly walked towards the noise. It took only a few moments to inform Paul that I was leaving him.

The announcement was factual and rather cold in its delivery and it was almost like I was having an out of body experience. It was the only way I could convey it without becoming emotional. I'd assumed a dominant stance and stated my position like a politician states a proposal in parliament. He looked stunned initially, but I believe he was probably as relieved as I was. There was neither a lengthy discussion nor a heated debate, just wide-eyed silence. I turned on my heel and went upstairs. I had no plan of exit and nowhere to go, and so the reality was that we lived together for several weeks after this. In that time, there were inevitable arguments and questions, but I kept my resolve and remained steadfast in my decision.

My situation was helped somewhat by a phone call I received from a girl I worked with, Michele. We'd always been friends; we connected. She was a warm and generous person who was married with three children and Paul and I would regularly attend barbecues and parties at their house and vice-versa. When I listened to her on the phone, I couldn't believe my ears. She told me that she too had left her husband and asked if I fancied a night out. Nights out weren't something I did - it had never been worth the hassle while I was with Paul. I only had to recall being at a conference which included an overnight stay and being embarrassed when the night porter approached me in the bar an, in front of my colleagues, informed me that my then boyfriend (Paul) wanted to know why I wasn't in my room! I said no to Michele initially because that was my usual response to such invitations.

Then after ten minutes, I realised I didn't have to answer to anyone anymore.

I called her back. 'I'm in'. I was finally free to do as I pleased.

Before long, I was grateful when the house sold and I could use some of the proceeds to set myself up in a swanky apartment which coincided with a new job as a Lean Consultant for a bank. I didn't know what a Lean Consultant was when I applied for the role and it appeared that neither did the two men interviewing, but we hit it off in the interview and on my drive home, one of them called to offer me the role. Things were looking up.

During this period of my life, I managed to stay reasonably in control of my weight by applying many of the tactics I had learned to date. I had many tricks in my toolbox by then. Tried and tested. I'd binge, starve and use laxatives at will and while I was unconcerned by the damage I was doing to my insides, I had developed a greater sense of pride in my appearance. I was a size 14/16 with a wardrobe of pretty clothes and long, blond hair and I was attracting attention from men. Overall, I was happy. My work was fulfilling and Michele and I would go out every weekend and we had the most amazing time, dancing for hours and burning tonnes of calories which were quickly replaced by the drinking of copious amounts of gin. We were having a ball and the stories I could tell are worthy of another book for sure. Most weekends I would meet a potential suitor and some of them I would get together with for a later date.

Michele suggested we should go to New York for a break together, and so we booked a five day stay and set off on our adventure. We spent a fortune in Macy's and Bloomingdales and visited all the sights. We'd start the day wearing heeled boots and by early afternoon needed to purchase trainers because our feet were so sore. I treated myself to a Louis Vuitton handbag using some of the proceeds from the house sale and I felt like a princess walking around the streets with a large carrier bag with LV blazoned on the front. We had purchased so many items we had to buy another suitcase to bring them all back home. It was liberating. And lots of fun.

From flirting with doughnut eating NYPD officers, and even receiving a marriage proposal from a Mafia Millionaire who lavished me with attention and cocktails, I felt alive for the first time in a long time. Michele and I didn't worry about what we were eating and I loved the large portions that were served everywhere particularly the huge ice-cream sundaes. We were sharing a room so I didn't have an opportunity to binge but I ate plenty during meal times and had lots of snacks whilst we were out shopping. It was a trip that proved good for the soul. My heart felt a little healed by the time we flew back home to reality.

Little did I know that life would soon take a very exciting turn.

There haven't been many occasions, where I have met a man and been instantly hooked.

That was until one night in Bristol.

I was out with some colleagues having attended a course and had decided to have some drinks in the evening by the river. The bars were vibrant, full of people having fun with music blaring from the sound systems and laughter hung happily in the air. I was feeling confident in my size fourteen jeans and a size sixteen blazer in military green, which highlighted my blonde hair brilliantly. My confidence was further boosted by the several gin and tonics I'd drunk.

We'd just taken a seat around a table in the third bar of the evening when I saw him. He was tall, at least 6' 2 and broad chested. His hair was blacker than black and his face and arms were tanned, turning his amazing smile dazzling white. I told myself I had to talk to him - it was a desire I hadn't felt before. He'd noticed me staring and smiled at me, which caused me to freeze and I looked away quickly. My inner voice was urging me to talk to him so I decided to throw caution to the wind and wander over to the bar area, where he was standing, to order the drinks. My confidence waned slightly. I stood next to him at the bar and I only managed to say hello. His friends were chatting to him and so I only drew a cursory 'hello' back from him.

I returned to the table. When our eyes met again - mine were glued to him all the time - I smiled. The group were ribbing me about being smitten by this man and I forced my attention away from him and engaged in conversation with colleague, Brett. Some ten minutes later Brett flicked his eyes sideways as if suggesting I should look to my right and when I did, there he was.

'Are you dancing?' he said.

I am told that the correct response to this chat up line is, 'are you asking?'

'I can't dance' was my reply, instead.

'With me you can,' he whispered softly.

He took my hand and led me to the dance floor. The legendary 'Come on Eileen' was playing - hardly the right song for a slow dance and yet we slow-danced like there was nobody else in the room. His name was Mike, but I would later refer to him as Soldier; he was a Sergeant Major in the army. We danced for over an hour which felt to me like minutes and I learnt that he was 43, though he didn't look it, and he was separated from his wife. At this stage I was only 27 so he must have thought it was his lucky day yet I thought it was mine. When Victoria came to find me to say she was leaving, I couldn't believe where the time had gone. I didn't want to leave, but was mindful that I didn't know my way back to the hotel. Soldier said he would see me back safely and my heart pounded as I quickly thought through all the things that could go wrong in this scenario. Victoria was pressing me for an answer and Soldier responded by taking my face in his hands and kissing me slowly on the lips. Every hair on my body stood on end.

I turned to Victoria, and reluctantly said I was coming with her.

I gave Soldier my number and walked on air the whole way back to the hotel, wishing I'd stayed and hoping he'd call.

He did, at 2 AM.

'You're beautiful,' was the only thing he wanted to tell me.

This was a start of a heady romance which continued to have me hooked. The lovely thing about this relationship is that Solider was hooked, too. We spent hours talking on the phone and we would spend weekends together at my apartment, where I would pretend I was into healthy eating and eat fruit for breakfast and chicken salads for lunch. We'd spend time walking around lakes, having meals together and had lots of fun in the bedroom and there was a connection between us that was truly unique, based on my previous experiences. I was on such a high that I actually had fewer thoughts of bingeing and appeared to be more resilient to the shame triggers. I loved Soldier's spontaneous side, from dancing with me in the kitchen to lifting me on to his shoulders before carrying me around as if I was feather light and not my actual thirteen stone in weight and although I cringed the whole time, I was happy. Really happy.

I was working in Cardiff a lot at that time and he would visit and stay with me at my hotel. He always looked so delicious. I'd be filled with pride as we walked around the town together in the evening sunshine. It was perfect. Or nearly. There was a fly in the ointment because Soldier was separated and had two teenage children. His wife was still very much in the picture as they were living in the same house, a situation I could understand of course having been there myself. And then on a night out in Cardiff, when the two of us were dancing to cheesy pop and a lady came up to us and said,

'You must have the happiest marriage, I've never seen a couple so connected.'

I realised I was head over heels in love. And so was he.

This euphoria was to come crashing down around me like a wave hitting a cliff.

After a particularly lovely weekend at my apartment, I drove Soldier back to Bristol on Sunday evening, before heading over to Cardiff ready to start work on Monday morning. We kissed goodbye and he walked into his house. Later that night he texted me saying his wife had gone crazy and trashed lots of his belongings. I was shocked and didn't really know what to say. We talked a few times during the week that followed and he mentioned how tough things were at home. She wanted him back and was making it crystal clear he shouldn't see me. On the Thursday of that week my phone rang, I answered it and was greeted by her voice. This wasn't something I was expecting, to say the least. We talked for half an hour and at times it was like chatting with a friend but then it was contrasted by an icy chill.

'At the end of the day he is a grown man and can make his own choices', I remember saying.

'At the end of the day the sun goes down, love' she retorted.

She was right. The sun had set and I was about to unravel once more.

It would be months before I would see Soldier again. We'd talk occasionally on the phone, but he had decided to give it another go with his wife. This had a profound effect on me. The incredible sense of rejection I felt, created a downward spiral of destructive behaviour once more. The bingeing was back with a vengeance and I went through a period, as I had in my late teens, where I would date every man that I could.

I had no idea what I was doing. I felt lost. Overwhelmed.

I was numbing, using the approval of men to banish the shame I felt because of the rejection. And while I understood that Soldier hadn't rejected me, he'd simply chosen a path that was right for his children, I missed him incredibly. I knew he wasn't really the right man for me but my fragile self-worth was so low that I felt sure that part of his decision was because I was fat and not good enough. I was never enough, it seemed.

And then, several months later, Soldier visited me at home and asked if we could try again. Just like that. But with the passage of time, the feelings I had for him, which were, I realise probably more infatuation than love, had lessened. The man who stood before me looked nice, but not as deliciously handsome as I'd recalled. He looked his age - something I'd never noticed before. We kissed and I didn't feel the same as I had before and so I told him it wasn't for me. We left on friendly terms and I was grateful for the time we had spent together.

My work was taking me all over the country, and I was asked to pick up a new project in Andover. On my first day I was introduced to a guy called Martin who I'd worked for on another project, but had never met face-to-face. He was very handsome and a real gentleman and greeted me with a handshake and a dazzling white smile. I immediately warmed to him. He was taller than me, slim and looked handsome in his suit, shirt and tie. His accent had a hint of Welsh which I found attractive and we spoke for a minute or two before I was moved on to the next area by my host. A group of us went out for dinner that night and though I sat next to Martin at the table, I hardly spoke to him, because my phone didn't stop bleeping with texts and calls from various guys I'd met during the previous weeks - something Martin is quick to remind me when we reminisce about the evening. When I got back to the hotel at the end of the night I regretted not spending time getting to know him and vowed that I would at the next opportunity. There was something very special about this guy who made me feel something I hadn't ever felt before, not with anyone. He made me feel both excited and safe and I liked it.

Later that week, the team were having a night out in town and I was invited along. My work colleague and friend Kristie was on fine form that evening and we were both drinking way too much and having lots of fun together. Kristie and I were always on the same wave length and I'd know exactly what she was thinking from just a look on her face. We brought out the best, or worst in each other and as a pair we were a force to be reckoned with.

I'd heard Martin was dating a girl who was much younger than me and therefore very much younger than him and this sent my competitive side into overdrive. I'd set my sights on him and so went over to chat to him in the bar. He was looking gorgeous in jeans and a fitted polo top and I'd already taken the opportunity to check out his bum earlier that evening.

'You know you fancy me, so you should call me and take me out,' I said at the end of our brief conversation. This was very brazen and coming from a place of complete insecurity masked as ultra-confidence.

'Should I?' he responded, not giving anything away.

I smiled and sauntered off with a cocky swagger.

On the Friday, I drove home and waited for him to call. By late evening he hadn't and I was feeling the rejection gremlins creeping in. Maybe he didn't fancy me, maybe I wasn't enough for him. What was wrong with me? There wasn't much room for rational thought in the sea of insecurity in which I regularly bathed! He might be busy, or he could be playing it cool or even might not be interested at all. I just had to know. I called a friend and asked for Martin's number so I could text him, an impatience driven by the need to end the feeling of low self-worth. He texted back quickly with 'Who's this?' later admitting that he knew it was me and was teasing. We sent texts backwards and forwards that evening and I was thrilled when we arranged a date for the following week.

Dating was complicated because we worked in the same area of the bank and our Line Manager was not keen on relationships at work. We therefore, decided to keep it a secret which is easier said than done as we had colleagues staying at the same hotel as me. Martin rented a flat in the town during the week and on our first date he collected me from the hotel in his car. I asked him to stop at the back of the hotel car park and I ran from the hotel door to meet him, ducking low in the passenger seat until we were out onto the country roads. We had an amazing evening with no silences and lots of laughter. We chatted about our previous marriages and Martin mentioned he had two girls. At the end of our date we kissed in the restaurant carpark. I felt an electric surge through my body. This man really was special. Martin pointed out the stars above us and I didn't want the night with this romantic, kind-hearted, thoughtful man to ever end.

Our relationship in the early days, was mainly played out in Andover because I was living in the North and he would return to Swansea at the weekends to see his children. After four weeks together, Martin arranged a special weekend, booking a fancy hotel in Bristol and asking me to pack a nice dress. I met him at the hotel, my tummy filled with butterflies and spent a lovely afternoon

43

together before getting dressed up for a night on the town. I wore a size 16 turquoise dress and some crystal strappy sandals and felt lovely, mainly due to Martin saying I looked beautiful. We enjoyed a marvellous dinner and then went to a few bars and clubs, dancing, laughing together and talking about everything and nothing.

We were on our way back to the hotel, noticeably intoxicated and loudly merry and before I knew what was happening, Martin had taken off his shoes and rolled up the legs of his jeans and was standing in the middle of the town's fountains. He was beckoning me to come in and so I did and we danced together with the water splashing onto our legs without a care in the world. I loved the spontaneity of it and I loved him. That night before we fell asleep embracing each other, Martin told me I would be his wife. I drifted off with a huge grin.

We eventually told our superiors that we were together and after five months we decided to move into together, renting a house in Swansea. This was the catalyst for another period of destructive eating habits. Not long after moving in to the house, I was coming downstairs one morning and slipped, sliding down the stairs on my back and feeling a sharp pain in my lower spine. The pain was so intense it sent me into a panic and my breathing quickened to a point where I was struggling for air. Thankfully my handbag was at the bottom on the stairs so I could reach for my mobile phone and call for an ambulance. I was taken to hospital where I would spend the next four days having scans which established a small crack in the base of my back. Martin was amazing during this time, continuing to work full time in Andover and travelling back to Swansea each evening to see me in hospital. I was eventually sent home with crutches and pain killers, which effected my mood and the lack of mobility descended me into a dark place.

I turned to one thing that was always there in times of distress. I would sit on the sofa watching shopping channels and eating sweets, chocolate and junk food I'd ordered from the online shop. I thought Martin had no idea about my eating habits, but several years later when I finally admitted about my binge eating he told me he already knew as he would find the wrappers hidden all over the house. I started to gain weight and at this point wasn't concerned with controlling it through my usual methods. I was in a depressed mist and was eating to feel better, to no avail. Depression wasn't something I could ever admit to in those days. I fought against it, determined to avoid the diagnosis. I didn't understand it as an illness and really thought it was a sign of weakness, of lacking. In truth, there had been several periods of my life that were burdened by depression and I really wish I'd sought help then.

Despite the challenges of feeling low and getting to grips with having two young step-children, my relationship with Martin was strong. He allowed me the freedom to be who I was and once I had recovered from the injury and got back into work, I started to lift from the depression. We'd both secured new positions at the bank, Martin in Bristol and me in Newport. The commute from Swansea didn't make sense and so we decided to move to Chepstow. We bought a lovely four-bedroom detached house and settled into making it our home. The house had a lovely feel to it and I felt safe and happy there from the outset.

We'd been living there for a month and were due to go on holiday with Martin's children. On the morning of the impending holiday, I woke feeling odd and somewhat nauseous. I couldn't put my finger on what was wrong with me. Then it struck me... I couldn't be, could I?! I did a pregnancy test and as the two pink lines appeared on the stick, I scrambled to check I'd read the instructions correctly.

I was pregnant.

A wave of panic flooded through my body. My head full of questions, I was in shock.

I sat on the bed for ages, wondering what to do. I'd always imagined that finding out I was pregnant would be a defining, jubilant moment in my life, but it didn't quite feel that way. I walked down the stairs to the kitchen to find Martin. He was preparing breakfast and I waved the stick in front of his face.

'What does that mean?' he asked me, with a puzzled look on his face.

When I told him, he gave me a big hug and said it would all be ok. My fears slowly fell away of course when I grew used to the idea. I spent a small fortune buying mother and baby magazines and absorbed the information written on the pages. The more I read, the more I learnt, the more comfortable I felt and despite periods of insecurity driven by the enormity of the situation, I started to embrace the fact that I was having a baby.

It also provided me with an unlimited licence to eat of course, and that's exactly what I did, wholeheartedly giving into the premise of 'eating for two'. It was as if I thought I had earned the right, and for the first time I was not apologetic about it. Suddenly, I wasn't fat - I was pregnant; and that meant I could eat whatever I wanted in front of people without being judged. Hilariously, even in the early weeks, I would stick out my already pregnant looking tummy, which was mostly fat rather than baby, and stroke it so people could see how pregnant I was, whilst munching on a cream scone or an ice cream in public.

During the pregnancy I gained over four stones. I was presenting symptoms of pre-eclampsia and needed a scan to make sure the baby was growing properly. The scan was carried out by a consultant, a lady in her thirties. She became quite irate as she attempted to get a picture of the baby by holding the Doppler against my tummy.

'Can you lift this fat up?' she said, referring to the flabby skin at the bottom of my bump.

Years of abusing my body had resulted in an unsightly overhang of skin and this was getting in the way during the scan.

'Obese mothers really do make this difficult,' she stated matter of factly, clearly never having heard of 'bed side manner'.

I felt the familiar wave of shame building up inside me.

'I'm sorry,' I muttered, desperately holding back the urge to cry.

I waited patiently until she was done not even hearing what she had to say about the baby. As soon as I was out of the scanning room I found the hospital shop, bought a large box of chocolates and devoured them the moment I got back to the car. It was yet another humiliating moment in my life and still I felt unable to change it.

Then one perfect night, during a Damien Rice concert, my lovely Martin proposed during the song 'The Blower's Daughter'. He presented me with a beautiful diamond ring and, looking lovingly into my eyes, asked me to marry him. I was heavily pregnant with Finley and everything about the moment was perfect. It was romantic and thoughtful - exactly like my husband to be.

Finley was born two weeks later than the planned due date, by emergency section following a very long arduous induced labour. I fell in love with him instantly and felt a bond with him like nothing I'd ever experienced before. Finley weighed just under 10lbs when he was born and doctors said he would never have been naturally delivered due to the small size of my pelvis. Having never been less than a size fourteen I had never appreciated my pelvis was so small and remained puzzled by this for many months.

Life at home with a baby was hugely different to the life I had been used to and the initial phase when Martin was also at home was lovely. I was learning how to look after Finley and dealing with the weird things that were happening to my body; all the reading in the world couldn't have prepared me for the feeling of breasts full of milk! Breast feeding didn't ever feel right for me, given my past, and therefore - much to the midwife's dismay - I didn't even attempt it and refused to let her persuade me otherwise. Before too long, the initial euphoria slowly subsided and I struggled with the boredom of being stranded at home.

I'd developed lovely friendships with some ladies from an ante-natal group and we met often to share stories about lack of sleep and the latest theories of weaning your baby. This was never enough to occupy my mind however and I found myself once again reaching for food as a way to cope.

The weight I had gained during pregnancy was going nowhere fast and I had a wedding to plan for.

Chapter Five

There is an old adage about the past which says that it will always catch up with you. My life was busier than ever with a baby and a husband to be and a wedding to arrange but the Past wasn't at all bothered with all that. It remained unchanged, looking on. Waiting.

The man who had abused me was still a part of my life albeit in a less constant way now that I was living a long way from my hometown. He would often still be at family events however and I would have to continue with the charade of being as polite as possible while wanting so much to confront him with what he'd done to me. His very presence would tear me apart inside and seeing him was always a sure-fire trigger for a period of out-of-control bingeing.

Martin and I had decided to keep the wedding small and invite some family members and close friends. I found myself one day driving north to deliver the invites and to inform those who weren't invited that it wasn't that we didn't want them to attend, it was more that we were trying to keep costs low. Being an Empath, I always felt the need to explain my actions and decisions. I decided I didn't want my abuser to spoil our day and spent the journey rehearsing my speech telling him that he and his wife would not be on the guest list.

Whilst driving to his home. I could hear my heart beating in my ears much as I had as a little girl when he had stolen my innocence from me. My usual forced friendliness in his presence was replaced by fierce determination– I had come here with a purpose. My goal was simply to explain that I wasn't inviting him to the wedding, using the excuse that we were keeping it small. I was holding Finley in my arms and as I started my rehearsed piece I was suddenly overwhelmed. I had had enough of remaining silent. Enough of suffering while he carried on without consequence. Enough.

For the first time in my life, I was ready to stand up to him. It was as if my body had been taken over by somebody else as I stated that I'd remembered everything he had done to me. As he glared at me, taking in my words, he began panting with anger and demanded to know why I was saying these things. With his rage showing through every line on his face, he pinned me against the wall by my throat.

'You're lying,' he muttered right into my face, his fingers clutched around my neck.

I looked him directly in the eyes, suddenly finding my back bone.

'I can still taste you in my mouth.' I spat, staring him down.

'Enough', I thought. 'Enough'.

He let go and held his head in his hands for a moment as he contemplated what to do.

'I never want to see you again.' I declared strongly.

They were my last ever words to him.

I have never reported him and I never will. It is a decision I have made to help me deal with the legacy of the abuse which is far reaching and complicated. I continue to this day to work on understanding the full impact of it upon my life and who I am.

This would prove to be the very last time I would see him but it was not the last time that the ugly aftershocks of shame associated with the abuse would strike.

The wedding date loomed large and was now three months away. Looking in the mirror, I felt disgust at what I'd become. I was over sixteen stone and due to a lack of exercise, was covered in rolls of fat. My hair was lank and my skin was dull. I urgently had to do something about it.

On one of my daily walks with Finley, I'd seen a poster advertising a meal replacement programme that promised to make life lighter by helping with the burden of weight loss. A consultant for the company had set up an office nearby and I suggested to Martin I might go along. At this stage, even my daily walks were akin to climbing a mountain and something had to give. The consultant talked me through the approach. Essentially, I would exist on meal replacement shakes and bars and all *real* food would be banished. The calorie consumption would be under 600 per day. As part of the programme I would have to provide a urine sample each week which would be tested to detect if I had stuck to the plan, an indicator called ketosis. The diet sounded like hell on earth, but it strangely appealed to me because all choices were removed and I wouldn't have to think about food at all. In addition to that, my need for approval would be satisfied because I would need to report in how well I had done via the ketosis test. The plan was £69 per week which was a lot of money given I was on maternity pay, but driven by sheer desperation, I decided to give it a chance.

Amazingly, through iron will power and determination, I stuck to the plan. After the first week I wasn't hungry at all and it was a struggle to consume the meal replacements - I'd often forget to do it altogether. I stopped thinking about food and wasn't tempted to binge at all. The weight was dropping off each week and my wedding dress was taken in several times during the final month.

I lost over four stones in three months, but because I hadn't exercised, my body looked dreadful under my clothes and I was unable to wear anything smaller than a size fourteen. I tricked myself into believing that my body was incapable of getting any smaller due to my 'big bones'.

On the day of the wedding, February 28th, 2009, I felt fabulous in a chocolate brown taffeta and silk gown. Because I'd lost weight so quickly, a lot of the guests were shocked at the transformation. Michele was my bridesmaid and she looked equally lovely, having lost weight on the same programme too. It was a really special day and unlike my marriage to Paul, I knew Martin was the right man for me and we had a beautiful, relaxed time. His speech made everybody cry. He talked about the fact that every time he told me that he loved me I would always respond with 'why?' I didn't hide my need for approval very well - and Martin, being kind-hearted, was always ready to provide me with validation. He went on during his speech to list all the reasons he loved me, adding that I had taught him how to love, which touched me deeply. We watch the speech every year on our anniversary, reliving the magic of that day.

Seeing our friends and close family together was dreamlike. The freedom of being at an event without my abuser being there was a huge relief.

The evening reception was a blast. Our friends re-enacted the Thriller dance, Martin & I danced to the Killers' 'Mr. Brightside' with his children and at one point the best man, Richard managed to fall asleep standing up. When Martin and I retired to our suite, the rest of the group gate-crashed a masquerade ball which was happening in another part of the hotel. It was an unforgettable night and a true celebration of our wonderful relationship. I felt so lucky.

We spent our honeymoon in Devon, taking Finley with us. We rented a cottage and had a chef come to cook for us. We indulged in cream teas and lots of lovely meals and I returned a week later ten pounds heavier. I couldn't get my head back into the meal replacement shakes and before long had gained back a lot of the weight I'd lost. This was inevitable of course, having survived on only 600 calories and then returning to eating large amounts of food again. While it was understandable it still served as a stick with which to beat myself.

As if the weight gain wasn't bad enough, I noticed that I was shedding hair. Every time I got up from my work chair there would be dozens of hairs on the seat and backrest. My hair was falling out and my hairdresser believed it was due to the extreme dieting I had undertaken in the months before. Over the course of the next few weeks I lost roughly half my hair. This had been the only part of me I'd ever truly liked. It was devastating and it would take over two years for my hair to return to normal. I vowed never to try meal replacement shakes again. This was another vow I made to myself that would inevitably land on the list of broken promises.

Soon I was back at work, working part-time, three days per week for the bank and having two days with Finley. He was such a happy little boy and the balance of work and being a mummy was working well apart from dealing with the challenge of having Martin work away from home. I missed him so much. It also meant there was nobody there to control my eating habits and so, inevitably, I found my way back to binge eating. To aid my bingeing habits, the local convenience store had installed self-serve tills which meant I could purchase chocolate muffins, sweets, crisps and chocolate bars and perform my own check out without the judgement of shop attendants.

Unsurprisingly, the weight started piling on. In desperation once again, and always ready for a quick fix, I was delighted when I was prescribed 'Orlistat' by my doctor. It is a pill that absorbs fat from your food and dispels it from your body before it is stored. They produce some pretty horrendous side effects, often meaning a

51

panicked dash to the toilet, sometimes not even being able to make it in time. The box stated that they should be used in conjunction with a calorie controlled diet, but I had other plans.

I had lost the plot again. Every two weeks I would have to return to the doctor's surgery to be weighed and would only be given more Orlistat pills if I had lost weight. And so, well versed as I was in trying to cheat the system, I'd resort to shakes and laxatives prior to my being weighed by the doctor. I'd then be rewarded with another box of Orlistat pills and would put myself through the same process again. It was a vicious and toxic cycle, all orchestrated by me.

Martin and I decided to try for another baby and within a month I was pregnant again. This time around the announcement was more of the defining moment I thought it should be. Finley and I surprised Martin by wrapping up a tiny baby vest with the pregnancy test stick which we presented to him when he arrived home from work. He was over the moon.

Once again, the pregnancy gave me an excuse to eat as I wanted and also meant I could stop using Orlistat. I craved mango and sushi and would eat this in abundance; my menu would consist of lots of junk, too.

At the end of pregnancy, I tipped the scales at just under twenty stones.

Coral was born by a planned C-section, two weeks earlier than her due date, weighing just over 9lbs. On the first night after the birth, my blood pressure was dipping very low and I was unable to look after Coral myself. I was aware she was crying a lot, but couldn't do anything about it. Her tears continued the next day and the only thing that consoled her was to be held. In the middle of the second night, a midwife came to me and said the only way to get Coral to sleep was to have her in bed with me. I was against this because I didn't want to create a habit, but after a further three hours of unsuccessfully trying to settle her in the cot, I resigned to having her in bed with me.

Coral was a difficult baby due to an allergy to milk, as we later established. When she was prescribed special formula at five months everything suddenly improved and she was a joy, but until that point, it was tough. Martin was working away during the week and I would spend hours walking with Coral and Finley in a double pram just to keep Coral from crying. This was beneficial for me from an exercise point of view, but it would quite often coincide with trips to the supermarket self-checkout. I'd purchase a box of cream cakes and eat them while I was walking, throwing the box into the park bin.

On one of these walks, Coral was crying so much I had to come back to the house. I remember standing on the driveway and crying because I didn't know what to do to make Coral better. I was sleep-deprived and probably depressed - though that was never confirmed - but at this stage I was most certainly in need of help. The assistance came from my next door neighbour, Sharon. She'd heard me through an open window and she gently took Coral from my arms, suggesting I take Finley to the park for an hour. Coral had stopped crying in Sharon's arms and seeing this I took up her kind offer, but as I walked away from the house the shame trigger struck.

I suddenly thought that Sharon must think I was a bad mum and that Coral mustn't like being with me as she'd stopped crying as soon as she left my arms. These feelings started to overwhelm me and I was in a state of panic. The first thing I did was go to the fish and chip shop and order two portions of fish and chips. I often bought two of everything. It was as if I thought the shop keeper would not think I was greedy if I was buying for other people as well. It was the same principle I'd applied on the market years before. Both portions were of course for me and I went to a quiet spot near the woods and devoured them.

Once again, my shame was numbed. For now, at least.

Chapter Six

Martin had been offered a new job in London which meant we needed to move to a location closer to his new office. I managed to secure a job with a credit card company and we soon landed in a small village nearby. A new job and a new community came with a set of new challenges. The children needed to settle into a different nursery and I found that the daily grind of getting them to childcare on time, adapting to the new job in a tough political environment and not having any friends close by was taking its toll. I felt like a swan swimming most days and was struggling to fit in with the culture at work. It was a very ego driven environment and rather than being focused on doing the right things for the customer it was somewhat focused on doing the right things for the superiors instead. The minutes at work seemed to tick by at a snail's pace and I was desperate to go home.

On my way home from work each day I would pass a McDonald's drive through. Martin was at home in the evenings and so my opportunities to binge were limited. I still hadn't confided in him about my relationship with food although he was well aware of it as I would discover later. He was still finding my sweet and chocolate wrappers stuffed in drawers and cupboards as he had years earlier.

McDonald's drive-through became my new friend and on most evenings I would order 2 meals with milkshakes. The fact that I could place an order from the car into a faceless machine seemed like my purchase was invisible. Other than the server, nobody else was aware of my purchasing. I would eat the meals whilst driving to collect the children from nursery, only stuffing the food into my mouth if I was sure the drivers around me couldn't see me. I would then have dinner with Martin in the evenings and would often convince him we needed a family sized bar of chocolate or a large tub of ice cream for dessert.

My calorie intake for the day was way beyond what I was burning and I was gaining weight quickly. None of my work clothes fitted properly and I had raw, painful red marks around my middle from the waist bands that would cut into me. My jackets would have a six-inch gap from edge to edge. I was utterly miserable and though he never said it, I believed Martin had stopped fancying me completely although he says this was never the case.

I'd been in my job for less than a year, when Martin found me in bed and in lots of pain. The pain was like the one I'd experienced when I had gall bladder problems years before. A trip to the hospital disproved that assumption. The doctor suggested I might have a stomach ulcer and referred me for a scan. As I had private medical cover, I decided to speed up the process by seeking a scan at the private hospital. The consultant there confirmed I did indeed have gall stones present in a small tube that is attached to the pancreas. He said that they should have been removed as part of the original operation, but it appeared this hadn't been the case. He also explained there was a shadow on my pancreas which may or may not be sinister and I was referred for more tests and an exploratory operation.

I was waiting for the results like a convicted criminal waiting for a sentence. While struggling to remain calm and patient, I realised that life was too short to waste it on being unhappy. On the day of the operation, I spoke to Martin and asked him to book an appointment with an accountant later that afternoon. He looked shocked and explained to me that I'd just had a sedation and needed to think about recovery. I assured him I was fine and at 4.00pm that afternoon we were sitting in front of an accountant, setting up a new business. My impetuous decision making had once again come to the fore and I was now officially an independent consultant...with no work.

The shadow turned out to be nothing serious, thankfully.

The following day I resigned from my job and the sense of relief was instant. I was not concerned about finding work, I was just desperate to escape the drudgery that was my current job. Within a week, I'd secured a six-month contract with a daily rate that would see my income double. The downside of this meant that every week from Monday to Thursday, I would be away from home, away from my children.

The enormity of this didn't hit me immediately – it snuck up on me a few weeks down the line. To help with the childcare, we employed a nanny who would stay at home with the children, reducing the number of days they would spend in a nursery. The children adapted to this situation perfectly making the decision easier. The reality however was somewhat more difficult. I'd leave home every Monday morning at 0630 and travel from Northampton to Bingley and wouldn't return home until 1800 on Thursday. Being away from the children was immensely difficult, especially as they were still so young.

I felt huge pangs of guilt.

And as ever, my guilt turned out to be an insatiable beast, which I fed and fed with heaps of food.

By now I was wearing size twenty-four dresses and I felt ridiculously uncomfortable. My feet and knees would ache under the strain of the weight and I would wear two pairs of Spanx under my dresses in a desperate effort to hold in my tummy. It didn't stop me from eating though. Each evening after work, I would go to the supermarket and buy whatever I fancied before skulking back to my hotel room and bingeing. I would hardly ever eat a normal meal, indulging on cake, pastries, sweets and chocolate instead.

I was half way through the assignment in Bingley and sinking further into a depression. I went to see a doctor. He recommended anti-depressants which had been prescribed years before and remained untouched in a cupboard. This time I decided to take them and with a new prescription I started the course. I also decided it was time to try and sort out my weight again. Having successfully done Slimming World before, I went along to a class in Bingley and tentatively stepped on the scales.

I was 18 stones and 4lbs.

I instantly felt the pangs of shame soaring through my body.

How on earth had I got to this point?

I vowed to sort it out.

I stuck to the regime and lost 8lbs. For a few weeks, I did well. But then the pain of being away from the children couldn't be ignored anymore and the lure of binge-eating was too great. I was

56

back at square one within weeks and stopped going to the class altogether.

I gave up. I'd had enough.

I accepted the fact that I was going to be fat. Forever.

The anti-depressants seemed to take hold. There's a reason why they call them 'anti-depressants' and not 'happiness increasers' - I felt like I was walking around in a fog and felt disconnected from everything. Martin said one evening that I had lost my sparkle, and I knew what he meant. It was like all of my shine had been worn away and I was now a duller version of myself. I had become my own shadow. It felt as if I was going through the motions on auto-pilot. The pills took the emotions away, making me apathetic and indifferent. I stopped caring about how I looked, what I said or how I behaved. I just wasn't bothered.

Although we liked the house we were living in, we found life in an established village quite stifling. There was always a drama unfolding and some of the villagers didn't speak to others. It was draining. That said, we were very friendly with a few couples and would hold dinner parties at our houses. I was very skilled at painting on the smiles and being the life and soul on these occasions. It was always an act and I pulled it off each time. Years of practice paid off, I guess.

Despite my inability to control my food intake or indeed my mood, I continued to do well on the work front. I gave it my all and appeared to be recognised as competent in every role I undertook. After the contract finished in Bingley, I secured another one and this time it was in Northampton. Before I started it, we managed to find the time to move to a lovely location, in the middle of farmland on the outskirts of a small village. We'd bought a fabulous house and I had a contract that paid brilliantly and just half an hour from home.

Things were looking up.

On my first day I also realised that the leader of operation had been my boss in a previous organisation. Initially, I felt embarrassed seeing him again because at this stage I was bigger than I had ever been. He didn't seem to notice, and if he did, he didn't say anything. Working for him again was great. He had always been supportive of my style and approaches and we set about improving the operations successfully. I enjoyed the project immensely. It didn't have an impact on the depression, though. I was still in its tight grip.

I continued to exist in the fog.

And then one day I just said 'enough'.

I stopped taking the pills.

This is something doctors warn against, but I didn't care about that. I wanted to 'feel' again, to stop being so numb and indifferent! My moods were all over the place during this period and I struggled to hold it together at work and home. I would pick fights with Martin, snap at the children and I'd feel impatient at work. At the end of each day I'd get in the car and once on the road, I'd scream at the top of my lungs to release the amassed emotions.

And then I'd eat.

Mundane tasks would feel insurmountable. When it snowed one morning, the unrealistic level of panic I felt at the prospect of driving to work was ridiculous. Everything had to be spotless, too. If there was a thing out of place at home I'd feel uneasy and restless. I'd spend evenings sorting through the children's playroom organising everything into boxes and containers and then I'd be freaking out internally if they messed it up. I was imploding and just didn't know what to do or where to turn.

I was sitting with a lady at the office, showing her how to do the new process I'd designed. She was a lovely, cheerful lady and as I usually do, I got chatting to her about her life outside of work. I have a genuine interest in people that stretches way beyond their role at work and I wanted to learn more about her. She told me about her children and I shared stories about mine.

'They'll be thrilled when the new one arrives' she said, patting my tummy gently.

It took a few moments to register that what her comment actually meant. I gulped back the familiar feeling of shame.

'Oh, I'm not pregnant, I'm just fat,' I blurted out as confidently as I could, putting on a fake smile. This self-deprecation felt like the most appropriate response – but I was dying on the inside. I shot a glance around the office to see how many people might have heard. I felt like the room was spinning around me as my head processed what was happening.

'I'm so sorry,' she said, visibly embarrassed about this faux pas, 'it must be that dress you are wearing'.

It wasn't the dress, it was my body.

I did look six months pregnant and it was no wonder she had thought it. I left the office within ten minutes of her making that comment telling her I had a meeting to attend. I hurried to the carpark and once safely in the confines of my car, I released the flood gates, allowing the tears to flow and living through the emotions. I sobbed and sobbed as I drove towards home. I'd left work far too early and had to text the boss to say I'd been sick and so had to leave in a hurry. When I arrived home, I was a complete mess, face streaked with tears, nose streaming and head pounding. I ran straight upstairs without acknowledging the nanny or the children.

I stood in front of the mirror. I pulled at the fat that covered my tummy and thighs.

'Look at the state of you' I said to myself with vicious disgust.

Something had to give.

I didn't share the ordeal with Martin but that evening I researched diet plans on the internet and told him I was going to try something new to lose some weight. By now he was used to me trying new diets; he simply said I should do what makes me happy and that he would support me in it. I ordered a cocktail of pills, carb blockers, fat blockers and appetite suppressants and signed up to a company called Diet Chef. This was a meal plan that provided three meals and a snack for each day of the week. The meals were vacuum-sealed and could be stored in the cupboard and would be heated in a microwave for a few minutes.

A few days later, a box of pre-made meals arrived together with an itinerary when I should eat them. The box contained enough food for a month and I paid £199 for the privilege. The various pills cost over £75 - I kept these hidden so that Martin wouldn't think I'd gone mad. I ate the meals and took a cocktail of the pills each day for less than a week before the binge urges set in. I just couldn't help myself. The desire to fill the emptiness was too great, even though I didn't even know what the emptiness was about anymore. I had a loving husband, gorgeous children, a great income and a lovely home. It made no sense.

One of the things that was interfering with my wellbeing was the continued need for approval and an ever-growing insistence on perfection. This was extending to my children and I was noticing that Finley would get mad with himself if he didn't get things right first time, to the point where he wouldn't even attempt some things in the first place. He hated getting dirty and thus didn't enjoy playing football. Coral was conscious about food and was already talking about her 'fat tummy', clearly mimicking what she had overheard from me. These things contributed to the expansion of the void which I 'happily' filled with food. Most of the first month's Diet Chef' food had remained untouched when I threw them out several months later.

Another epic failure.

Next, I experimented with hypnosis in a desperate bid to get my eating under control. Given the success I'd had giving up smoking with a 'how to give up smoking book', I thought the same approach might work. I read several books, listened to recordings and even paid £75 per session for three sessions with a lady who claimed to make me see food differently. She had me imagining myself surrounded by a pink bubble and floating along a line going out into my future. Alas, none of it worked. It didn't work because I didn't want it to work. My mind was closed to the prospect I could conquer the food demons because I was reliant on them. I had committed whole-heartedly to giving up smoking. My relationship with food was a tougher nut to crack. I wanted to escape its strangling clutches but I had no idea how to exist without it.

My contract was nearing completion and I was offered another via a consulting firm I'd known for a long time. The contract was short, just six weeks and it was in Warwick, about an hour's drive from the house. The piece of work required a review of cleaning operations. This was a scary prospect as I didn't know the first thing about cleaning, having always worked in financial services. I decided to take the risk. I wasn't going to pass on the opportunity like I did back on the RAF expedition.

I met with the team on a sunny Monday afternoon in April 2013. At this point I weighed over 19 stones and felt sluggish and uncomfortable in my skirt, top and jacket, all of which were too small but I was relishing the challenge of getting stuck into something new. I was due to work until midnight to observe the cleaning team in action and look for opportunities. My size hindered this process immensely. My feet and knees ached and I was hot and annoyed, moving from floor to floor with the cleaning operatives. After a few days struggling physically with the project, I was about to have another 'that's it, enough' moment.

The previous weekend I'd travelled up North to see my beloved Grandad. He was still the light of my life and my hero. I loved him dearly and we were still as close ever. Despite an extremely healthy lifestyle throughout his 81 years, Grandad had been battling cancer for over two years. He'd lost so much weight he was a shadow of his former self and knowing he was weakening, I wanted to spend time with him. We had a lovely afternoon chatting about old times. I was glad to reminisce and look back at a time when I had been happy as a child. I had always been happy when he was there. As I was leaving, Mum took some photographs of us together and it was these photographs that provided the wake-up call I needed. I looked enormous and this gave me the kick I needed to search for a personal trainer online.

I met the trainer a few days later and we discussed what he was looking to achieve with me. He took measurements and I was mortified to establish that my waist circumference was 52 inches and each thigh measured 28 inches. Not sure which one was more embarrassing: my sudden awareness of these figures or him knowing about them! He gave me a sheet which outlined what I should eat. It followed Paleo principles (basically as non-processed and natural as possible) and felt quite doable. It stung when he said that before long I wouldn't need to wear tent-like dresses; I told myself he was trying to motivate me.

We booked a session for the following day and I decided to call him The Terminator. I worked with him for five weeks and lost 21lbs. He would weigh me every week – I didn't use any laxatives, salt water, fasting or anything similar this time - and he was always thrilled with my progress, which of course appealed to me and fuelled my need for approval. He had me pushing tyres around the garden, dangling from the TRX and bear crawling. It always felt like an extreme effort and I would defiantly refuse to do a lot of the things he asked of me, not being used to pushing my body to that level. The exercises that I did follow through on had a clear effect on my physique. I felt better in my clothes and people from the cleaning team started to notice the changes.

On 14th June, five weeks after I'd last seen him, Mum called at 9.30 PM.

'Grandad is poorly. He's telling you to hurry up', she said.

My heart sank. I left immediately and drove the 3 hours to his home. The 18 hours that followed were extremely difficult. He was in so much pain, struggling to catch his breath, laying there helplessly. This was peppered with moments of joy when he would open his eyes and smile or tap his fingers to the music that was playing on low in the background.

As the final hours of his life loomed, I was struggling to hold it together. I was desperate to binge to numb the extreme sense of loss I was already feeling. I kept taking trips to the kitchen to find biscuits or make sandwiches that I'd eat quickly in the bathroom. I didn't want to be doing this but I couldn't stop it. I made sandwiches for everybody else and Mum got short with me saying 'I'm not hungry, this isn't the time for food'. I totally understood that for anybody normal this would be the response and of course I then felt ashamed of myself and ate most of the sandwiches on my own to block it out. At times like this when food was the last thing on most people's minds, it was the first thing on mine.

When Grandad took his last breath, I was holding his hand and I was overwhelmed with emotion. It was the most devastatingly beautiful moment I had experienced. This beautiful man, who had given me every opportunity in life and taught me how to strive and achieve whilst remaining humble and kind, had left me, forever. A piece of me died with him that day.

This moment was followed by strange sense of calm and despite the curtains being drawn, the room seemed to be filled with light. An hour later, as the undertakers carried his body from the house, I felt him with me. All around me family members were grieving and yet I didn't cry another tear that day. I felt a sense of peace and I knew he would always be by my side.

When Mum and I arrived back at her house, she switched on the radio and the Eurhythmics song 'There Must Be an Angel' was playing on the radio. I looked at my Mum and she suddenly looked like a little girl. My Grandad was her everything, having brought her up alone from the age of ten when her Mum, my Nan, had left the family home to be with her Millionaire. She was exhausted from the months of caring for him and broken from the grief.

The funeral was a tough day and I struggled to get the words out when I stood and delivered the eulogy. The sight of the coffin and the realisation that this meant I wouldn't see him again suddenly hit me and the tears flowed as I read the piece I'd prepared. Mum was incredible and graceful that day and I was immensely proud of her, as Grandad would have been.

And whereas one story ended, another continued.

When the cleaning project concluded, I remained with the same company. They asked me to pick up another project looking at security which was based in Northampton and therefore very close to home again. I settled into this quickly, but was back on a slippery slope, finding the Paleo principles hard to maintain. Catching up with my old friend McDonald's was just so much easier. The grief was knocking at my door and I was struggling to find the motivation. This meant when the weekly weigh in was looming, I would either go back to starving myself or I'd cancel the session. The weight was creeping up again and I was using every excuse in the book. One day the trainer was due for a session and he didn't turn up. I text him but he didn't reply and I didn't hear from him again. The Terminator gave up on me, because once again I had given up on myself.

I stopped exercising, but didn't want to end up back up over 19 stones; so I was back at it, searching for a quick-fix answer to my battle with the bulge. I continued to take the pills and experimented with the 5:2 diet. This meant eating normally for 5 days of the week and taking in just 500 calories on the other two days. The trouble with that was my 'normal' was not in line with most peoples. My 'normal' included 2000 calorie binges on top of my usual daily intake of food. I tried to get back into Slimming World again, managed to lose a bit more weight and felt good for a short while.

December 2013 brought the completion of the security project. I'd managed to improve the operational performance significantly and got myself a good reputation with the leaders. The security firm was part of a much larger group which employed over 50,000 people in the UK. As the project was concluding, the Managing Director for one of the divisions, asked me if I would consider a role as Business Excellence Director for the support services division which included cleaning, security and facilities management. I'd built strong relationships with the leaders of security business already and I felt part of their team. I jumped at the opportunity and got ready for a January start.

Over Christmas, I indulged heavily as per usual, eating everything and anything. On Christmas Day alone, I must have consumed over 5000 calories – I was stuffed more than the turkey! I loved Christmas and spending quality time with the children. It was even more special knowing that I'd got a secure job starting a week or so later. In between Christmas and New Year, I felt ill and couldn't put my finger on what was wrong. I thought the sickness might be due to eating excessive amounts of rich food, so I tried to cut down and ate hardly anything for a few days.

On 30th December I found out I was pregnant. I couldn't believe it.

Five days into my new job in early January, I lost the baby.

This was the second miscarriage I'd had, having one a few months after giving birth to Coral. Being so new to the job, I didn't take any time off. I simply buried the feelings, pretending I was okay and used pain killers to deal with the pain, explaining to a few colleagues at work that I'd had a small procedure carried out which was causing me to be in pain. And, as usual, I used food as my crutch.

I weighed 19 stones and 5lbs when I signed up to the Cambridge Diet. It was a similar concept to the meal replacement shakes I'd tried previously and I told myself I would commit to it for a few weeks to help me lose a stone. I had to go to the Consultant's house to be weighed and collect the milkshakes and bars for the week ahead. The lady was warm and friendly and explained that she wasn't on the plan at that time but she said it had worked well for her in the past.

I was pleased to see that the milkshake came ready mixed in tetra style cartons which meant they would fit in well with my working day. The diet meant I would be consuming just 600 calories a day again. I stuck to the plan for three weeks and managed to lose over a stone in weight which I was delighted about. Beyond this, I struggled. I tried a hybrid approach of having a Cambridge plan shake for breakfast and then salad for lunch and dinner, but the lack of calories and usual shame triggers meant I was soon incorporating binges.

I was living a double life.

At work, I'd developed strong friendships with my peers and we would often have nights out, during which I would always opt for the healthiest meal on the menu. I couldn't let my colleagues suspect I had a poor relationship with food, could I? And that was even though I was wearing size 20 dresses.

Going into work was a real pleasure. Despite being bigger, I was putting lots of effort into the way I presented myself. I spent a small fortune on clothes, shoes and bags and would wear new outfits every week. I received compliments from my colleagues about the way I dressed and I seemed to be doing a great job at hiding the mess I called my body that existed underneath my shiny new outfits.

If only they knew of the constant turmoil that was going on inside their apparently happy-go-lucky colleague, who smiled easily and laughed generously while the cruel Merry-Go-Round of self-criticism and self-doubt seemed never ending.

Chapter Seven

In November 2014, I got a text message from the Company's MD that said I should be at the office the following morning for a meeting. Confused, I rang a few of my fellow colleagues and established we had all received the same message. We tried to understand what that might mean. I was worried about it and instantly calmed my nervousness by stopping at the service station and buying two family sized bars of dairy milk chocolate which I ate on the way home. I discussed the text message and my accompanying sense of foreboding with Martin and he said whatever it was, we would find a way through it.

The next morning, I arrived at the office, and the first thing I noticed was the car belonging to the Chief Executive Officer parked outside. I then saw the Group HR Director in reception and knew something was amiss. The MD for our division was in the executive suite when I arrived and as I took a seat at my desk, he joked about his golf swing and demonstrated the action of hitting the ball. I took this to be a positive sign. He was jovial, so surely nothing bad was going to happen.

The leadership team was called into the boardroom and the MD, CEO and HR Director were sitting in a line at the head of the table. The MD explained that he was leaving the business and was looking forward to a break before finding a new challenge. He thanked us for our hard work before handing over to the CEO. He explained that the support services division was being merged with the catering division and that the Operations Directors for each of those businesses were safe. It meant that while three of my colleagues were ok, the rest of us who held positions in the support functions, were put at risk. We were told that we would each have an individual meeting later that day with the Group HR director.

I could feel the emotion building inside me. I loved my job and this felt like the ultimate rejection. I'd never been in this position before and I really did not like it. My first instinct was to get outside so I could cry without my colleagues seeing me. I called Martin who was his usual beautiful reassuring self and said we would go for a dinner that evening and talk it through. Next, I rang my mentor who ran a consulting firm and he assured me he could give me work straight away. I began to feel a little calmer about the situation. I went back into the building and found some of my colleagues in the staff restaurant. We discussed the shocking nature of the announcement and its impact. As we delved into the details, we slowly unpicked the last few months and recognised the signs of this coming.

I was desperate to eat.

'God, I need chocolate,' was something I never said in front of people. Until now.

One of my colleagues, got up, hurriedly bought me a Kit-Kat and I ate it in front of them all, not really caring, just needing the numbing effect.

I had my meeting with the HR Director, and I was told that I would be in competition with a guy who had been in the business for 30 years. Realistically, I knew that the business wouldn't pay redundancy to somebody who'd been in the business for 30 years over somebody who had less than a year's service. The conversation was pointless.

I decided to take matters into my own hands. I rang the MD for the Catering Division and asked for a meeting with him. I also rang the MDs of other divisions in the company. I had several meetings over the next week or so and a few weeks later found myself sitting next to the Catering Division MD at a Christmas party, having convinced him to give me a role as Operations Excellence Director alongside the guy with the 30 years' service who would continue as Business Excellence Director. I was given a team of 12 and we set about making things happen.

I did well in this role and was respected by the MD. I liked him, too, and worked hard to deliver and to impress him that way. A few months after joining his team, he told me that the Business Excellence Director was leaving and he wanted me to take on all his responsibilities, including marketing and culinary development as well as customer experience and systems – all of which I had no idea about at the time. I jumped at the chance and though I felt totally daunted at the prospect I was confident in my ability to succeed. I worked extremely long hours to fit everything in and couldn't have been readier for my August holiday in Lanzarote.

Flying was always a bind. I could just about fasten the seat belt around my middle and felt embarrassed that the tray wouldn't move all the way to the down position because of my tummy. My ankles would swell during the flight and I'd spend most of the time eating. I'd buy large bags of peanut M&M's and boxes of Pringles at the airport and eat the hours away until we landed.

Holidays always brought me down to earth with a bump and would inevitably end in tears. I'd have to get my flesh out and it always felt excruciatingly painful to do so – emotionally and physically - and I would grow increasingly anxious each morning, trying on different outfits and trying to squeeze my tummy into shorts. The complex that we stayed in had a small patio area directly outside our villa and the garden led onto a shared pool area with sun loungers framing it. I had brought swim dresses with me and several sarongs and if I was venturing beyond the patio I would wrap the sarong around my middle.

Martin would bring a sun lounger onto the patio so I didn't need to sunbathe with the other holiday makers. I felt so self-conscious about my size and that was only amplified when comparing myself to other women. One lady in particular – her name was Fiona - had a stunning body. She had two children and yet was super slim with a lovely tan; you wouldn't know she had been pregnant at all. I would often see her in the morning, popping out for a run while I was stuffing my face with a chocolate croissant. I would watch her with envy as she jumped around in the pool playing volleyball with her children, wearing a tiny bikini, whilst I was stuck to the sun lounger, not wanting to move or draw attention to myself. I wasn't engaging in playing games with my children in the way I longed to do and instead would munch through large bags of crisps and huge baguette sandwiches. I'd then squeeze my bloated tummy into a dress and eat a three-course meal in the evening.

On returning home a weigh-in revealed that I had gained nearly a stone in two weeks and I was tipping the scales at almost 17 stones. My work clothes were bursting at the seams and in desperation I made a call to the Cambridge Consultant and collected some meal replacements from her that afternoon. Within a week, I'd lost ten pounds and felt a lot better, being less bloated.

I was further cheered up when I was asked by my boss to pick up responsibility for Strategy. This meant another string to my bow and I started to work much more closely with the MD and I learned a lot.

With work going well, I decided to try and make an effort to exercise again, having seen how amazing Fiona had looked on holiday. A Google search helped me to find a personal trainer in the area and I booked an appointment with him. His name was Del Wilson.

Del arrived at the house and I warmed to him immediately. He was quiet and humble and didn't make me feel bad about my size. He talked about the types of workouts he would design and that these would be focused around kettlebells and rowing, his two favourite things. Del competed in kettlebell competitions and was the world champion in the veteran class. He certainly didn't look his age, which at that point was 49. He explained that he wouldn't be able to help me with nutrition because he wasn't trained in this so I decided I would follow the paleo principles and once again set off with gusto.

The first sessions were hard. I would wear large t-shirts and tracksuit bottoms and by the end of the session I'd be bright red. I hated the noise that my breathing made and would regularly complain about this, insisting we had music playing to disguise my breathing. Every week Del would ask me what I weighed and at first I was able to report that the weight was coming off. I got below 16 stones for the first time in years, but as with so many occasions before, this was short-lived and I spent the next few months losing and gaining weight. I persevered with the exercise, though, and became stronger as time progressed. I slowly realised that exercising meant I could eat without gaining too much weight and whilst I wasn't always committed to the idea of a workout prior to it, I always felt great afterwards.

I was thrilled when I was able to complete a 5000-metre row. This was a battle of will, and I was determined to complete it even though I was gasping most of the way through and had blisters on my hands at the end. I did it and managed to do so within 26 minutes. I was also becoming very good at kettlebell lifting and found I could lift heavy weight for prolonged periods of time, managing six minutes of continual clean and press lifts with a 14kg bell. Sadly, I was not applying the same level of commitment and drive to the eating side of the things and continued with my dangerous cycle of starving, bingeing, dieting and taking fat reducing pills in an effort to lose weight. I snapped at Del one evening when he asked if I'd had success on the scales that week.

'I am not going to lose weight, ok?' I said with an icy tone.

He never asked me again.

One Sunday, Del suggested we try a bleep test to assess my fitness. This essentially meant running set distances and reaching the finish line before the bleep. The bleep would get quicker over time meaning I would need to run progressively faster. I wasn't overly enamoured with the idea because I detested running. I was too big to run and my belly and breasts would jump up and down, making me feel self-conscious. Del said he would run it with me and my competitive side kicked in, so I gave it my all.

I'd reached level 4 and was almost done when my foot got caught in a divot in the lawn and I felt my ankle snap.

The pain was instant, but the panic about it was the main problem. I have never been good with pain and I was immediately overwhelmed by it. Martin was out with the children and Del did his best to calm me down. I managed to hop into the house by holding his shoulder and by the time we got there, my ankle was already enormous. I spent the day doing ice and elevation routines, convinced it would just be a sprain. The next morning my foot was badly bruised and swollen to three times its size. I reluctantly went along to the hospital. An X-ray revealed that I'd chipped a bone and the doctor confirmed that the tendons were severely damaged. I was gutted. I was due to host a James Bond-themed Awards Ball, organised as a thank you for the leaders and managers in the division at work. I'd spent months with my team arranging every detail of the event, including outfit planning - a very expensive dress and some super high heels, so it compounded my utter frustration at the injury.

As well as the awards dinner, there was also a conference which my team had worked hard to ensure everything would go to plan. I'd booked the Olympic medallist rower, Greg Searle as the motivational speaker. He and I had spoken at the same conference a few years prior, and being honest, I missed most of his talk because I was panicking about my own talk and kept going over the details in my head. This time around I was determined to hear what he had to say. Greg is very tall and was towering over most of the team. I was hobbling around on crutches and wearing jeans, converse and a pale pink blazer. Lots of people had told me I looked great that day, including Greg but I remember feeling incredibly embarrassed that I was fat and unfit standing in front of an Olympian. When I heard him speak, his words penetrated my soul like nothing else had for a long time. He talked about the commitment needed to succeed and how often it demanded sacrifices but the rewards were worth it. He talked about changing coaches and initially how hard it was to alter his tried and tested regime but how in the end, it had improved his performance for the better. For some reason, in that moment, I translated what he said into my own life, thinking about needing to radically change the way I approached weight loss, because so far, whilst it had delivered short term results, I didn't ever get to the end goal, sustainable weight loss.

On the night of the event I swapped my heels for flip flops and used crutches to hobble around. Not my idea of the dream ball footwear, but the night was successful and everybody seemed to enjoy it. Despite the painful ankle, I did as well. I was blown away when I first saw the martini bar and the amazing 007 themed room. It looked stunning and the team had totally transformed the restaurant. I hosted the awards with a colleague who is a complete comedian, and we bounced off each throughout the evening. Despite going to bed at midnight, the next day I was exhausted and my foot was swollen and sore. On the way home I tucked into the chocolates I had been given and by the time I'd got home, they were finished.

Exercising was an obvious challenge and I had to focus on upper body and abs work with Del. My eating was all over the place as usual and by the close of 2015, despite the consistent training, I weighed over 16 stones and most of the hard work over the last four months had been undone.

I had also resigned. It was one of my in-the-moment-choices which had occurred at the December Exec Meeting. There'd been a number of decisions made during previous months which were not aligning to my own ambitions or my personal values. Throughout the morning as I listened to the various topics, I decided I would leave. I didn't have a job to go to, but I knew it was the right thing to do.

At break time, the MD asked me what was wrong. I was never adept at hiding my feelings and it often showed in my expression. I said I would speak to him the next day; he didn't let go and I eventually disclosed that I was resigning. During another break we spoke about it further – he tried to convince me that I was making the wrong decision. However, I stayed true to my word and submitted my written resignation the next day. He barely spoke to me again after that day and the final few weeks before my gardening leave were dreadful. I hated that he felt I'd let him down. Whilst I don't regret my decision, I do feel sad that my relationship with the MD was damaged as a result. He had always championed me and I learned a great deal from him. I hope one day I will put it right. I also miss some of the colleagues I worked alongside because in such a fast-paced business, bonds are created which are strong.

Within a few weeks of resigning, I'd accepted a position of Managing Consultant with a consulting firm that I had been a client of for many years. The MD had been my mentor and I liked and respected him. The assessment process had been challenging and had included several meetings with the various Directors and a half-day session with an occupational psychologist. I worried what she might make of me and whether she would pick up on my addictive behaviours.

She recommended me without any advisory notes. Phew!

I spent Christmas with my family and it was beautiful. My parents, sister and niece spent four days at our house and Martin's parents and children came for New Year. As always, eating and drinking was the main activity and I attempted to eat my bodyweight in chocolate. I bought huge boxes of posh chocolates from Hotel Chocolat and actually had to order twice because I'd eaten the first order before Christmas had even arrived, secretly taking the empty boxes to work with me to dispose of them. Despite eating huge amounts of food in front of my family, I also chose to do some secret munching, too, fuelling my habitual need by eating cake and chocolate in the bathroom. Once again, I turned to laxatives, carb blockers and fat binders throughout the season to try and control my weight.

Another year had been spent battling my demons. I was 37 years of age and felt utterly beaten once more. Stuck. Powerless to the overwhelming feeling that I just wasn't enough.

But.

Life was about to change in ways that I could never, ever have imagined.

The Sun was finally about to appear.

Autobiography in Five Chapters

Portia Nelson

I

I walk down the street.
There is a deep hole in the sidewalk
I fall in.
I am lost...
I am hopeless.
It isn't my fault.
It takes forever to find a way out.

II

I walk down the same street.
There is a deep hole in the sidewalk.
I pretend I don't see it.
I fall in again.
I can't believe I'm in the same place.
But it isn't my fault.
It still takes a long time to get out.

III

I walk down the same street.
There is a deep hole in the sidewalk.
I see it is there.
I still fall in...It's a habit
My eyes are open; I know where I am;
It is my fault.
I get out immediately.

IV

I walk down the same street.
There is a deep hole in the sidewalk.
I walk around it.

V

I walk down another street.

PART TWO

A BIG GIRL'S JOURNEY TO LEAN

I believed that my pain would be the source of my trauma forever, then suddenly I realised this one thing: All of my scars and all of my wounds were also the source of my understanding. I wasn't breaking; I was being built.
Jenna Galbut

Chapter Eight

Some people call it a 'Moment of Clarity', others an 'Epiphany' - a single second when your life changes for the better. When the path ahead opens up and you get to see a view that has been obscured for most of your life. Sounds great, doesn't it? My ah-ha! moment wasn't quite like this. It would take a little while for the penny to drop, the door to open and for the view to open out ahead of me. Looking back, I think it was more of a slow exhale. The burden I'd been carrying around with me had simply become too much for me to bare but again, I wasn't aware of this. I was about to catch up with myself, however. It was the 21st January 2016 and the start of something magical.

Prepping like a boss' The Body Coach called it. I'd been in the kitchen for three hours and had used every pot, pan and utensil I owned, cooking foods I'd never heard of before. I was faced with a mountain of plastic containers filled with prepared meals for the week ahead and an even greater mountain of washing up as a result. Though exhausted from the relentless task, I felt a sense of accomplishment. I'd prepared eight different meals in multiple portions, and had painstakingly weighed every single ingredient to ensure I followed the plan to the letter. I'd only have to heat things through rather than scratch cook for the remainder of the week and I was set up for success. The most striking thing for me, was the sheer volume of food I was allowed to eat in just one meal. I stared at a bag of raw spinach, weighing 200 grams and realised that a whole bag would be consumed with each meal. How on earth would I manage all this spinach in one go?

My friend Nicola had suggested we sign up for The Body Coach plan in December 2015. It was a clean eating and exercise plan spread over 90 days which promised amazing transformations - how many times have I heard that before. I'd never heard of its creator, Joe Wicks. He was – and still is - an Instagram sensation, but at that time I didn't have an Instagram or Twitter account and was oblivious to his fame. He'd written a recipe book called 'Lean in 15' which was based on snappy cooking demonstrations he uploaded onto Instagram. His personality is his unique selling point. His boisterous, upbeat messages were highly infectious and he'd built a huge following as a result. Joe had since devised the 90daySSS plan - shift shape and sustain - and I visited his website several times over a number of weeks wondering if it was all too good to be true. I actually thought it might be a scam set up to extract money from gullible and vulnerable people! How wrong I was.

I was desperate to lose weight yet again and thought I might as well give it a try. I tried everything else, why not add another to the list.

I had to submit three photographs of myself, a front, a side and back view of my body in underwear or a bikini. Great joke. There was no way I was exposing my flesh to faceless strangers; and so, I took a selfie wearing pyjamas and submitted that instead and soon I received the plan via email. It contained almost one hundred pages of information.

I printed it out and spent a few days trying to understand the content. This plan was to cover the first 30 days and was referred to as 'cycle one'. There was a short section that outlined the exercise requirements and then a longer section with a myriad different recipes. Some were to be eaten only after a workout and the rest were for all other times of the day. Snacks were also prescribed alongside several different vitamins. The one word that was standing out all the way through was spinach (Popeye would've loved this plan)!

It struck me immediately how different this plan was, and at that time, 'different' equalled 'difficult'. I kept putting the document into a drawer because it felt insurmountable before taking it out again the next day and have another flick through the information, trying to conjure up the courage to start. I was so consumed by the fact I might fail again, I couldn't find the will to begin.

Eventually, I succumbed. I decided to start the plan on the first day of my Gardening Leave. I'd have a few months off work to really give it my all this time! I was required to input my starting measurements and bodyweight and at the same time I even submitted revised photographs, this time with me wearing my underwear. I asked Martin to take the photographs for me; sucking in my tummy

77

as hard as I could as he took each one. When I looked at the images on my phone screen I couldn't believe my eyes. I had rolls of fat adorning my back and cellulite decorating my upper legs like swathes of hideous wood-chip wallpaper. My upper arms were puckered with layers of unsightly skin and despite knowing I was big, I was not prepared for the cold reality of it. The sad thing was, I'd already lost over three stones in weight so I could only imagine how much worse I must have looked at my biggest. I struggled to understand how Martin could find me attractive. Even my legs, which I had always thought were my best asset, looked a lot bigger than I'd realised.

This could have been a severe shame trigger, plummeting me in to the depths of a binge.

This time something snapped.

I became angry with myself and decided something drastic had to change. I'd had these moments several times before but this time it felt different. I'd hit the bottom of the pit and I suddenly felt a fierce determination to rise. I thought about my 9-year-old self and all she'd endured in her little life. I told her to hold on tight. We were going to figure this out together. I decided to approach this new challenge with the same determination as I applied at work when successfully securing fantastic roles. The thing that appeared to be at the heart of this success was self-belief and positivity. If I could apply these principles at work, I wondered what would happen if I applied them in a personal capacity to help me gain control of my poor relationship with food?

I was starting an exciting new job, I knew that I was talented and successful and yet I never felt worthy and this needed to change. I looked around at the most successful people I knew and realised they all had one thing in common - they took health and wellbeing seriously. If they could do it, why couldn't I? Why couldn't I be one of those women who loved exercise and drinking green juice? It suddenly all seemed so simple. The only thing that was standing in my way was me. I had to believe I was worthy. I needed to change the way I was thinking. I needed to start thinking like a slim, healthy, fit person, and then I had to behave like one.

And so, the journey began. I buckled up and started to apply the 'Fake it till you make it' philosophy. An online search revealed a book on Positive Thinking by the author Justin Albert and while I wasn't a fan of so called 'self-help' books, this one was short, so I gave it a go. I powered through the book in an evening. It set out a practical strategy for changing the mind-set, using a number of tools, one of which was self-affirmation. This was a short statement or mantra that I could repeat to myself throughout the day, therefore training the unconscious part of my brain to pick up on my more positive voice and start to believe it. In essence, 'what we think we become'. I wrote some affirmations in my journal and started to practice them every day, including a favourite one I still use daily:

I enjoy exercising regularly and eating healthily to give me the body I deserve and desire.

With the meal plan in my hand, I set out to purchase the ingredients required in the recipes, turning my kitchen counter into a colourful Borough Market stall display (with a hefty price tag of £170!) as I'd needed to buy things I had never used before. I foolishly planned a menu for the week that included twelve different recipes and as my protein allowance was high, I would often eat two chicken breasts for one meal, it was an expensive affair. I would learn over time that there were ways to reduce this initial ridiculous spend, by shopping at Aldi and cooking a smaller range of meals using options such as omelettes and turkey mince recipes.

Sundays would become my dedicated prep day. I would spend a few hours each week cooking meals for the week ahead. This kept me on track and meant I was never tempted to opt for a takeaway when I couldn't be bothered to cook after work, and rather amazingly, 'prepping like a boss' made takeaway a more cumbersome option!

So that was the food side of things covered, next to tackle was the crucial element of exercise in The Body Coach Plan. I was introduced to 'HIIT', or High Intensity Interval Training to be precise, and although I'd been working out with Del, my personal trainer, since August and had increased my fitness slightly - nothing prepared me for this!

I'd tried to avoid cardio as much as possible and would strive to influence Del to stick with kettlebell workouts because I hated how my flesh would jiggle and how out of breath I would become if I was jumping around. I'd tell him my ankle was bothering me and, which was partially true, but it didn't mean I couldn't do cardio, it just meant we had to choose cardio carefully. However, with my newly found motivation, developing positive mind-set and a fierce desire to succeed, I was up for the HIIT sessions. Del suggested we do the workouts on the rowing machine to ensure I didn't put too much pressure on my joints, particularly my ankle. Rowing between 130 and 140 metres in 30 seconds was exhausting. I'd be gasping for breath and totally in need of the 60 seconds rest after each row. My face would be beetroot red and I would complain about the sound of my breath as I huffed and puffed like an old-fashioned locomotive.

Each session became a mental battle of mind over matter. 'It's only thirty seconds', I'd huff. 'Only five more sets to go', I'd puff through the sweat, recovering. After each session I could eat a refuel meal, loaded with carbohydrates and included one of my favourites, overnight oats, made with Manuka honey, berries and protein powder. The huge portion meant I would feel full for hours afterwards which was a new sensation for me, even though I had often devoured heaps of food before starting the plan. It made me aware that calorie does not equal calorie; a healthy meal full of nutritious substance fuelled my body incomparably more effectively than empty carbs consumed without a second thought.

I settled into a routine of eating three meals and two snacks per day and exercising five times per week. During the first thirty days, all of the meals I had to eat were made from a series of recipes that I could choose from throughout the week. The food measurements worked out for me - I didn't have to think too much, it was straightforward, easy and thus couldn't justify any excuses. Providing I weighed the ingredients precisely, I should lose weight. This felt counter-intuitive; the portions were so big I thought I'd be gaining weight rather than losing it. So many of us are programmed to think the only way to lose weight is to restrict calories yet this approach was encouraging eating an abundance of nutritious food. I'd travel everywhere with mountains of plastic nutritiously filled

80

tubs. If I was staying away in hotels for work, I would phone ahead and ask if I could store food in the fridges, stating that I had special dietary requirements, and they were all accommodating. The first few days went effortlessly – the novelty of the plan ensured the smooth sailing.

Then came day five.

You think you already know what's about to happen, right? I did too.

But not this time!

I dug deep and pushed through. Every fibre of my being was screaming 'cake!!!' because my body was craving sugar while my mind desired the usual numbing sensation it had been conditioned to receive. So, I applied the same deliberate practice of positive mental attitude to my eating as I did to exercise. Nothing was more important than this and after a few very tough weeks, I started to enjoy the new way of eating and the daily affirmations were taking effect. Boom. I saw the little nine-year-old me smiling back a little more often when I'd look in the mirror. 'You can do it!' she seemed to whisper.

Being off work on gardening leave, I had lots of time on my hands initially. I would take myself out for long walks in the fresh air. Despite not needing to get up early, I would find myself getting up at 6AM, pulling on tracksuit bottoms and a huge fur lined hoodie and going out into the dark morning. Whatever the elements had to offer, I would embrace it, walking at pace and practicing affirmations. Del had advised me that walking was a great way to burn fat which provided even greater will. At the end of each day my Fitbit would be registering over 15,000 steps - three times more than my usual working day step count!

I was burning fat and feeling awesome.

Nicola, who had started the plan alongside Lynsey, another friend of ours, set up a chat room on Facebook to compare notes. With me being a few weeks ahead of them, it was funny to listen to their initial thoughts on the plan. They were experiencing the same doubts, concerns and feelings as I had initially and it was lovely to be able to share my knowledge, advising them which meals were good, and, my most important advice, that 200 grams of spinach is a lot easier to stomach when wilted!

Lynsey told me about a Facebook group which was for people who were following the plan. It took me a few days to pluck up the courage, but eventually I decided to join. I was instantly hooked; it provided a platform of knowledge, tips and tricks for life on the plan and I was amazed at the transformation photos posted by people in the group. I felt a real sense of solidarity with these strangers.

Week three of the plan was a tough one for me. In the first week I'd lost a few pounds and then for the next two weeks nothing at all. I was starting to feel the rush of disappointment and couldn't understand where I was going wrong. I had followed the plan to the letter and this time I really had, yet it wasn't delivering results. As I had for most of my adult life, I was standing on the scales every day, sometimes twice until I read a post in the Facebook group which suggested that the scales were not a useful indicator of success on this type of plan and that that they should only be used once per month at the end of the cycle. As I continued to read through the posts, I found people were feeling the same as me and the other members on the page were reassuring them that this was normal. There was only one thing for it - I would ask Martin to hide the scales. I would no longer be negatively influenced by them, so I persevered with my daily affirmations and stuck to the plan.

On day 30, I woke up and was excited to take my measurements. I was thrilled when the tape measure told me that I'd lost 19 inches and 5 kilos! It had all happened in the final week and I couldn't believe it. There wasn't a cat in Cheshire smiling more than me! I was immensely proud of myself for surviving thirty whole days without a binge and even more so that I had stuck to the plan completely and eaten healthy, nutritious food.

When I studied the updated photos that Martin had taken I could see an immense difference.

Then the self-doubt started to creep in.

The image in the photos was still hideous. In that moment it felt like my efforts had been in vain. My inner voice was trying to convince me that I would never get the body I desired because I was so very far away from it.

I believed her.

I was at the foot of a very high mountain and needed a bottomless pit of energy to climb it. Even given the results after thirty days, I didn't know if I was able to muster it up. Feeling deflated, I wrote a half-hearted post on the Facebook page which stated that I'd completed cycle one and ONLY lost 5kg. I took a screen shot of the before and after measurements from the Body Coach website; out of shame, I cropped my actual weight out of the image. I didn't want anybody to know how heavy I was. Unlike most of the members who posted in the group, I didn't post my before and after photographs. I would be mortified if anybody ever saw these.

However, even being so low, I stayed strong in the moment of self-sabotage and didn't yield to a binge. This was transformational progress.

The response to my post was hugely encouraging with so many people taking the time to congratulate me and help me see the weight and inch loss in a positive light. This response lifted me; I guess it provided the external recognition I craved. At this point I hadn't recognised that a need for approval was one of my core stories, but I now realise that social media validation was a wonderful asset and an enabler to my early journey in the absence of my own self-belief.

I began to adapt to a new way of life. Of cultivating a new relationship with food and felt confident to make a few tailor-made adaptations to the plan. I already knew that pasta, rice and bread made me bloated and therefore avoided these, opting for oats, wraps and sweet potatoes instead. To mitigate any bloating, I drank peppermint tea and consumed lots of water to which I would often add a drop of sugar free squash, even though it wasn't included in the plan, I figured that since I had given up drinking six glasses of diet coke and several lattes each day, a few drops of squash should be perfectly acceptable.

The weight training introduced on cycle two was making a difference to my shape and I could feel muscle growing underneath the layers of fat and even though I would still get out of breath which I despised and would make me feel embarrassed in front of Del, I persevered. I was lifting heavier weights each week and this provided a sense of achievement as I documented my progress.

When Del wasn't around, I would put as much effort into my training as I did when he was with me because I recognised that missing a rep or two would slow down my progress and I would be the one who lost out. This gave me the drive to push through when I was getting tired or fed up with the high volume of repetitions. And of course, I always had my little cheerleader whispering in my ear.

When I reflect on my state of mind at this early stage in my journey, I am curious to try and understand what was so different to every previous attempt to stop binge eating. My honest belief is that I was thinking fundamentally differently. This was a forced practice of affirmation, positive thinking and visualisation and it was having a dramatic impact. This coupled with the dawning realisation that I could eat an abundance of nutritious, tasty food and not have to starve to lose weight, was giving me the drive to carry on. The Body Coach plan truly was a revelation to me and was a far cry from the low fat and very low-calorie diets that have dominated the market place for decades.

Midway through this second cycle I tried on a pair of jeans which I hadn't worn in a long time. I'd bought them in New York and I'd loved them when they fitted back then. To my surprise, on this occasion they fastened effortlessly; feeling delighted, I combined them with a V-neck sweater and red scarf and took a full-length selfie. Rather than looking round, I looked tall and elegant and whilst I was still heavy I didn't look 'fat'.

I posted my photo in the Facebook group with a caption explaining how happy I was. A few hours later Nicola sent me a message to say she had tweeted about my jeans success and the Body Coach had seen it and retweeted the message. I had no clue what any of that meant! Nicola suggested I should create a Twitter account and check it out for myself. Not knowing what I was doing, I set about trying to create a profile, which turned out quite intuitive and easy to do. Within a few minutes @coxange78 was live – not the most exciting or creative of handles, much to Nicola's dismay. She'd suggested I should go for 'The Lean Lady' because I delivered Lean improvement in a business capacity and was on a lean journey, but that didn't feel appropriate. I might practice Lean, but lean I was not.

Before I knew it, I was at the end of another thirty days and a weigh-in confirmed I had lost another 5kg. I had eaten mountains of food including carbohydrates which I'd always classed as the devil's food and yet the weight had fallen off once again. The photos, whilst still difficult viewing, revealed significant change. The fat that hugged my back like several rubber swimming rings, had been replaced by much smoother skin and my legs were shapely. This time I felt brave enough to post my progress pictures in the Facebook group. I'd been reading a book by Brene Brown called 'The Gift of Imperfection'; in it she described how in order to grow, we need to be prepared to be vulnerable and with that advice in mind, I found the courage to post my before and after cellulite-laden photographs in all of their glory. I was overwhelmed with the response. People were using words like 'phenomenal' and 'inspirational' and pointing out the reduction in back fat and how much more toned my legs looked. I was thrilled and it gave me the drive to carry on.

By the end of cycle three I'd lost another five kilograms and was feeling slimmer than I had felt in years. I was elated with the results of the ninety days. I'd lost 9.5 inches from my waist and 9 inches from my hips. I felt like a different person and had boundless energy. More than this though, I had escaped the seductive draw of the binge cycles and managed to complete the whole ninety days without eating anything that hadn't been prescribed in the plan. I'd powered through every workout like a stream train and I was feeling fitter with more energy and a newfound zest for life.

I submitted by final results to the Body Coach and posted in the Facebook group with the following testimonial:

GRADUATION
Wow, I've done it! 94 days and it's been mostly amazing.

My weight loss journey has been life long, with the most recent mission starting in 2013 weighing over 19 stones to now (yes, it's taken a while)

My colleague Nicola recommended TBC before Christmas and I signed up half-heartedly thinking it would be as ineffective as the 'protein world' fad diet we'd tried a few months before. How wrong I was! You get out what you put in so once the plan was in my hands I promised to give it my all.

WHAT I LOST

15 kgs
28.5 inches
Cellulite
Wobbly thighs
Back rolls
A wardrobe full of size 20 dresses
The heart sinking feeling when I look in the mirror
Big knickers
None of my cup size! Yes, I still have boobs 😄

WHAT I GAINED

Tons of support from my coach and the Facebook group
Inner Confidence (rather than outer confidence)
Size 12 jeans
Legs that I love, they are damn sexy!
Amazing skin
Education about fuelling the body
A love of weights
A home gym (spent too much!)
A body I can now see wearing a bikini for the first time ever

WHAT I DID

Training 100%
Had the odd square of choc or sweetie
150 crunches every day during c3
Walked 1000km during the 90 days
Took my rowing distance in 30 seconds from 131 to 152 metres
Gave up coffee and Coke
Abstained from alcohol
Drank sugar free squash with most of my water (slapped hand)
Found a love of peppermint tea
Had Lizi's granola 5 times a week

Tried to keep positive throughout
Used the FB group for support
Posted a lot on social media to stay accountable
Stopped weighing myself every day. Yay
Laughed a lot!

WHAT I DIDN'T DO
Eat bread or pasta ever
Take BCAA during cycle 3
A single burpee
Weigh things during cycle 3
Compare myself to others
Cry
Have cheat meals
Have post cycle days off
GIVE UP

I am totally and utterly thrilled with my results. Yes, I still have bingo wings and a tummy that needs lots of work but in 90 days the impact is overwhelming. I feel sassy, sexy, full of energy and damn proud of myself.

Tonight, I am going for a meal with my amazing husband and although I won't have alcohol, I am going to treat myself to affogato dessert. Then back on c3 tomorrow until SAS arrives which I intend to do until August.

I love Joe Wicks, I love the plan, I love my coach and I actually love Angela Cox! Thank you to the Body Coach for making it such an enjoyable ride.

What is clear from reading this testimonial is I was still not in a place mentally where I felt able to share how shocking my relationship with food had really been (note the lack of the word 'binge' in the post). It would take a while to get to that place.

I posted a short message on Twitter with the 'before' photo of me wearing a blue spotty dress, with a very shiny bloated face and large stomach and the 'after' photograph of me wearing a new dress and heels, looking healthy and more in proportion. My post on Facebook was so popular my phone notifications didn't stop all day. The post attracted more than one thousand likes and reading the comments felt quite surreal.

I went to bed that evening feeling as high as a kite. I'd managed to complete a plan that had delivered amazing results. I was feeling good and little did I realise it at the time, but life was about to get even more exciting!

Chapter Nine

I woke the next day and flicked through my phone to browse the usual applications. When I opened my Twitter account I was astounded to find four private messages from Joe Wicks himself. This was coupled with hundreds of other notifications that I was struggling to process while rubbing my eyes to make sure I was actually awake. Joe had written to me saying he had seen my transformation, read my testimonial and found it to be one of the most inspiring he had ever come across. He sent several messages because I wasn't responding and he was eager to share my photographs with his followers. I'd opted for an early night and had been oblivious that this had been occurring while I slept!

Impatient for a response from me, Joe had fired ahead and posted my photographs and testimonial in the Hall of Fame on his website which was linked to Instagram and Twitter. He sent me a final note: 'I hope you don't mind'. He said mine was the only transformation photograph he'd ever posted of a person wearing clothes rather than underwear and the response was crazy - it was the 'most liked' transformation to date. I was shaking as I hesitantly wrote back to him with a huge 'thank you'. He replied and we exchanged a few messages throughout the day - I really couldn't comprehend it. It was all very surreal. I signed up to Instagram using the same handle I used for Twitter (@coxange78) and spent some time reading through the hundreds of messages posted under my photographs on Joe's wall. Everybody was being so kind and supportive and I felt like I was in a whirlwind of success.

Fresh from this high, I signed up to the SAS plan which is a thirty-day rolling follow-on plan by the Body Coach. The SAS plan was similar to 90daysss and included weight training, HIIT workouts and set recipes to follow throughout the month. Joe asked me to keep him informed as to how I was getting on. Midway through the plan I wasn't happy with the results and was having another self-sabotage wobble. I thought I was consuming too much food on the plan and my weight loss had slowed down so I wrote to Joe and asked him for help. To his credit, he wrote back, gently telling me that my body needed the calories and I should stick with it. He confidently advised me to trust him, and the plan, and lift as heavy weights as I could manage.

Joe had launched an Instagram competition to celebrate having one million followers. I didn't know anything about it until I saw posts from people in the Facebook group saying they had won tickets. A few days after these posts I received a private message from Joe saying he would like to meet me and asking for my email address so he could send an invite to the party. To say I was thrilled was an understatement! I now had an opportunity to thank the man who had changed my way of thinking about food and I was beyond excited. I asked a lady from the Facebook group to join me as my guest. We'd never met before, but as soon as we did on the evening we got along straight away. She'd always supported my journey and had done equally well on the plan so I thought she deserved the treat. I'd travelled to London wearing skinny jeans which was a total first for me. I'd always avoided them believing they were un-flattering but I was learning to embrace new styles to go with my new body.

I bought a dress from Oasis for the party. It was a wrap dress with navy and white vertical stripes and was very striking. I felt amazing initially but once there I was slightly overwhelmed and a little uncomfortable. Most of the guests were much younger than me and certainly much slimmer, making me feel anxious and conscious about my size. Every fibre of my being was telling me to leave and although I hadn't touched a drop of alcohol since the turn of the year and it was now mid-May, I desperately wanted a gin & tonic to calm my nerves. I'd recognised that drinking alcohol would slow my progress so had avoided it so I once again resisted the urge and drank water instead.

The party was being held in a small bar in Soho and the two hundred guests crammed the space with little room to move. Joe had advised that the food being served would be of the junk variety, something he refers to as 'guiltee' food. There were burgers, chicken wings and garlic bread, cupcakes, popcorn and sweeties but I didn't eat anything and I wasn't remotely tempted. It was lovely to recognise some of the girls from the Facebook group who had inspired me with their amazing transformations, looking gorgeous. We chatted and compared stories about our time on the plan.

A smiley lady took to a raised platform at one end of the room and announced into the microphone that Joe Wicks would be arriving shortly. An eruption of excited screams filled the room. He was dressed in jeans with a striped t-shirt worn under a leather jacket and his trade-mark floppy hair fell softly around his face. He was immediately inundated with ladies lining up to talk to him and take selfies. I waited patiently, sipping on my water and trying to hold my tummy in, all the while practicing affirmations in my head. After ten minutes or so, Joe spotted me and said, 'it's Angela, give me a hug, you're amazing'. I was thrilled he had recognised me and we chatted for a few minutes before I gave him a present and a card by way of a 'thank you'.

My friend and I left the bar for a while to get some clean food from a restaurant across the road and I shared the selfies of Joe and me on Instagram and on the Facebook page where people began sharing my excitement. Returning to the venue, Joe and I had the opportunity to chat once more and I was touched to hear how much he loved my positivity and how well I had done completing the plan. He suggested it was inspiring lots of men and women to do the same. I felt a genuine sense of pride. Little 9-year-old me, beamed. We left the party well before midnight and I slept with a huge grin on my face. I'd met Joe Wicks, a genuine man with heaps of humility and a desire to help others. A week later he sent me a private message on Twitter to thank me for the card and the present and said the note I had written had touched him.

As I approached the end of the thirty-day SAS plan I posted in the Facebook group stating that I intended repeating the 90-day plan. This seemed to set hares racing and lots of people thought I was bonkers and they made it clear that the 90-day plan wasn't designed to be repeated. Even the team at Body Coach HQ couldn't tell me that it would work a second time, but I didn't care. Something inside me was telling me it was the right thing to do, so before I'd even submitted my SAS plan results, I signed up and paid for another 90-day plan, designed for my new body. I submitted the SAS results and had lost another 2kg. Once again Joe posted my photos on his pages -

this time he shared my Instagram handle with the caption 'Inspirational Woman Alert'. My phone went into meltdown and within half a day my Instagram follower-ship had increased by six thousand.

Whilst the vast majority of the comments on his post were positive and congratulatory, a couple however, weren't. This would be my first experience of trolling. It was sadly not my last and while Joe said I must ignore the haters, I found it difficult. I was being accused of faking my 'before' photographs and while a lot of people may have the resilience to brush this off, I struggled. It was all consuming and I couldn't focus on anything else.

The ultimate win in this situation however, is that I didn't turn to food. Fuelled by my progress, I felt strong enough to save myself from a binge. Once again, I remained stoic to my mission and instead, I appeased myself by writing to the people who had written the posts to tell them how they had made me feel. This would become a coping strategy for me for several months and one that overall served me well.

A lot of advice written about trolls states that you shouldn't respond to them, 'Don't feed a troll' they say. I soon learnt not to do this publicly but found that by writing to them directly it turned me into a real person in their eyes and this often derailed them. I am sure for some it provided entertainment too, but it made me feel better and I was able to let it go. In this instance one of the men I'd challenged was so hugely apologetic I actually ended up helping him for several months with his own lean journey.

And when I wasn't dealing with trolls or supporting others on their plans, my journey continued. I started to log my HIIT workouts in a journal upon starting the second 90-day plan. I would post a selfie in my exercise gear alongside a photo of the HIIT workout written in my journal. People in the Facebook group started to use my journal extracts for their own workouts and I started to receive positive comments, encouraging me to write them in a book!

The Trolls weren't so keen.

'I am sick of this! It's like the Angela show around here', it read one day under one of my Facebook posts in the group. Despite my daily affirmations, I was still very much in need of validation and I'd

92

become used to the praise I would get from others on the page just as I had when I was a child at school. The criticism would throw me off balance, every time. My immediate reaction was to stop posting, but I realised that sharing my journey was keeping me focused and honest therefore stopping might destabilise me. I kept quiet for a few days and my inner voice, Miss. Meddler, had a field day, trying her best to knock me off course, but I silenced her and told myself I deserved the right to share my story.

That weekend, a girl from the Facebook group asked me to set up my own page. She said she loved my workouts, but couldn't always find them amidst the hundreds of posts. I immediately responded with a note to express my doubts. I genuinely thought that nobody would follow, but she persisted and joked that I could have my own 'Angela Show' away from the Nay Sayers who lay in wait!

Could I do it, I wondered?

YES, yes I could!

All I needed to do was figure out how to set up a group. I emailed Sarah a few times and together we figured it out. I named the group. 'A Big Girl's Journey to Lean' was born. Hardly the catchiest name, in hindsight and I often get teased about how it doesn't exactly roll off the tongue, but it did explain what the group was about, which at that juncture, was a personal blog about my journey.

Once the page was set up, I posted about it in the other Facebook group and to my surprise, people started to join! By the end of the day, there was over one hundred members. Sarah agreed to be an Admin and two other ladies wrote to me and volunteered, too. I had an Admin Team made up of wonderfully supportive Sarah, kind hearted Lizzie and, while she was new to the plan, there was something about her I really liked - Natalie. Even at that stage I knew that I wanted a mixture of styles and personalities in our admin team and I was confident that between the four of us we could manage the page.

The confidence was short-lived and within days I was panicking slightly and feeling the pressure to perform like an acrobat at the circus. If all of these people had joined the group, I needed to give them something to read and connect with. I discussed the page with Martin that evening. He is always full of great ideas and helps me believe I can make things happen and while I have never been overly creative, I am strategic and thought if I could surround myself with the right people, I could turn ideas into something that can be delivered in reality. Martin suggested I should find a way to allow people to interact. I remembered how in the other group they had done something called Transformation Tuesday which had proved a hit. What I needed was a similar theme for each day of the week which would prompt people to share stories and support each other. The daily theme was born, and continues to this day.

Some themes are more successful than others. 'Share your Story Saturday' is always great and the stories will often be heart wrenching, joyous or both. 'Set a goal Sunday' challenges people to focus on the week ahead and set out what they would like to achieve. 'Talent Tuesday' is fabulous because it allows members to share the things at which they excel - Cake baking, garden design and various crafts feature heavily. We even learnt how to make a chicken out of a tea towel which was filmed by Lizzie, who would give any Blue Peter presenter a run for their money! 'Twerking Tuesday' was hilarious and we had dozens of members posting videos of themselves twerking. 'Flex Friday' fills the page with lots of flexed muscles. It's all about good, honest, feel-good fun and motivation. We often ask the members to come up with ideas for themes, too, and they are always forthcoming.

With the themes in place, the page started to fill with posts and I set about trying to respond to each and every one. I wanted people to feel valued and to provide recognition for the time they'd taken to post. The page was growing at an exciting rate and each time I posted about it in other Facebook group I would get a deluge of requests to join, definitely aided by the fact I'd learned how to post a link! It wasn't long before I received a note from a member of the admin team of the other Facebook group to say I was not allowed to post about my group anymore. By this time I didn't need to, because other people were doing it for me.

It was very clear from the outset that I wanted the group to be a positive, motivational place, free from judgement or bitching. I'd seen negativity in other groups and also a 'preaching' culture which meant individuals would tell others what they should and shouldn't be doing. I was keen that the ethos of this group would be about supporting others, by showing respect for people and role modelling behaviours rather than dictating or chastising. I wanted our vibe to attract our Tribe! I thought about 'A Big Girl's Journey to Lean' in a work context asking myself 'If this was my business or a team I led, how would I approach it?' I concluded that the leadership style I adopted at work could be transferred onto the way I led the group. Initially that meant creating a culture that allowed people the freedom to operate within a framework of core values. I recognised that I needed to devise a set of those values for the page and to share them to manage people's expectations. It didn't take me too long to come up with the following:

Positivity – No Self Sabotage

I would often read posts which started with phrases like 'I hate myself' or 'I'm such a failure'. I wanted to breed a culture of positivity and self-love and so whenever a member posted in this way, I would ask them to think about how they would write the post if they were talking about a friend. I'd use gentle nudging and suggestion rather than a forceful approach and then ask them to think about rewriting the post coming from a place of self-love rather than self-sabotage. Rather than saying 'I hate myself', they'd write 'I want to learn to love myself again and I'm looking for advice'

Accountability – Take ownership of your own journey

I'd learnt pretty quickly that nobody could lose the weight for me. I could be guided, supported, taught and encouraged but ultimately, I had to get my workout gear on and do a workout and I had to eat well. If I didn't do that, there was nobody to blame but me. I had to be accountable and own the decisions I made and I felt this provided a foundation for my journey. I therefore brought this to this premise to the group too.

Sharing – Be prepared to share your successes and struggles

This was designed to encourage people to take part. Instead of lurking on the side lines, step into the arena and put yourself out there as others do. If we all join in then there are more examples to learn from, more role models to follow and more friendships to make.

95

Respect – No rudeness or mean-spirited comments
I wanted members to feel supported and to post freely without fear of being judged. Respect for people is incredibly important to me and if mean comments are posted they are removed and I write to the person who posted both the original post and the rude comment. If the comment is extreme then I will remove the person from the group. Harmony is key.

Laugh out loud – because it makes you feel good
The ground needed a fun side. Inspirational and motivational is at the heart, but this can come with a cheer, too. When members post about their jeans falling down in the supermarket queue because they have gotten so loose, their legs hurting so much after leg day that they can't climb the stairs or their smoothie maker exploding and sending smoothie flying around the kitchen, we laugh with them.

Scroll on – if a post isn't for you, move past it
Encouraging the premise of saying nothing if you don't have anything nice to say or ignoring a post if it is not appealing to you, scrolling on is again about harmony. It mitigates against arguments or disagreements which can disrupt the group and create ill feeling

With the values in place, I felt confident the group would remain a positive, vibrant, joyful place that would provide members with moments of escapism amidst a busy day. A sanctuary of optimism and inspiration.

We set up something called 'Target Practice', which was a challenge set every Sunday and would encourage members to spend five minutes per day exercising a certain body part. It captured people's attention and lots of members got involved. In less than a week, the page had one thousand members, including many of the ladies I had got to know in the other group, and a few weeks later, on 17th July our Tribe had reached 2000. I was thrilled and so very proud.

Chapter Ten

With the page growing and work keeping me busy I decided I needed more helpers to manage the surge of posts that were occurring each day. Soon, Emma, Bev, Brooke and Suzie joined the Admin Team, and together we kept the page updated every day. We spent a lot of time in our admin chat room discussing posts and devising strategies to help people who were struggling.

I had finished cycle one of the second 90-day plan and submitted my results with another 3kg loss. Once again Joe Wicks posted my pictures and this time the negative comments were more plentiful. The year before I had been named one of the Top 25 Inspirational Lean Leaders in Europe by the Lean Management Journal (LMJ). Some of Joe's followers had obviously seen this on the internet and had jumped to the conclusion that the 'lean' meant I was a health and fitness expert rather than the actual meaning which was linked to business improvement methodology. I was being berated because people thought my results were a scam.

Simultaneously - and I didn't help this situation - a handful of people from the other Facebook group started a thread stating that my 'before' picture was taken before January 2016. This was true. The photo was actually taken in July 2015 at the ceremony for the LMJ award. It was, at that time, the only 'dressed' full length photo I had that represented my starting weight for the Body Coach journey. Whilst it had been taken in the July, I was still wearing the dress in the January and I weighed 4lbs more at the start of the first Body Coach plan than I did in the July before it. What I learned in this scenario is that people sometimes like to bring you down. I was discouraged it was coming from people who had seen my journey from the outset and who'd I'd supported during their own struggles.

I started to worry about how the negative jibes were affecting me and wondered why it was hurting so badly when I read them. Equally I wondered why the praise I had been receiving had felt like it mattered so much. I strive to preserve harmony in all aspects of my life and connection with others is important to me. Posting my journey had changed from something that I'd found joyful to something I was suddenly perceiving as emotionally draining and stressful. I continued to challenge the people who were attempting to knock me down; at the same time, I realised I would have to find a different way to effectively deal with situations like this moving forward.

If I wanted to continue to post about my journey outside of the safety of my own group and thus, my comfort zone, I would need to do it for reasons of my own accountability and learn that if praise was received, it was a lovely side effect; and if criticism came, then ignoring it would be the appropriate reaction.

People have often told me that I need to develop a thick skin but that's no mean feat for an Empath like me. It is who I am, and while I might indeed need to develop an edge to make me more resilient, what I have come to understand is that feedback in any form tells me less about myself and more about the person who is giving it. Whilst I can think about this logically in the cold light of day however, in the moments where the feedback is being received, the emotion often overrides the logic and I feel genuinely devastated. In these moments, I have to remind myself that on the whole I am supported whole-heartedly and have a few followers who have been with me since the outset. I am so grateful to them and for them.

Mid-July saw my first video post to the group as part of a 'Film Friday' challenge. It was a video I recorded using my phone to thank members for getting involved. I posted it, nervously, and because of the response, found the confidence to post another one within a few days - a video of me doing push-ups as part of another challenge.

Social media works in the same way as real life. Just as we are influenced by our colleagues, friends and family, we are affected by our social media idols and followers. What I found is that if I tried something, took a brave step and showed my vulnerability, then others were encouraged to do the same. When I asked the Admin Team to follow my lead and film videos of themselves, while they didn't exactly jump at the idea, they eventually found the courage and did it. Looking back over the catalogue of videos that are now being created, it's amazing to see how each of them have grown in confidence and self-belief.

Cycle two was much easier second time around. My body was responding well to the carbohydrates and I was enjoying the German Volume Training, lifting heavier weights and gaining strength. On 19th June, I posted a picture of myself wearing a bikini. I'd never worn a bikini before and this was a huge leap of faith for me. I studied the photo before I posted it, with a positive head, determined to see the good things rather than the bad. I'd spent a lifetime vetting photographs - that's if I had allowed myself to be in them in the first place. Almost every time a photograph was taken of me which included more than just my face, I would immediately hate it. I wouldn't remember the joy of the occasion, focusing on how awful I looked instead. I have missed out on countless photographs with my children, because I would instantly delete them from the camera, or rip them up. I am thankful now that my parents and family members kept several photographs, so I can truly track my progress. So, despite not being fully in love with my body yet, I could see the tone on my legs and I had great boobs and I tried to focus on these parts to feel a sense of accomplishment. The response to the photograph was positive. Many people were telling me I could wear a smaller bikini - something I wasn't in agreement with - but it gave me a lovely confidence boost and I was pleased I'd taken the risk.

At this point I'd only shared underwear photos within the confines and virtual safety of the Facebook groups. These groups were closed - only members of the group could see the content. There had been a heart-stopping moment a few months before where I inadvertently posted my 'before' and 'after' underwear collage photo as my Facebook profile picture. I realised the second it happened and what followed was a panic-induced scramble to remove it. Why is it always in these moments that Facebook doesn't work properly? I pressed the delete icon at least a dozen times, but the photo stayed put, daringly staring at me. The five or so minutes that it took to change the profile photo seemed like days. I was mortified that my colleagues, friends and family members could have seen me in my pants! I was even more horrified that the photo had already attracted comments from several people, despite it being online just for a few minutes. I still felt a sense of shame about the way I had looked and this could have sent me into a binge cycle -

99

instead I chose to read the comments and saw that people were hugely supportive. What I came to realise is that whilst I felt ashamed of my 'big girl' photos, I didn't look like that anymore; equally I'd achieved great things with that coating of fat on my body and convinced myself that I should be proud. This gave me the impetus to allow Joe to post my underwear pictures for the first time and when I saw them on his Facebook and Instagram pages I was biting my lip, waiting for the response. I read celebratory posts from old friends and colleagues and winced only slightly that they could see me in my pants. I noticed that, once again, overall people were overwhelmingly supportive and so I was equally delighted when Joe then went on to ask me to record a video testimonial for his page. It was something new that he wanted to try and I was the first person he'd asked. I felt honoured and nervous. I'd not done my hair or makeup that day and was still in my training gear from my workout but I decided to just go for it; unrehearsed and without any real thought I recorded a quick video into my phone and sent it to him. He was delighted and it was posted on his page a week or so later. The number of views it received made me wish I'd done my hair and makeup before creating it!

I was on holiday in Lanzarote for two weeks in August during cycle three and managed to stay on target for the whole holiday. My seat belt fastened easily on the plane and I spent the flight drinking water and only eating my prescribed snack of olives. I chose appropriate meals in restaurants using the pick and mix principles and I followed the training plan. I'd scheduled a couple of treats during the holiday, such as ice cream or a dessert and to allow for this, I did some extra HIIT sessions on rest days to boost my metabolism and went for long walks with Martin while the children were in the kids' club. I felt good on holiday, wearing bikinis and even ventured beyond the balcony and out onto the sun loungers around the pool. Each evening I would take lots of photographs with the children and I wouldn't delete any of them, instead I'd post them proudly on Instagram which now had almost 8000 followers. I'd play with the children around the pool and even went on the waterslide at a water park wearing a bikini - something I had never done or even considered doing before. I felt slightly self-conscious while doing it, but the beaming smiles from the children made it so worth it.

I was thrilled to return from holiday and for the first time, I powered through. Once again, I graduated with honours. I'd lost 3.5 kg during the 90 days which took my weight loss since the beginning of January to 24kg. My waist had shrunk by 13 inches overall. I posted my photos and my testimonial on Facebook and on Instagram:

SECOND GRADUATION

I cannot believe how quickly this 90 days has gone. I've now done the plan twice with a month's break in between when I followed the SAS plan.

It has been so much easier the second time around. It just feels like a way of life now and it's so easy to follow.

All I need to think about is three meals and two snacks per day and it certainly beats existing on milkshakes, tracking points, counting calories or eating cabbage soup which I have tried so many times before. I love the 90-day plan not only because it delivers visible results, but also because of the things you can't see: -

How much fitter I feel
How I didn't feel self-conscious on holiday
How I automatically choose a healthy option from a menu
How I feel full of energy even after a 14-hour day
How I feel 28 rather than 38
How my kids are getting involved and see me as a role model

THE STATS
During this 90days I've lost 3.5kg and 13 inches.
Meaning overall since I started in January I've lost 24kg and 45 inches and gained collar bones, hip bones and muscles!!! Lovely muscles.

I have committed to my journey 100% and have never missed a training session. I've not had alcohol since I started in January and I've only had a handful of treat meals, choosing to stick to the plan, even on a recent 2-week holiday. I don't feel deprived though, I embrace it because feeling like this is better than any burger and chips or cocktail. Those that don't believe Joe's plan works just need to look at my progress and thousands of others who have done it to see that it does, especially if you give it your all and make it your way of working.

During this 90 days I've had some firsts: -
I've discovered I love burpees
I've bench pressed 40kg
I've got into size 10 jeans
I have size 12 tops
I wore a bikini and strutted around
I went on a water slide with my kids
I set up a lean community on Facebook, A big girl's journey to lean
I felt happy in my skin

I have been fat since I was a child. Yo-yo dieting all my life, at my largest I was 19 stone 5lbs. I have done every weight loss plan going and sometimes I was lucky enough to get down to a size 14, but never a 10/12 and never with tone and definition that I have now. And, I'd always put the weight back on. Not this time though, this time I've learnt I don't need to starve to be lean. I need to fuel my body and exercise and it's a formula I can live with. I love the training and with the help of my PT, Del, I've mastered the techniques so I only need to use him occasionally now. It's a sustainable plan and one I thank you for, Joe Wicks. You and your team are incredible. Some people have asked why I needed to repeat the plan, it should just be 90 days. Well being realistic, if your starting position is 101kg you can't get to your goal within 90 days. The plan delivers results, it's flexible and set out for you so I wanted to follow it whilst I ensured the lean way of life became habitual.

Next step for me is to repeat the plan for a third time. This time I'm doing it to support my husband who is inspired to do the plan, too. We'll kick off in mid-September and I can't wait to go again. My goal is to get abs, or as close as I can get after 2 c sections and years of yo-yo diets. If determination delivered them, I'd have them for sure. I also want to start training for and competing in kettlebell pentathlons and enter some running events! So plenty of goals to keep to me focused and lean!

So, there it was in black and white, I'd committed to doing the plan AGAIN!

Chapter Eleven

The Facebook group had continued to grow at pace and by September it had 9,000 active members. It even had its very own hashtag, #BGJTL, which people had started to use on Instagram. The daily themes were still going strong and the majority of posts were in line with the group values. When this wasn't the case, one of the admin crew would delete the post and write to the individual explaining why.

One of the themes was Tikiboo Tuesday. Tikiboo Fitness is a brand of fitness gear that the page followers raved about, including me. I had several pairs and loved them; their funky designs made my legs look slimmer. The theme required members to post pictures of themselves wearing their Tikiboo leggings and lots of people participated. Unbeknown to me, my Mum wrote to Tikiboo about the theme. I cringed slightly when she told me, but several emails were exchanged with the owner Faye and she was turned out to be lovely. She offered a discount code for the group which we were all delighted by. Faye was so pleased by the response that I became an official brand ambassador. Me! An ambassador for fitness wear - something I never dreamed would be possible!

Some of the original admin crew members had stepped down due to lack of time and new members had joined, chosen carefully for the way in which they interacted with other members. We welcomed the funny and motivational Hannah or 'Bob' as we call her who would become one of my closest friends, the inimitable and wonderful H and Gavin, who had been through his own Body Coach transformation and was extremely supportive and inspiring.

Martin decided to sign up to the plan this time too and I was thrilled to bits, even though it made the prepping doubly difficult because we both had different food weights. Having both of us on the plan would help me with accountability. I also decided to add another aspect to sharing my journey by recording daily vlogs. These would be three-minute videos recorded each evening to outline what I'd eaten, how I'd trained and what I'd learnt about myself throughout the day. I decided the platform for sharing the vlogs would be YouTube and I set up a channel called 'A Big Girl's Journey to Lean'.

My first few vlogs were terrible. I didn't realise that I should hold my smart phone horizontally and so the early vlogs had columns of black at each side of the screen. To attract more views, I would post the links to the vlogs on Facebook and Twitter. I am still amazed that my first attempt has had 1700 views! In addition to my daily updates, I recorded some recipe demonstrations, which people loved, and videos sharing top tips video including how to prep like a boss. The vlogs grew in popularity and within a month my channel reached 1000 subscribers who would regularly watch and leave comments and likes and a few who would privately send me truly heart-warming messages.

Never one to rest on my laurels, I created a training journal after some encouragement from the Admin Team so that I could continue to write out my workouts in the 'old school' way I loved. I continued to do this as it was easier to refer to during my workout than the notes on my phone screen and the act of physically writing down my workout the night before prepared me mentally for it. With a little help from my friends by way of suggesting printing companies and designing a logo, I ordered 360 copies. On the night they launched, they sold out in 24 minutes! The feedback was incredible and it was superb to see people posting their workouts written up on the journal pages. While they were popular, they really took a lot of time and effort and combined with everything else I was doing at home and at work, it was proving stressful. Whilst the demand for the journals continued, I decided it wasn't worth the hassle. Embracing the words of Roy T Bennet who said that 'Great things happen to those who don't stop believing, trying, learning and being grateful', I moved into September ready for new ways in which to challenge myself.

First up would be a 5k run! I disliked running immensely, because despite being a lot smaller at this point, my breasts were still large and my tummy would jiggle around as I ran. I also didn't seem to have the stamina for it. I did however, want to raise some money for Cancer charities and signed up for a Pretty Muddy 5k in Milton Keynes, despite not having done any training. I announced it on the group and one of the members, Gaelle, decided to join me. I met her at the venue, wearing head to toe pink. We'd never met before and yet we hugged and chatted like we knew each other for ages. Gaelle is an amazing runner and recently ran 100k on one day so she vowed to help me round the track as up to that point I had never completed a 5k. I found it relatively easy and because it was interspersed with obstacles, it was great fun, too. Gaelle's support was invaluable and we talked all the way around the course whilst trying to dodge the mud that was being fired at us from large shooters. We were freezing by the end of the race, but came down the final slide holding hands and smiling. I'd raised £700 for Cancer Research, survived my first 5k race and met a fellow Leanie.

The Facebook page was going from strength to strength and began to garner attention from journalists interested in my story. A lady who was casting for a Channel 4 show got in touch, having seen my transformation on Twitter and wanted me to get involved in a programme that was focusing on losing weight through fitness. While it was an exciting prospect and I was flattered by the interest, I also knew that the timing of the invitation wasn't right for me. I didn't feel that I'd quite reached where I wanted to be before sharing my journey more widely, so I declined and instead turned my attention to ways in which I could support my Leanies further.

On 11th September 2016, I posted a picture of myself in workout gear with the words 'LIVE HIIT THIS SUNDAY at 0930' emblazoned across it. It was another hair-brained scheme thought up in the middle of the night. I'd decided to live-stream my Sunday morning HIIT routine into the Facebook group, so that others could join in with me. Not being a fitness expert, I asked Bev – one of the first admins of BGJTL group - to join me as she was a qualified fitness instructor and could make sure it remained safe. I asked H to come along to do the filming and answer the questions on the live feed. I hadn't met Bev or H before in person, so the prospect of having them stay over at my house on the Saturday night was a little daunting but we'd spent so many hours in the chat room over previous months, it felt like we knew each other rather well.

H had a great suggestion that alongside the Sunday morning HIIT, we should stream a live chat session into the group to answer people's questions and while I found the idea a little scary, we decided to go for it and advertised it in on the page.

H arrived at my house on Saturday afternoon followed soon afterwards by Bev. It was like meeting old friends and I appreciated having them there with me. We had dinner together, chatting relentlessly and checking in on the page. The excitement was building up and people were posting to say they were looking forward to the chat. I felt sick and kept pacing around the house, much to H and Bev's amusement. We prepared the room trying to get the lighting right and deciding on the perfect seating arrangements.

At 9 PM we started streaming and Bev immediately took the lead as our very own Holly Willoughby! The live screen shows you how many people have joined the chat and I felt the butterflies fluttering in my tummy as the numbers grew. People with familiar names started to type questions and we did our best to answer them between us. Members were mostly interested in the Body Coach plan and how we had found it, as well as how I'd managed to repeat it. They were asking about the mind-set techniques I had adopted and even what lipstick I used. The Admin Crew had joined the chat to support us and were being mischievous asking silly questions which had H in fits of silent laughter.

We had such a lovely time and the three of us felt that we had great chemistry, even though we had only met in person that evening. We were live for an hour and the chat attracted more than 2000 views. When we switched off, we paused in silence until we'd confirmed the stream had definitely concluded and then we burst into laughter and recalled some of the highlights. There was a real, positive energy in the room. We huddled around the laptop and watched the whole thing, viewing through half-closed eyes as if we were watching a horror movie. We'd missed multiple questions so spent time answering them as posts so that people would feel valued. It was encouraging to see we knew so many of the members by name along with their stories. This community was certainly engaged and connected and I felt proud of every single member.

We went to bed before midnight, knowing we had to be up early the next morning to prepare for the HIIT. I was in a quandary over what to wear and was experiencing the sick nervous feeling once more. Not only was H in charge of filming and music, she also took on the challenge of keeping me calm! Bev and I ran through the moves in my kitchen. We'd included twenty different moves and would do each one for 30 seconds with a 30 second rest in between. During the rest period, Bev would demonstrate the next move. We set up the mats outside and then... it was time!

We were live and we were welcoming everybody to our HIIT session. It felt surreal and I had a few moments of worry, thinking what my tummy would look like as I bounced up and down on camera or if I'd be able to keep up with full push-ups for 30 seconds. I practiced affirmations in my mind to calm my nerves and get my positive head back on. H was interacting with the members and us, saying hello to people as they commented and telling us how many people were on and ready to work out with us.

'Emma Neal is ready' H said.

'Jackie's watching from her bed and says Hi'

There were a lot of people watching from their beds which instantly made us laugh. We started and Bev got stuck in straight away. The moves were full on and included push-ups, mountain climbers, jumping jacks and high knees. In between each move Bev showed the audience the next move and I got my breath back. We had a ball and Bev was a star. She was shattered afterwards having done all of the demonstrating and I was exhausted from pushing myself to the maximum. The feedback coming from the members was amazing. Hundreds of people had joined in with us and hundreds more had watched. As we tucked into our well-deserved protein pancakes, we watched it back and laughed the whole way through.

People quickly started asking for more workouts, but being conscious that I am not a fitness expert, I was uneasy about it. I spoke to Del and he agreed to help me film some workouts for the YouTube channel. We had a great time making the first video which was a kettlebell strength and conditioning workout and was well received with over 7000 views. Encouraged, I felt I wanted something that was more accessible to beginners. I wanted the workouts to be aimed at people who were bigger and/or had never exercised because one of my frustrations with 'Beginner's' workouts

108

is that they are often compiled by experts who have never been overweight. They can't put themselves in the Beginner's shoes and know what it feels like to attempt a burpee and listen to your tummy fat slapping against your thighs or the crushing sensation you feel internally as you attempt to bend over and touch your toes. I wanted to create a workout with these challenges in mind that would allow people to improve their fitness and complete a workout without having to give up halfway through because the bar had been set too high. I was keen for it to have levels of progression, too, so anybody attempting it more than once could work up to a more advanced move.

I wrote down all of the moves and came up with a low-impact and mid-range version of each one. If for example, the mid-range version was high knees, the low version was marching. When Del read the list, he laughed and stated that it looked a bit too easy. He and I have a great relationship and we can discuss things openly. He drives me mad sometimes, I drive him mad and then we laugh about it, so I stuck to my guns and he agreed to give it a go. That's one of the things I love about Del, he has a lot of humility and is prepared to try alternative approaches. It worked in the same way as a HIIT workout, with 30 seconds of work followed by 30 seconds of rest. We recorded it in the garden and Del had worked up a little sweat towards the end which I do not fail to tease him about ever since. He uploaded it to YouTube that afternoon and the feedback came rolling in. Our first beginner's HIIT has had more than 15k views and comments such as, 'Thank you so much for this. I've been battling with other videos and this was brilliant', made it all worth it. Del and I have filmed several videos since and they have all been well received, with only the odd negative comment from the Troll Gang.

As September drew to a close, I reflected on what had been an unforgettable 9 months, full of personal and professional milestones. I looked forward to what the last few months of the year had in store for me, never imagining that not all of the experiences which lay in wait, would be happy ones.

Chapter Twelve

October 2016 was another great month. Martin and I were powering through the Body Coach plan without deviation. I hadn't missed a workout since I started in January which felt like an amazing Non-Scales Victory. Nor had I had coughs or colds which was a blessing and the only 'treat meals' I'd indulged in were at the end of each cycle. I was due to take a holiday at the end of the month and wanted to look as good as I possibly could do. Martin had settled into plan too and I had started to see a difference in him. He'd been a few stones overweight prior to starting the plan and had been miserable with it. Now he had a newly found spring in his step and his regained confidence was highly attractive. Having shared goals was certainly bringing us closer together and I loved it and him.

Once again, I'd invited new admin members to join the crew to help deal with its ever-increasing size. Donna had been an inspiration to me during the first few months of my journey and when she'd posted her photographs on the Facebook group, I was in awe. I felt we had a lot in common and I loved how positive she had been as a member of the page. I was thrilled when she accepted the opportunity to join the admin crew and she did so just in time to help us celebrate achieving 10,000 members. In less than three months we'd hit a milestone I didn't ever envisage and it felt like winning the lottery. I was extremely proud of the team and the community as a whole. I felt I'd built something special.

Life had certainly changed a lot since January, and as if I needed another reminder, I found myself receiving a Twitter message from a lady at Bella magazine who wanted to write a story about me. I'd sometimes read Bella in the doctor's surgery and seen the weight loss stories and while the magazine seems to embrace all that is cheesy, I was always super impressed with the men and women who'd lost weight. I'd featured in Woman magazine when I'd lost weight before my first wedding when they'd written an article about my weight-loss with slimming world and published photos of me wearing wedding dresses. I'd cringed reading the write-up, because it was very twee and so I spoke to the lady at Bella and expressed my concerns. She was extremely reassuring and promised that I would be provided with a full read through of the story before it was published. We discussed the story over the phone and she asked lots of questions. She asked me to send in photographs and we had a few further calls to clarify details. The magazine was launched just before Christmas. I laughed a lot when group members started a trend of going into shops, opening all of the Bella magazines on my double page spread and taking photographs of them. The perfectionist in me was a little upset when I saw that they'd used a photograph of me weighing 17 stones, but stated it was me at 19 stones. I felt this was misleading but the Admin Crew said I shouldn't worry about it. It was amazing to be featured and great to read some of the posts and letters that followed. We attracted new members too, who had read about the group through the magazine.

As my holiday loomed, I decided to write a holiday plan to keep my head in the game. As I'd done in August, I'd planned to have a handful of treats and wanted to make sure I put in a few extra workouts to allow for these. I also wanted to maximise time with the children so rather than spend an hour at the gym in one go, I split my workouts in half and did part in the morning whilst the children were still chilling in bed and half in the late afternoon, when they had some screen time after a day in the sunshine. We'd then enjoy a lovely family meal together at a nice restaurant.

I learnt that having a plan and posting about it on social media helped me stick to it. Every day on holiday I'd do the work and then post my selfies as usual. Regardless of who was watching, just by making public statement of intent, I had to deliver against it. 'Make a plan, share a plan, keep a plan' had become a mantra.

I generated some criticism for this approach from some of my followers which was disappointing. A handful of people thought that I should relax as I was on holiday after all! Others were harsher and called me 'pathetic' but I no longer felt that I had to overindulge in food and drink to have a good time, something that had become an affirmation during my journey. Exercising made me feel good and kept my body toned. I'd come so far, and simply didn't want to go back to feeling the way I did. It was always difficult dealing with comments like these and I tried very hard to get better at dealing with them but the truth was, that it still mattered what people thought of me. I had thought that I was improving the way I reacted to criticism. Or was I?

At the airport on the return leg of the holiday, this would be truly tested when everything turned upside down. It was a day I never want to repeat.

That morning as we took our last breakfast in the early morning Lanzarote sunshine, I casually flicked through the posts on the page and one post stood out for not being aligned to the group's values. It was a very long post and was entitled 'Sunday Sermon'. It had been posted by a regular poster, but had a very different tone to her usual posts, coming, she claimed, from a place of tough love (with an emphasis on the 'tough'). She was essentially saying that people needed to get a grip and that if they were succumbing to cake then they were failing and not giving 100% commitment. They should stop whinging about what they can't do because nobody wants to hear it. It was on the wrong side of self-righteous and made for rather uncomfortable reading. The problem I have with posts like this is that the lady was standing on the moral high ground and telling others how they should behave. One person's failure is another's success – it's all a matter of perspective - and therefore I have already encouraged people to share their individual approaches, but not mandate their approach as 'the only way'. I popped into the admin chat and asked the other admins to take a look. We were all uncomfortable about the content, but had noticed a few members had written comments on the thread such as 'I couldn't agree more' and 'here, here.'

As the morning progressed and we travelled to the airport things started to escalate. Members were posting to say that they felt upset by the content of the post and we received a few complaints. In hindsight, I should have taken the step to delete the post but at that stage I didn't. Instead I commented on the post stating that we are all different and whilst this ladies approach worked for her, it didn't mean it was right for everybody.

I wrote a post which explained that the group always supported those who were struggling and we encouraged members to reach out so that we could help them but a few members I didn't recognise started to create conflict on the Sunday Sermon post and in the end, just before I boarded the flight, I deleted it and wrote to the member who had posted it originally to explain why. It was then that I would come under further criticism for being a dictator who wouldn't allow people to have an opinion and for not allowing freedom of speech. One or two of the comments were plain nasty and personal. I took the decision to block these members from the group. They were right. I didn't allow freedom of speech if it was on a level that caused conflict or created hurt or unrest. Other groups were like that and it always made me feel uneasy but 'BGJTL' was about harmony, support and a place of sanctuary and I would vehemently protect that like a lioness protects her cubs.

As the plane took to the sky I felt sick. The situation had been difficult to manage. The Admin Team were in a state of flux and I was now offline for 4 hours. I knew there would be further fallout whilst I was in the air and I was urging the time to pass by quicker. The knots in my stomach were twisting and I tried my best to keep distracted by playing games with the children and reading magazines.

As soon as I could, I checked in with the Admin Team.

I suddenly felt cold and it had nothing to do with returning from the sun into the November weather. There waiting for me were screen shots of threads that had been posted in another group. In between each screen shot were the reactionary words of the Admin Team.

'Oh my god, I can't believe they are talking about her like this'
'She has helped these people'

The thread had been posted in a Facebook group I hadn't heard of before by one of the women who had been blocked. At least a dozen people were involved in the thread and a lot of the posts were mean. Many of the people getting involved were people who had been with me since the start of my journey. They were all having a lot of fun kicking around my character and reputation like a bunch of school boys kicking a tin can around the playground. I was way too robotic. I was desperate to be famous. I wouldn't let people have an opinion. I was pathetic because I took selfies all the time. I was even more

113

pathetic because I did a tutorial on how to take a good selfie. I was a show off. I was self-obsessed.

It made pleasant reading, as you can imagine. They continued to criticise every part of me and my life.

'There's no denying she's done well, BUT she is getting too big for her boots. Who does she think she is, doing live chats?'

'She's got a great body BUT she is totally obsessed and isn't real like the rest of us'

'Yes, she's followed the plan BUT it's easy to lose weight if you have money'

'Oh, if only it was that easy' I thought. Yes, I am lucky to have a good job that pays well but I work long hours as a result and spend time travelling around the country. My financial status has never made it easy for me to lose weight. If that was the case, I'd have been slim for most of my adult life. It was a ridiculous comment to make, coming from a place of total misunderstanding and ignorance.

The comment that hurt the most, though, came from a lady I admired greatly. She was beautiful and we had always supported each other. She'd sponsored me for the 5k race and I was considering her to be a member of the admin crew. Martin had bought me a tennis bracelet in Lanzarote. It was made from cubic zirconia stones and hadn't cost very much at all. I posted a picture of it on Instagram with a thank you note to Martin. As I continued to read the thread screen shots I saw that this lady had written,

'The diamond bracelet was the last straw for me. She shoves it in people's faces'

I felt crushed.

I was reading all of these comments whilst trying to collect the bags and make our way through passport control. Waves of heat were radiating through my body and the airport surroundings seemed to blur into a fog.

I was 9 years of age again, feeling hurt and lost and misunderstood.

Martin was aware that I was distressed and concentrated on occupying the children so they wouldn't suspect anything was wrong. I couldn't focus on anything but the words written on the page. I wondered how many bystanders had read the thread and

114

formed an opinion of me. Occasionally my logical mind took over informing me that it really didn't matter what anybody else thought, that people have opinions and these are entitled. That the most important view was my own and if I could look at myself in the mirror and know I was a good, honest person then none of these opinions or judgements counted. I could listen to them if I felt it would enhance how I lived; otherwise I could discount the information. Unfortunately, though, my logical mind is often overruled by my emotional self and I am back to letting the critical arrows penetrate my core before I know it.

The Admin Crew were upset and they were trying to deal with the repercussions from the morning's events. Normally when we delete a post, other people start new threads stating how upset they were when they read the original post. It's the ripple effect, but it unnecessarily exacerbates the situation. The crew were busy deleting these posts and writing to the members to explain why.

I decided I wouldn't act on most of the comments I had read. A lot of the people, - whilst I had helped them previously - didn't mean anything to me and I attributed their behaviour to jealousy or projection. I did, however, write a very brief note to the lady who'd commented about the bracelet. The message was read but there was no response and so I decided to block her from all of my social media platforms. As we travelled home, I thought about what my next step would be.

That evening I posted a note on to the group and turned off commenting. I didn't want to encourage negativity by opening up the floodgates and turning off commenting prevents this. Writing how I felt was therapeutic and I wanted to make it clear that I found this type of behaviour unacceptable.

Even though many might counsel me to stay quiet, I have never been one to take things lying down. I am turning comments off on this post and would ask you all not to respond in any way. I know that the vast majority of this group believes in the group values and are here for the right reasons and for those that do, I am truly thankful.

Trolls in my opinion take many forms and I am saddened that it appears we have them in this community. I have blocked a handful of people today having read a vile thread that took place elsewhere. Sadly, it involved members of this group including people I have gone out of my way to help.

I understand that if you put yourself out there you have to expect this, but I don't expect it from people I have helped. People who only this week were writing to me for support.

Yes, I brag about being a size 10 after years spent in a big body

Yes, I post selfies and did a tutorial that makes me a laughing stock

Yes, I post my achievements and 'ram it down people's throats

Yes, I involve my husband and he must be long suffering

Yes, I am driven and have an iron will which mean I am not friendship material

Yes, I love myself and show off

Yes, I post my new clothes which is sickening

Guilteeeeeeee

But I also have a heart and a thin skin.

I have a family who have read these vile words and feel it too.

I have a team who work hard and are reeling from this.

I have a brain which tells me these people are not with it.

If you are on the page and you harbour these ill feelings for me then leave. You are not welcome. I've had a gut full of it.

I have no intention of stopping to support the thousands of people who find this page a safe-haven.

Writing this has restored my equilibrium and tomorrow, normal service will resume on the page.

I wasn't lying about my equilibrium. I felt a sense of calm after I had written this post. I was grateful that this time, a stressful situation hadn't resulted in a binge. At least this is a Demon I have put to rest, I thought.

A few months later, I'd just finished my morning workout when I received a note from Bob in the Admin chat. She said the tennis bracelet lady had got in touch with her stating she had been trying to reach me to apologise. She went on to say that at that time she had been in a bad place; she'd been reflecting on the year and the one

116

thing she'd regretted was how she had treated me. She said I hadn't deserved it. As soon as I read the words I felt better.

Some of the Admin Crew were saying I should ignore her. My personal view is that it takes a lot of guts for a person to apologise and forgiveness is generally the best option. The situation had played on my mind several times since the incident and I was thrilled that she wanted to put that right. The relationship was tentative for a few months and I tried to make her feel at ease by unblocking her from my accounts commenting on her posts, so she could see that the forgiveness is genuine. We now engage often and I am pleased to have her back in my world. She is a lovely lady and I value her support.

It was a tough day. We learnt a lot as a team. I learnt a lot as an individual. I started to realise that I couldn't mitigate against these incidents occurring. The more things went well for me, the more it seemed to happen. I could either let it consume me or I could let it go and I tried hard to do the latter. A few months later I was at a conference and a speaker said the only way to avoid criticism was to do nothing and say nothing. Neither of those options were appealing to me.

I simply accepted that there are people in the world who won't like you.

And that's ok.

Chapter Thirteen

As winter set in casting darkness over the mornings and evenings, I struggled with motivation. I'm a sunshine fan and have no problem springing out of bed to exercise if it's light and the sky is blue, but I find it more of a fight when it isn't. To combat this, I devised a strategy. I was on the 3rd round of the 90daysss plan so I was very familiar with it, I just needed to make sure I did it. I would exercise on Saturday and Sundays when I wasn't working and didn't need to get up too early. I'd do the remaining workouts on midweek evenings, or, if I was working from home, I'd train at lunchtimes. This meant I rarely had to crawl out of bed at 6 AM to workout. With the plan for the week nailed down, I would document the workouts in my journal, coming up with HIITs that were different each day and complementary to the weights workouts. If it was leg day I would focus the HIIT workout on upper body and abs, combining moving planks, bicycle crunches, triceps dips, push-ups and renegade rows. If it was arms day, the HIIT would be full of leg exercises. The variation kept it fun and interesting.

The day before a workout I would get my kit ready and leave it somewhere visible. I was loving colourful training gear and even though nobody could see me in my garage, I always wore great outfits. Getting geared up seemed to help my mind-set. I invested in a daylight-emulating light box and I would switch this on as soon as I woke up and have it on for an hour each evening to artificially extend the day. It really seemed to help me.

I have always worked out at home - unless I am away with work then I will venture into a gym, although I've only done this during the latter part of my journey, as I didn't have the confidence at its beginning. Martin and I cleared out the garage and initially I purchased a weights bench, some dumbbells and a barbell with plates. This collection has been added to extensively over the last year; each time I sold some of my bigger clothes, I'd invest the money in gym equipment. I also saved fortunes not buying wine and prosecco and takeaways every week. I now have an impressive array of kit, albeit all cobbled together without any real thought. It includes dumbbells, kettlebells, barbells, a bench and a squat rack plus cardio equipment such as a treadmill, cross trainer, battle-ropes and a spin bike. I also have a skipping rope which was as cheap as chips and ideal for raising the heart rate. There is a sound system in the garage but I rarely listen to music when a train, preferring instead to listen to podcasts and audio books so I can learn as I lift.

The garage is a great place to be during the summer months; in winter though, it can be freezing cold. This could have been another perfectly logical reason not to exercise, but instead of giving in to the excuses, I bought a heater and a cheap fleece jacket to wear whilst I was warming up. If it was really cold, and on days were I was working shoulders or arms, I would bring the dumbbells into the house and work-out indoors.

These small rituals really helped me to ensure I didn't miss a workout throughout the winter months. I found that it was simply a matter of adjusting my routines to fit the circumstances. The old saying 'Where there is a will, there is a way' is very pertinent; I've added to it with 'Where there isn't a will, find the why'. When motivation dips, as it sometimes and inadvertently does, I remember the reasons why I am doing this in the first place and that is to be a fabulous role model for my children.

I'd decided to have a Christmas Party for the Admin Crew as a way to bring everyone together, to meet most of them for the first time and to thank them for the time and effort they put in to the page. I arranged it for 4th December and we advertised it as 'Christmas at the Cox's' in the group. The whole Admin Team would come to my house for the party and we planned to live-stream into the group throughout the evening. We were excited to meet each other and were already getting into the Christmas spirit, talking about our party dresses and in H's case, her suit. We'd decided to film a live HIIT the following morning and Del had agreed to come along and help us.

For Target Practice in December, I came up with the idea of doing an Advent Calendar. Each day, one of the Admin Crew would film a festive video with the exercise for the following day. They would stand behind a door with a number on it and when the door opened, they demo the move and talk to the group. We had such a giggle out-doing each other's videos, wearing festive outfits, hats and adding animation to the videos. The members appreciated it too and lots of them joined in.

On the day of the Christmas party I once again felt nervous but I busied myself shopping for food for the guests. I was wearing a pair of size 10 jeans which were gaping at the back so I posted a picture showing this on Instagram. I couldn't believe that size ten was too big having only ever been able to get down to a size 14 on previous weight loss attempts. Of course, these things are relative, as I have come to understand. Sometimes I can try on two pairs of size 10 trousers from the same shop and one style will fit and the other won't, but I'd had these jeans for few months and could tell I I'd lost weight since the last time I'd worn then. What I also noticed as I looked at my decreasing frame in the mirror is that the skin on my tummy was becoming looser by the week. If I was standing and not moving I could make it look nice by breathing in and standing tall but if I was to jump up and down, it would jump up and down with me. If I was working out in a hotel gym, I would wear Spanx to disguise it - ridiculous, but true. In that moment, looking in the bedroom mirror, I felt deflated. I'd put in so much hard work and yet the abuse I had inflicted on my body was still evident. I pulled my jumper over the skin and, giving little 8-year-old me a very caring look as she looked back at me, I focused my attention on the fact that I had amazing legs and my bingo wings had banished, so there was plenty to be grateful for. I practiced some affirmations and successfully silenced Miss. Meddler. For now.

When I heard the first car on the driveway, my heartbeat quickened with anticipation. I took several deep breaths to calm myself and went to the door. Nat looked like Lara Croft in her coated leather jeans and crop top. She was lean and had abs to die for. I loved her immediately. H and I had a big hug and then I saw Bob. She was just as I imagined her to be from her photographs and had flawless skin and a youthful complexion. We hit it off straight away and I scalded her, with a smile, for bringing mince pies. I'd prepared all sorts of yummy clean food and she had brought cakes! The three of us spent time chatting about everything and anything and it was

120

like old friends meeting, even though we had not seen each other in real life before.

Donna and Bev arrived next. It was a joy to meet Donna for the first time. She was petite, slender and elegant. Bev had dyed her hair blonde since we last met and she looked full of vitality. Suzy and Pete arrived shortly afterwards; Suzy was tall and slim with a huge smile and Pete was lean and a little shy. Immediately it struck me that they were a great couple. Everybody gelled perfectly and the kitchen was filled with noisy excitement as we chatted and laughed about the antics we'd experienced. Del was the final guest to arrive and he and Pete had a good catch up whilst the girls got ready for the party

I'd bought a sequinned dress from French Connection. It was a great shape for me and I felt good. We had live chats scheduled throughout the evening with different members of the Admin Crew joining me for 30-minute slots. Those who were not on the chat were busy trying to make us laugh. Many of the members joined the chats and the atmosphere was electric. Half way through the evening it occurred to me that I was at a Christmas party and I hadn't had any alcohol, yet I was as high as kite with joy. I'd also managed to stick to clean food and it served to remind me once more that I really didn't need to overindulge or drink to have a good time. My daily affirmations were working!

Our final instalment that evening was a rendition of Slade's 'Merry Christmas Everybody' which was sang by the whole crew. We were dancing and wearing Santa hats and the members were posting comments like crazy. When the laptop had been switched off we looked at each other in disbelief, acknowledging what we had achieved without saying a word. BGJTL was special; the sense of community and belonging was touching people in a way I had never experienced before through social media.

The next morning, we woke bright and breezy – well, some more breezy than others, depending on the previous night's alcohol consumption - and we prepared for the HIIT. Pete was filming for us and I had designed a workout with 3 levels (beginners, intermediate, and advanced) so that everybody watching could join in. It was absolutely freezing, but we donned our Santa hats and Tikiboos and

121

Bev took us through a warm up. Over 1000 people joined us for the Christmas HIIT and we laughed all the way through it. Once the live feed had been switched off I broke the news to the team that we were doing a second workout Del had designed for the YouTube channel. This one included kettlebells and the team were less than impressed.

'Think of the calorie burn' I shouted as we got underway. They grudgingly joined me.

When we'd finished, we were well and truly done and in need of some breakfast. I'd made a large vat of overnight oats with chocolate protein powder and banana. We tucked in to warm bowlfuls of goodness as we tried to defrost our extremities. It had been an amazing 24 hours and it was one I hope we would repeat. Surrounding myself with like-minded people is one of the many secrets of my success and the Admin Crew feel like they will be friends for life.

December was packed full of parties and social events which meant lots of opportunities to wear lovely dresses. I felt like a film star when I wore a long black fishtail gown for the work Black Tie Dinner and Mr. Cox said he was so proud to have me on his arm - I was equally proud of him. He'd been giving his all to the Body Coach plan and he looked hellishly handsome in his tuxedo. During the event, the MD played a video that celebrated the achievements of the year. I hid behind a menu card when I saw a special mention for the outstanding work I did in my spare time and an extract of one my vlogs was played. I hadn't told many people at work and now they all could see it for themselves. All the same, it was lovely to know that the MD was supportive of what I was doing.

Throughout the silly season I managed to abstain from alcohol and avoid indulging in the myriad of festive treats that seemed to be present everywhere I turned. I kept telling myself that if I made the choice to eat them, it would set me back and I concluded that my mid- and long-term goals were more important than the immediate pleasure of a Cadbury's Roses chocolate.

On 23rd December I submitted my results for the third round of the 90daysss plan. I'd lost another 4.5kg. Once again, I posted my graduation testimonial,

THIRD GRADUTATION

On 21st January I started my journey with the Body Coach. Today I have completed the 90dayssss plan for the third time and combined with a month on the SAS plan means I have done 10 cycles in total over 11 months. Never in my wildest dreams did I think I would get the results I have and I will be forever thankful that Joe Wicks devised a plan that works and is sustainable.

THE STATS
29.5kg melted - From 101kg to 71.5kg
4.5kg during final 90days
56 inches lost
14 inches from waist
5 inches from each thigh
From size 18/20 to size 8/10

I have never been smaller than size 14 for all of my adult life and have spent many years on very low calories diets which wrecked my metabolism and meant I was constantly yo-yo-ing between 123kg & 74kg. Well no more. I have developed a love of exercise. I've built lean muscle mass and I've learnt how to fuel my body. Moreover, I have tested my mental strength and I am so proud of myself for eating clean, not drinking alcohol and training hard for eleven months.

People ask why I did the plan 3 times. Joe's plan only needs to be done once to teach you the principles. For somebody like me who had a shocking relationship with food, I wanted a little longer to establish the good habits and break the poor ones. Having the structure of the plan has helped me achieve this. I honestly know I will never go back, something I have never felt confident about before Body Coach.

Speaking of confidence, I am now filled with it. I am wearing clothes I have never thought I could such as skinny jeans, zip up *boots and bikinis. I no longer feel sick when I walk into a room full of strangers and I am happy with my body and my mind.*

I am fit for the first time ever. I can run, I can jump around, I can lift heavy and play with the kids and its fun. I enjoy it.

MY TOP 5 NON- SCALE VICTORIES
Wearing a bikini for first time ever
Doing 39 push-ups in a row
Being able to look at my tummy in the mirror
Fitting into a size 8
Having strangers say they would never guess I'd been bigger

Apart from being proud of myself for smashing the plan this year, I am also delighted to be helping others. Mr. Cox has joined me in the latest 90 days and he has smashed it and is looking rather delicious. I am so proud of him!

I help people through my FB group, A Big Girl's Journey to Lean. There are 13500 members in the group and many of them joined the body coach plan as a result of the inspiration they find there. I've vlogged about the entire 90 days on You Tube too. Knowing other people are transforming because of my journey is so rewarding.

I've got my share of haters which is a shame but I am learning you can't please everyone and I know it's more about them than me. I am maybe achieving what they can't. My Nan always said when people try to bring you down, stand fast, dig deep, smile and work even harder! So that's what I'll do.

I only occasionally have treat meals, usually at the end of a cycle or once or twice on holiday. So, I am looking forward to having Christmas Day totally off plan and eating whatever I like. I'll be back on it between Xmas & New Year trying the lovely recipes from Joe's books. I haven't had alcohol all year and plan to continue with that because I don't miss it at all.

My next step is getting to grips with macros and build some further muscle, keep working on my abs and take on some fitness challenges. I will succeed and keep smashing it in 2017. It's all about small incremental improvements now.

If you are thinking of trying the plan, my advice would be **GO FOR IT!** *Be stronger than your strongest excuse and this will change your life. If I can do it, anybody can. It's life changing.*

I recorded a second video testimonial for the Body Coach and this was loaded to his Facebook group. This time it was over three minutes long and shared my experiences from the 10 months I'd followed the Body Coach. Joe said it was natural and authentic when he saw it. I don't think he will ever fully appreciate the impact he has had on my life. One day I will meet him again and try to articulate it.

I'd fully established that having a plan was a good idea for me. I'd successfully completed three iterations of the 90daysss plan and was thrilled with the results. I wasn't quite at goal and needed something new. The Body Coach plan is amazing because it works out the macro-nutrients that you need to eat each day. It also ensures that if you follow the training and eating plan precisely, a calorie deficit is created, meaning you lose fat. One thing I realised is that whilst I understood the types of foods I needed to eat to stay lean, I hadn't learnt anything about how to track macro-nutrients (macros) and so felt a bit lost. I downloaded the MyFitnessPal app and tried to work it out; however, I am the type of person who likes to understand something fully in order to feel like I can succeed. There were many other plans being followed by members of the group. Two that captured my interest based on results were Trinity Transformations' Trinity plan and Sustain Nutrition's Sustain Plan.

I love the two boys who founded Sustain, especially James (AKA Big Nose) Walker. They are very human and support women through their plan by personally coaching them on a daily basis. The Sustain plan didn't teach macro tracking though, and I was keen to get this skill-set under my belt. The Trinity plan sounded ideal. It was a 90-

day plan, combining full body resistance workouts with a step by step guide to tracking macros. The founders, Rob and Ben have a unique approach to their work which focussed on mind-set, and after contacting Ben for more information, I felt confident that it was the plan for me.

And so, the next stage of my journey was decided.

From 1st January, I'd be joining Trinity Transformations.

Chapter Fourteen

Christmas was amazing, filled with family time and fun. Food did play a part, but it didn't take over like it had in previous years. I didn't spend days making calorific treats, cakes, fudges and trifles. Instead I decided I was taking Christmas Day off plan, meaning I would eat whatever I fancied and for the rest of the holiday I would cook recipes from Joe's 'Lean in 15' books to keep it healthy. I enjoyed some chocolate for the first time all year on Christmas day and I had roast potatoes, dessert and cheese.

People often remark about my 100% approach, saying I am rigid and don't enjoy life. It doesn't feel like that for me. I've spent years eating exactly what I wanted and it left me with a body I despised. I looked upon my new approach as me being kind to myself and my body, nurturing myself and striving towards my goals. I didn't feel deprived or like I was missing out because I was eating good quality food and had endorphins flowing through me like liquid gold. I didn't have alcohol and as a result, didn't wake on Boxing Day morning with the usual hangover. In fact, I felt so good that Martin and I ran a 5k. This was the first 5k run I had ever done. The Pretty Muddy run was 5k, but that had been interspersed with obstacles. I have always had a mental block when it came to running, believing I was too big to run. The 5k was tough, but not insurmountable and I felt so amazing when we'd completed it.

On New Year's Day I started the Trinity Transformations Trinity Plan. The first week on the plan was called the Diet Makeover. There was a list of food provided and it was essentially made up of single ingredient foods with a few surprising additions such as dark chocolate and nut butter. I would be allowed to eat freely from the list. I found this rather daunting because I'd been used to having the portions prescribed; this also presented a challenge because it meant I would need to come up with recipes totally by myself. There were four workouts to undertake which looked fairly easy on paper, but in practice were quite the opposite. Trinity introduced specific tempo for each lift. Interestingly, the workouts didn't include any cardio or

HIIT workouts because Trinity believe these interfere with the building of lean muscle mass. This was something I would need to adapt to because I had grown used to and enjoyed the HIIT workouts I'd done throughout the Body Coach plans.

The final element of the first week was to engage in meditation for ten minutes each day. I'll be honest: I struggled with it. Try as I might, my mind wouldn't switch off, galloping a thousand miles per hour and processing work stuff, as well as making me feel self-conscious and, frankly, a bit silly for just sitting there with the sole purpose of calm mindfulness. I decided instead to repurpose this time and made it about positive thinking and affirmations. I'd spend quality time being kind to myself and manifesting my thoughts.

I enjoyed the first week on the plan and sent a breakdown of what I'd eaten to the boys. According to their feedback, I could incorporate more carbohydrates into my nutrition. Again, this was something different to my previous routines as I'd been used to eating carbs only after a workout. However, I decided to embrace it and did some research to understand which food sources contained high amounts of carbohydrate without having to revert to bread, rice and pasta. I choose to eat oats, shelled hemp seeds, chia seeds, medjool dates, rye bread and banana as my main carb sources and found several amazing recipes to include them.

Doreen, Sarah and Shelley had been incorporated into the Admin Crew. Doreen was an avid watcher of my vlogs and had always supported members with comments which is what being an admin is all about (contrary to the popular belief of being there only to delete posts). I was pleased to have her on board. Shelley is a Personal Trainer and we'd formed a relationship back in the early days of my journey. I was thrilled when she agreed to join because I knew she would work well with other members of the crew and being a triathlete, she could inspire people, who were already fit, to take their journey to the next level. I'd known Sarah since my early twenties when we'd worked together. I'd discovered she was a member of the page by accident one day when I noticed that she had liked one of my posts and so I wrote to her. We share a similar story - she has battled with food demons her whole life, too. When I found out she was following the 90daysss plan, I was over the moon and just had to have her on the crew. The BGJTL community had over 12,000 members now and was still going strong.

Having a birthday in early January is not much fun - people are generally partied out after New Year, therefore it has usually been quiet in terms of socialising with friends and family. Martin always works hard to make it special and had booked a spa day for me. The idea of going to a spa had never appealed to me prior to losing weight and I would avoid it like the plague. But finally, aged 39, I was thrilled to go and a happy to wear a bikini. That said, there was still the occasional moment of insecurity when Miss. Meddler tried to take over and make me want to run for the changing room. I was learning that no matter how good my body looked, if I didn't control my inner critic, I could still feel like the big girl. In a certain way, my inner critic WAS the big girl who just couldn't come to terms with the fact that I was getting further and further away from her. She wanted to keep me safe from the outer world, in which I was thriving by now, through injecting her old ways of thinking into my mind from time to time. I have come to accept and understand her. She was no longer in control.

At our Christmas party, I shared with the admin crew that I fancied doing some motivational speaking. Bob then suggested I should do a seminar and sell tickets for it. I protested profusely about the idea, but since she was adamant, I agreed to think it over. Before I knew it, I actually started to plan the first BGJTL seminar. I'd found a venue in Milton Keynes with the capacity to hold 200 people - not that I expected that many to come, anyway, but the Admin Crew were optimistic. Lorraine from the group had kindly agreed to set up access to a ticket purchasing site which would make the administration of the tickets sales easier. I asked each one of the Admin Crew to practice a five-minute presentation of their own journeys using a skeleton framework. This included an overview of their own lean journey, why they had started it and what was next for them. I wanted each of them to have a part to play on the day. Pete came up with the idea that we should all pose in exercise gear in front of a black backdrop and he would create a poster by superimposing our images onto a background. We could use this to help advertise the event. We giggled a lot as we each loaded our images to the admin chat for the others to see.

I focused on my own presentation. Pete produced a branded slide deck using the content I'd provided. I wanted the whole thing to be photos and pictures and then I would add the commentary on the day. I also invited a guy called Neil Marsh to the seminar. Neil had started to follow me before Christmas and had commenced a vlog stating me as his inspiration for doing so. He had set himself a goal to run 2017 miles during 2017 and was sharing this journey with his followers. I loved his spirit, his positivity and the fact that he had lost a lot of weight, too, albeit not through the Body Coach Programme. I asked him if he would present at the seminar which was a risk as we'd never met, but I could tell from his vlog style that he would be great.

A few months previously, one of the group members, Sarah, wrote to me to say she was leaving the group because she had Cancer. I was devastated for her and the news had of course come as a cruel blow to her and her family. Though we'd never met, I had been inspired at how positively she approached her fight with the big C and decided I wanted to raise money for Cancer charities using the seminar as the vehicle - having Sarah as my inspiration as well as my dear Grandad and other friends and family members who were battling or had battled with the disease.

I decided a charity raffle would be a good idea and with the help of the Admin Team, we set about contacting companies we thought might donate. We were inundated with responses and very generous donations including plans from Trinity Transformations and Sustain Nutrition and signed books from Joe Wicks. We had over 30 raffle prizes! I set up a charity site and posted a link to it on my social media pages. I asked that if people had been grateful for my help this year, and if they were financially able, would they please donate £1. Within a week there was more than £1500 raised.

The day of the ticket sale came. 200 tickets were available.

200 were sold. Within 25 minutes.

I was stunned. The analytics showed that people were travelling from all over the country as well as from Aberdeen, Edinburgh and Wales. I suddenly felt enormous pressure to ensure everything went well. Fortunately, there was still time to ensure this was the case. I asked the admin crew to practice their talks and upload them to our chat, so we could give pointers on what worked well and what didn't. This proved to be invaluable and the team, whilst they hated it to start with, took a lot of value from the practice. I, on the other-hand, didn't practice at all. I would usually rehearse intensely for this sort of thing, but for some reason, I was procrastinating.

Trinity continued and as the weeks progressed, I learned more about macro tracking. Week three introduced calorie counting which felt a bit 1990s and I approached it with an eye roll; however, the boys are right when they say how easy it is to overeat if you are not keeping track of your calories and overeating on clean foods is still overeating and can cause weight gain. It made sense to me and I started to track everything meticulously.

The following week I moved on to keeping tabs on protein amounts before finally incorporating carbs and fats ratios, too. The approach was fairly pragmatic and stated that I should aim to hit the targets within a five percent tolerance. My macro targets were set at 25% protein, 36% carbs and 40% fats. To make life easier, I loaded recipes into MyFitnessPal in advance. This was an arduous task initially, but one that would save me loads of time in the long run. Each evening I would plan my meals and snacks for the following day to ensure my macros were in line with the target. This was much easier than tracking throughout the day and suddenly realising you didn't have enough calories left for dinner.

My calorie amount was increasing slightly week on week to ensure that when I reached plateau, I could reduce my calories down again without getting into dangerously low-calorie territory. Reducing calories at the point of plateau would give my metabolism a boost and get me back into fat burning mode. Midway through the plan, my calorie intake was 1800 per day and I was enjoying a lot of carbs from sources I had never or rarely eaten before my lean journey had commenced the year before. I even had started to experiment with food. I was making dishes such as chia seed puddings and baked oats and sharing my recipes on Instagram.

Chia Seed Pudding
200mls coconut milk
3 tablespoons chia seeds
2 tablespoons raw cacao powder
1 tablespoon lacuma powder
Handful of raspberries
Incorporate all ingredients into a snap lidded jar and leave in fridge overnight

I'd been researching vegan superfoods having followed some people on Instagram who were making amazing vegan recipes. I didn't have any intention of becoming a vegan full time but plant based products appealed to me. I established a relationship with a company called Sevenhills Wholefoods. They offered a discount code for the group and sent me samples of their products to try in my dishes. It was fantastic because I got to try so many things I'd never known existed like Incan berries, cacao nibs, coconut sugar and maca powder. Followers were very interested in the recipes and I was thrilled because the experiments with new foods and flavours gave me a feeling of more energy.

My mind-set was becoming stronger every day. I was gaining strength from the way I was beating the food demons and I was working hard to stop worrying about what other people thought of me. This was aided by the affirmations which were changing my self-talk and providing me with a feeling that I was enough.

I'd lived my life adding caveats:

'I'll be worthy when I've done xyz'

'I'll be more lovable if I lost a stone'

And yet what I had come to learn is that weight doesn't define who I am or make me feel any differently about myself. What makes me feel different is what I choose to believe about myself. If I tell myself constantly that I am beautiful, I am worthy, I am enough, then even if I feel like I am lying to start with, over time these things manifest into truth. These new beliefs are compounded through deliberately practicing the positive self-talk and have nothing to do with body composition.

This positive approach would come in handy when I experienced another horrendous day in the company of the trolls.

'I hope you don't mind me saying so, but your arms look really big in your latest vlog'.

I laughed when I read it at first but then Miss. Meddler stepped in and started her games. The thing about criticism is it always penetrates deepest if it's about something I feel insecure about. I'd worked so hard to get my arms into shape, banishing the bingo wings and losing over 4 inches from each bicep. I felt confident in showing them off and for the first time I was relishing wearing sleeveless tops. This new-found confidence was sketchy, though, because I'd not practiced it for very long and therefore this person's words were able to throw me off balance. I wrote back to saying that it wasn't the best thing to say to somebody who had lost lots of weight'.

'You just can't be criticised because you are always so perfect'

I decided to block this person and worked hard to just let the comments go. I concluded that I didn't believe my arms were big and therefore this person's opinion didn't matter. It took me several excruciating hours to get to that point though. Blocking somebody was equally painful, but in the end, I decided that the best way to deal with negativity was to remove it from my life when I could.

And then, like a left hook from Mike Tyson, along came blow number two. This time it was on my YouTube channel. I'd received a few unpleasant comments from this woman before and so knew what to expect, but I read on. And on. And on.

I was gloating and showing off. I was fame hungry and brain washing people while at the same time jumping on Joe Wicks's bandwagon.

And on it went, full of poison and bad language. This woman was angry and it seemed that she needed to let me have it.

When I read things like this about myself, I take a huge step back and sadly question everything I do. Maybe that's the point. That's what Trolls want. To pull the rug from under you. Derail you. Hit you where it hurts and if you've reached this far into my story, if you've understood what has shaped the person I am, then you will understand the damage it does, even temporarily.

My husband reminded me that

'They say a little knowledge is dangerous, but it's not half as bad as a lot of ignorance.'

True. I have indeed experienced many episodes of trolling and each time I take stock and think about the feedback. In this case I decided the feedback was completely useless. It might be her opinion of me and I felt sad that she had formed it; however, I recognised it was shared neither by the majority, nor by me. People who followed my vlogs and were members of my group were generally doing so because they found my journey helpful. I reminded myself that I couldn't please everyone and that I could make a conscious choice to let go of this situation. And so, after a few hours of licking my wounds, I decided not to delete this woman's comment and carried on regardless.

Trolls are insatiable characters however and so, as if those blows hadn't been enough, along came the kick in the teeth, this time delivered by a medley of women. I actually couldn't believe it when I opened my Facebook chat and read a message from a lady who'd been a member of the Facebook group for a long time. She told me that members of an unofficial 'Trinity' group were making fun of me. They didn't like the fact that that Rob and Ben were using my vlogs as part of their marketing campaign, with my blessing. The women had started to record vlogs acting as if they were me, but poking fun and being mean in the most childish of ways. I was sent a screenshot of the conversations and established that several of the women were actually members of BGJTL. I blocked them and went to bed that night feeling severely bruised and also quite angry.

People harboured real animosity towards me in a way that made me feel dreadful and it was happening often. I'd seen quite a few posts from people saying that if you put yourself out there, you need to expect trolling but I think this is sad and it represents one of the pitfalls of social media. I practiced positive self-talk until I fell asleep.

The next day I woke ready to carry on, remembering once again that the only way to avoid criticism is to do or say nothing, neither of which were outcomes I favoured.

Standing in the mirror, ready to face the day, I found her there as she always was - little girl Me once more but rather than my comforting her this time, she seemed to be whispering, 'You can do this.'

I breathed out. Smiled back.

Yes I can.

134

Chapter Fifteen

The BGJTL Motivational Seminar was a very big deal. I felt the weight of expectations on my shoulders and I was determined to ensure that everyone would take something away from the day. The night before I met the Admin Crew at the venue and we spent a few hours setting up the room, filling goodie bags with the freebies supplied by various companies and setting out the raffle. My beloved Bob couldn't make it and I really missed having there but she sent us all her best wishes and was sure that the day would go amazingly. Oh, I do hope so, I thought! I'd bought a tree intertwined with twinkling lights and we called it the 'BGJTL wishing tree'. Attendees would be asked to make a wish on a paper heart and hang it on the tree for it to become true.

H had come up with a musical intro for each of the speakers and she had done a voice over for each one. My song was Little Mix's 'Salute' and H did a full-on X Factor style intro, roaring:

'Ladies and Gentleman, welcome to the first BGJTL Motivational Seminar, please welcome to the stage, Angelaaaaa.... Cox.' It was magical. When I heard it during the practice run, my arms prickled with goose-bumps and I protested that it was all a bit too 'showy'. The Admin Crew insisted we had to keep it, and though I struggled with it and cringed, I was thrilled that H had produced something so slick. The Admin Crew love to have a giggle, but they also know that I like things to be professional and credible and they respect that. I was hugely appreciative of the effort they had put into the event and their individual presentations.

When everything was set up, we went to the bar and met some of the attendees who were staying over the night before. It felt bizarre putting faces to names – even though I had seen their profile pictures before - and feeling a natural affiliation with these total strangers. The conversations flowed naturally. Like old friends picking up seamlessly from where they'd last left off.

The seminar was due to start at 09.30 AM. In the preceding hours, I was like a bumble bee trapped in a jar. I couldn't keep still and was flitting from one thing to another, checking details and trying to ignore the fact I hadn't practiced my talk. Even now, with only hours to go before the event, I was still undecided about how much of my journey I was willing to share and to practice the talk would have meant committing to it. I would 'wing it' and see where my heart led me. The Admin Crew had everything under control and had even found time to go to the gym that morning. I was too focused on the details of the day to think about exercise. I was getting updates from the Admin Crew via the chat group and I could tell they were high with adrenaline. H arrived at 7.30am and came bounding into my hotel room like Tigger. She was always so chirpy in the mornings and having her around made me feel instantly calmer. She was able to restore my equilibrium and I was thankful that she was part of the team. H had brought Lizzie along (one of the first members of the Admin Crew) and it was a delight to finally meet her. She looked as beautiful in real life as she did in her photos and her warm hug was most welcome. They were both excited to find out what the day had in store and went off in search of the others.

Alone again, I pulled on a pair of size 8 black jeans and a black BGJTL t-shirt which had my name printed on the back in bright pink. Shelley had arranged t-shirts for each of us to aid easy identification. I felt slim, which was a positive start to the day. I looked in the mirror and took a moment to remind myself how far I had come by holding my blue spotty size 20 dress against me. I told myself that I had earned the right to tell my story and as people were willing to listen, I didn't need to be nervous.

It was wonderful to see some new but familiar faces and some whom I considered friends even though we'd never met. I had been beyond thrilled to receive a message a few days before from Sarah, the inspiration behind the charity fund raising, to say that although she'd recently had surgery and had been feeling unwell from the chemotherapy, she desperately wanted to be there. I was blown away once more by the resolve of this incredible woman and when we saw each other, just stood and hugged. I could do this I thought. For Sarah. For my Grandad. For nine-year-old me and all the amazing people who'd gone out of their way to make it that day, each one of them, I was sure, battling their own demons. I could do it for them and for us. Feeling inspired, I went off to get changed.

The Admin Crew were busy engaging people in the various money raising activities and Martin, Finley and Coral were selling raffle tickets. I was on my own. The nerves were kicking in and I was feeling overwhelmed. Whenever I feel this, I try to get a grip by breaking down the task ahead into bitesize pieces. This helps me to dilute the feeling of being overwhelmed. In this instance, the only thing I needed to focus on was bitesize piece one which was to get into my dress and heels and bitesize piece two, to make it to the stage without falling over. Once I was there, I could focus on the other bitesize pieces. Removing the enormity of the situation and purely focussing on the few minutes directly ahead of me helped me to calm down.

I was getting changed in a small office next to the main room. I was conscious that people were walking past and could see into the room through the glass panel in the door, therefore I huddled in the corner as I removed my jeans and top, hoping nobody would see me in my bra and pants. I then laughed at myself - they'd seen me in my bra and pants on several occasions on the page! I'd chosen a maroon coloured, leather pencil dress which I teamed with the nude Louboutin heels that Martin had bought me for Christmas. I wiggled my toes into the sky-high Louboutin's - a choice I instantly regretted as I had an hour of standing ahead of me and had to try and make it to the stage without falling over and hurting myself horribly. As I stood in the corridor waiting for my cue, my heart was beating like the bass drum in a marching band. It was so loud I could hear it ringing in my ears and I could literally feel the blood pumping around my body.

'You're going to smash it, just be yourself' I was telling myself over and over whilst trying to shush Miss. Meddler who was busy convincing me I was going to make a spectacular entrance by falling flat on my face.

When I heard H's voiceover and the Little Mix music boom over the sound system, I thought I might actually be sick. I swallowed hard and pressed my knuckle, an NLP anchoring technique I'd picked up along the way. Pressing my knuckle is the mechanism

137

which triggers the confidence vibes and thankfully, it worked marvellously.

'Ladies and Gentleman, please welcome to the stage, Angelaaaaa…. Cox!!'

I walked into the room and instantly felt the warm and accepting nature of the audience. I was immediately grounded by their big smiles and standing ovation. This allowed me to make it to the stage without falling over on my heels - almost like I was being carried - and as soon as I made it, I felt ready. Despite the lack of practice, I now knew I would be just fine. I was telling my own story, I knew it like the back of my hand and I was the only person who knew what was coming next, so if I missed a bit or decided not to tell it all, nobody would know.

The next hour passed by in a blur and when I looked out over the sea of faces, many had tears rolling down their cheeks. My heart had led me to tell some of the more impactful elements of my story and talking about the abuse for the first time was liberating for me and clearly emotional for the audience. I'd told a handful of people about it previously, but this was the first time even the Admin Crew had heard this aspect of my journey and how it had contributed to − or rather shaped - my relationship with food; but equally, how I was determined to re-write the future.

At points, the room was filled with laughter, particularly when I presented my 'Ode to the Trolls' which heard Lily Allen's song 'Fuck you, fuck you very, very much' blaring from the sound system. The audience broke into rapturous applause and clearly enjoyed this moment.

I'd been on stage for an hour when I heard myself saying the final words 'And that was this big girl's journey to lean'. As the room erupted into claps and whoops, I stood feeling both elated and yet emotionally drained (and with very sore feet from the ridiculously high heels!) I had delivered the whole talk without any notes and spoken directly from the heart. It had felt effortless and I was suddenly amazed at how easy I had found it to be so open with complete strangers. I guess the months of sharing of my journey on social media prepared me for this. I'd been so saddened afterwards to learn that several people in the room had experienced similar ordeals

138

and in some instances, I was the first person they had ever told about them.

I took my seat in the audience and listened to the Admin Crew relay their stories. It occurred to me that we'd all faced difficulties and challenges along the way and I was sure that most of the audience probably had too. Life can be tough and we are marvellous, strong creatures who seem able to cope with whatever it throws at us. For some the coping mechanisms become addictions and these might be with food, alcohol, cigarettes, drugs, exercise, perfectionism, cleaning – basically anything that will provide a crutch to help us on our way. As each member of the Admin Crew spoke, I recognised that what many of us had been able to do was consciously identify the crutch, but more importantly, identify the root causes making us require the crutch in the first place, which was one of the keys to success. It was emotional listening to the individual journeys and I am sure there wasn't one person in the room that day who couldn't resonate with something that was divulged.

We'd arranged a 45 minute break to give people chance to meet each other and 'network'. During this session I was inundated with hugs and kisses from members. I was acutely embarrassed about the fact that people were queueing up to have a selfie with me. I felt a bit silly and kept saying:

'It's just me, you don't need to queue. I'll come and find you'.

And yet people were saying how much I had touched their lives and how my story had been a catalyst for them to spring into action. Whenever I hear this, it always makes me feel proud. I realise that there are many other people in this world who have achieved sustainable weight loss and I am not special in that respect; however, many have tapped into my story and been inspired to follow, which is a huge honour to me.

The seminar had been a success. Neil Marsh had told his amazing story about how he battled with his weight and now runs a fitness business and puts himself through all manner of challenges. I had closed the seminar with my ten top tips for getting lean. When we sat in the car after the event I put my head back on the seat and breathed in deeply. I had just stood in front of 200 people and told a story of successful weight loss; if you'd have told me I'd be doing that 18 months previously I'd have told you that you were bonkers. The icing on the cake was that the BGJTL community and all of the wonderful companies who donated prizes had raised £5400 for Macmillan Cancer Support.

H and a lady called KT, who would go on to join the Admin Crew and become a very special friend, had filmed the event and later created an 'after-movie' which featured the highlights of the events to the Little Mix song 'Salute'. It was such a lovely gesture and a great way to re-live all aspects of the day, those I had witnessed, and those I hadn't.

I expected to be incredibly emotional during the act of telling my story and I was surprised that in reality I wasn't. I was happy and proud that I was able to hold my resolve.

Afterwards however, I sat in the car on the drive home and I was suddenly hit by the enormity of what had occurred. It was then that the tears began to flow.

Chapter Sixteen

I grabbed at the handfuls of skin on my tummy and sighed with displease.

I was half way through the Trinity plan. I had lovely lean legs, a great bum and defined shoulders. My face was a nice shape and I still had my boobs. I was conscious that I didn't really want to lose any more weight, because I didn't want to lose my curves. I'd always strived to be slim but my goal wasn't to be so lean that I could see my every muscle. That said, however much I was in love with my body - and with most parts I genuinely was - I couldn't get past the look of my tummy.

I'd always had an overhang for as long as I can remember and after two C-sections it had only deteriorated. It started from one hip and hung down all the way around to the other. The hanging skin over my C-section scar was so damaged it resembled cottage cheese. I couldn't bear to look at it. My belly button had become a long horizontal line and the skin above my belly button was loose and jiggled when I moved. The more weight I lost, the looser the skin became and I felt and looked deflated.

I was doing more than 500 abdominal exercises every week, lifting heavy weights, eating clean, drinking water and body brushing daily. I'd used firming creams and massage techniques.

Nothing would improve it.

I would look decent in a bikini if I was standing still. I could hold in my core and because the muscles were strong would look lean. My pants would hide the overhang and, provided I didn't move, nobody would guess that I was hiding so much skin.

But, if I relaxed my core it would wobble. If I jumped, it would jump with me. If I did a push up, it would hang down to the floor. If I took down my pants, I suddenly looked like the big girl again.

The sight of the overhang instantly made me look 2 stones heavier.

I had to do something about it.

Ruth had joined the admin crew and was an instant hit. She had lost five stones by walking over 20k steps each day. She had also had a tummy tuck. I remember seeing her 'before' photos on Instagram and she showed a photo of herself bending over and the loose skin hanging down. That photo was like a massive smack in the face to me, in a good way. I was so relieved that I was not the only person who faced this challenge.

I started to look up photos of tummy tucks on Instagram and then progressed to watching abdominoplasty operations being performed on YouTube. The procedure looked incredibly brutal and I wondered what the pain must be like afterwards. Essentially you are cut from one hip to the other hip along the bikini line and then from hip to belly button and back to the hip. This produces a large piece of skin which is then removed, retaining the belly button on its stalk. The skin on the upper abdomen is then peeled back revealing the abdominal wall. When a woman is pregnant, the size of the baby often tears open the abdominals creating a gap between them. During a tummy tuck these muscles can be repaired by stitching it back together using permanent nylon threads. The skin from the upper abdomen is then placed back over the abdominals like a bed sheet and pulled down to meet the hairline. A hole is created for the original belly button to poke through and then the belly button and the skin edges are stitched and glued together. The words 'tummy tuck' make it sound so simple, but the operation was far from it.

One of the elements I didn't like was that afterwards, drains were left in the tummy and pubis mons for several days to reduce swelling. This idea filled me with dread. I'd had a drain following the gall bladder removal years before and still recall the sickening sensation I felt when it was removed. The sight of the drains poking through the skin made me feel queasy too. Further research informed me that there was a method of tummy tuck that was drain-free, but this approach was not as widely used by surgeons because of a complication called seroma. This is when a build-up of fluid can occur in the cavity between the muscle wall and the skin. Despite the potential complication, I was convinced that drain-free would be the type of tummy tuck for me. My core was very strong and I was able to lift extremely heavy weights, hold a plank for over 4 minutes and do full sit ups with ease, so I was convinced I wouldn't need muscle repair. This appeared to be the element of the operation that caused the most pain afterwards and I was pleased I wouldn't need it.

I did some research into surgeons and found a handful who performed drain-free tummy tucks. One of these was called Mr. Ahmad and he worked out of a number of private hospitals in the Cambridge area including Nuffield which was an hour's drive from my home. I rang his secretary, Nicky, and we chatted for over half an hour. We clicked immediately and she was able to fit me in for a consultation later that week.

On the day of the consultation I pulled on my skinny jeans and knee-length boots. I never got tired of the feeling that wearing knee length boots gave me. It was one of those Non-Scale Victories that I had been yearning for as long as I could remember. I'd purchased long boots twice before and both had elasticated uppers because leather uppers wouldn't fit over my chunky calves. I remember breaking a pair of boots in a shoe shop once by trying to force them to zip up. I was so mortified, I put them back on the shelf and left the shop pronto, closely followed by guzzling two cream cakes from Greggs next door. The pair I wore for the consultation were soft brown leather off the peg from Ralph Lauren and to zip them up over the denim felt like winning the lottery.

As soon as I met him, I knew I'd be in safe hands. Mr. Ahmad was warm, friendly and extremely humble, given his role and seniority. He explained to me that he had been practicing drain-free tummy tucks for over ten years and in that time, had only had one episode of seroma. He asked me lots of questions about my history, my family and my reasons for wanting the operation and he appeared surprised to learn that I had been so overweight. He commented that I was extremely lucky that the rest of my body had responded so well to the exercise as a lot of ladies would require thigh, arm and breast lifts after such weight loss. I explained to him that I would like the scar to be very low sited and would like him to use a method called quilting stitches to ensure the scar didn't rise up. He knew what I was talking about and appeared surprised that I had researched so heavily. I also said that I didn't want muscle repair. He smiled slightly and said:

'Ah but you'll need it Mrs. Cox'.

He asked me to undress to my underwear and he and a chaperone came into the room. I stood awkwardly in my pants and bra trying to hold my tummy in. He asked me to lie on a bed and he poked the skin on my tummy. He then asked me to do sit ups whilst he pressed down onto my abdominals.

'Very strong muscles you have' he said, whilst my need for approval danced with joy.

'But you will need muscle repair. There is a 1cm gap and repairing it is advisable, because it will enhance the overall shape'

This news was not so good.

'But that will make it very painful' I moaned.

'You'll want the best possible results' he stated in a way that meant I couldn't disagree.

'I would also recommend some liposuction to the flanks to ensure we can create a lovely waist line' he said.

I'd never really had a waist. I was a classic apple shape and carried most of my weight on my torso so the thought of having a waist was appealing. My only goal, though, was to lose the loose skin and to have a scar that was not visible if I was wearing pants. I reinforced these particulars and we agreed on the approach, taking the surgeon's advice to include liposuction. Mr. Ahmad would send me a quote and the operation was provisionally booked in for 26th April 2017.

I was as high as a kite on the way home. I might finally be free of the skin that I felt was holding me back. Martin was totally supportive and said he wanted me to be happy.

I decided to commit.

It was also around this time that I received an email to say that I had been nominated for two Venus Women's Awards. One was Influential Woman and one was Inspirational Woman. I was both shocked and thrilled at the same time. It was initially unclear who had nominated me, but I later discovered it was submitted by the BGJTL Admin Crew. I didn't think too much more about it until a few weeks later when I received a call to say that I had been named as a Semi-Finalist in both categories. This was wonderful and I posted the news on the group - everybody was thrilled, telling me I

144

would be a winner for sure. I was asked to meet the judging panel for both categories. There was a single judge for the Influential Woman, a solicitor and two judges for Inspirational Woman, both were Professors at Reading University. I couldn't meet either face-to-face due to work commitments and set up calls instead.

I didn't feel a connection with the solicitor. She was very nice, but I felt she was in a rush and didn't really get what it was I was doing via BGJTL. The conversation lasted no longer than twenty minutes. The ladies from Reading University were the opposite and seemed hugely interested; we chatted easily for at least an hour. I came away from both sessions feeling like I'd done the best I could in the circumstances presented and waited for the next steps.

In the meantime, I continued to put my heart and soul into Trinity and my body was shaping up week after week. I had another holiday to Lanzarote coming up and wanted to look my best. It was also vital to be as lean as possible going into the operation.

Just before I left on holiday, I attended the Venus Awards Finalist Announcement. It was being held in Reading and I asked my colleague Robin to come along with me. It was fabulous to see so many wonderful women being recognised for their achievements in a plethora of categories. The first of my categories to be announced was the Influential Woman. Being recognised as influential is remarkably humbling. It's one of those titles you would never give yourself and I hadn't ever considered that I might fit the bill as I didn't think I'd done anything remotely influential. Whilst I had already told myself I wouldn't be a finalist based on the lack of rapport I'd felt with the judge, I was still disappointed when my name wasn't read out as the finalists were announced. Robin tapped my arm and whispered,

'You have done brilliantly to get to this stage'.

I smiled gently, wishing I believed that.

I took it to mean I had failed.

I know people might read this and think it's ridiculous but it's how I have lived my whole life. To not win is to fail and that's how I felt at that point. I grew up believing that only 100% was enough. Whilst I sat pulling at my fingers and trying to eliminate the hot, flushed feeling of failure from my face and chest, I was aware that

145

the Inspirational Woman was being announced. This time I heard my name being called and found myself walking up to the stage to collect the finalist certificate. I smiled huge, genuine smiles for the camera because I was totally thrilled to be a finalist in this category and I caught sight of Robin taking pictures of me with pride. Eighteen months ago, I could never have dreamed of being nominated for these types of awards, let alone be a finalist for Inspirational Woman, and here I was.

When I shared the news with my followers, not one mentioned the fact I wasn't a finalist in the Influential Category. They were just thrilled with the results overall and lots of them commented on the Venus page. Reading through the comments I realised how much of an impact I was having on several lives and this clearly conveyed the message that regardless of an award, I was inspiring others and that was a phenomenal privilege.

I was a winner regardless and that was the best feeling in the world.

Chapter Seventeen

The week before the operation was long and emotional. I'd returned from an amazing holiday in Lanzarote where I had stayed healthy and exercised daily. Spending quality time with Martin and the children had been fabulous and I'd had several moments during the break when I'd reflected on how lucky I was and how much happier I felt in my skin. Martin and I had done HIIT workouts every morning before breakfast and the children had joined in, helping to keep time and counting the reps. It was such a joy to see how our change of lifestyle was impacting the children. They are so positive about exercise and eat much more healthily now.

Before leaving for holiday I'd completed the Trinity plan and was thrilled with my progress. I could see a real difference from the weight training and I felt strong and toned. My shoulders were looking chiselled and my quads were popping. I had gained an inch on my waist which the boys had told me to expect due to the increase in carbohydrates; but overall, I was over the moon and had happily worn a bikini on holiday. I'd not run around in it however, due to the loose skin.

When we landed back in the UK just a week before the operation, the enormity of what was ahead hit me like a sledge hammer. My brain just wouldn't switch off and whilst on one hand I was filled with excitement, on the other I was a bundle of nerves due to trying to process the myriad of 'what ifs'. I was also grappling with an astounding aspect that I hadn't bargained for. I was suddenly terrified of letting go of the Big Girl.

I'd spent my whole life being an expert at binge eating, overeating and being the Big Girl. I was good at it, brilliant in fact, and it had always served me 'well'. Being the Big Girl was safe - it shielded me from harm and kept me in the background. Becoming leaner and sharing my story had thrust me into the limelight and whilst I was comfortable with that, there was still a minute part of me that knew I had the opportunity to revert to the Big Girl, should I want to. This was like my comfort blanket and whilst I didn't require it to make me feel safe these days, it was there, tucked away in case I ever did.

The impending operation made me face the fact that the comfort blanket needed to be thrown away once and for all. I have been a thumb sucker my whole life and when I was born I started to use a literal blanket, which I would rub between my fingers and right thumb whilst I sucked my left thumb. It was quite specific and no substitute would suffice. My mum recounts a story where I screamed for over an hour because I spotted my soaking wet blanket hanging on the washing line one day after being laundered. When the time came to finally bin the blanket, it was like having my right arm removed. I continued to suck my thumb, but learned not to need the blanket - because it just wasn't there anymore.

I envisaged this situation would bring about a similar outcome. Investing in an expensive operation was one thing - and one that I battled with because it felt so self-indulgent - but equally, the physical aspect of the operation would make it difficult to go back to overeating. My skin would be stretched tightly and eating excessive amounts of food would be a definite no-no.

I had to make a vow to myself that the comfort blanket was no longer an option and the Big Girl, who had been such a major part of my life, could no longer be relied upon. This meant trusting that I had the capability to sustain a healthy routine for the rest of my life and making a pact that I would commit to that as my payback for the investment I was making. It might sound straightforward, but this was a huge emotional barrier to overcome and it gave me many sleepless hours in that last week.

In the lead up to the big day, I took photographs in all sorts of positions and they made me feel exactly how my 16 stone Body Coach photos had the year before. I'd taken them with the apron of skin on show, not holding my core, lying on my side, leaning forward and doing push-ups. I had not seen photos of myself like this before and whilst I was aware of what the skin looked like in real life, seeing it on the photos put me back in the mind-set of the Big Ggirl again. To help me prepare mentally, I shared my photographs on Instagram and in the group. People were mostly shocked, because they hadn't seen the extent of the skin in my usual standing poses.

Several of them said that they could, for the first time, understand why I decided to have the operation and of course there were a handful of people who stated that I was shallow and doing it for cosmetic reasons and one lady who announced she was unfollowing me because she no longer saw me as an inspiration based on the decision to have surgery. I let this all go. I had to. There was too much at stake.

For once I genuinely didn't care what anybody thought.

It was I who was living with the skin. It had to go.

On the day of the operation, Martin and I drove to the hospital, mostly in silence. Throughout the hour-long journey, I was working through scenarios in my mind and Martin knows that it's best to leave me to it, occasionally giving my leg an encouraging, warm rub when he heard me let out an involuntary sigh.

I reported to the hospital reception desk at 11am and I noticed Mr. Ahmad and Nicky were having a meeting at a small table. I waved and they returned the greeting; Martin and I took a seat nearby. Within a few minutes, they came over to where we were seated and I jumped up and gave them both a hug. We chatted for a while and I shared with them how excited I felt that it was finally happening. Mr. Ahmad took Martin and me to a consulting room and took photos of me in my underwear as 'before' images for comparison later. We signed the consent forms and he said he would see me soon.

We were taken to a private room which would be my home for the next few nights. The room was light and airy and there was a hospital gown folded on the bed. The nurse came in and measured me for compression stockings and suggested I change into the gown and the fabulously unattractive mesh knickers. When I'd changed, she returned and helped me pull on the ridiculously tight compression socks which needed to be worn during and beyond the operation to prevent blood clots.

I was ready - at least in terms of the attire, anyway. I unpacked my bag and laid out the arnica pills and bromelain tablets which, according to my extensive research, were meant to help reduce swelling after the operation. I brushed my teeth and then brushed them again not only because I was hungry from not eating for 15 hours, but also to pass the time. Martin kept reassuring me that everything would be ok.

Mrs. Smith came to see me. She was the anaesthetist and was referred to respectfully as 'THE Mrs. Smith' by Mr. Ahmad. This had immediately filled me with confidence about her competence; meeting her only cemented that. She was a very calm, quiet lady with a mass of curly hair and she was very professional, but kind too. She was impressed with my diet and exercise regimes and said that I was a 'model patient'. It was lovely to hear that.

It was after 2 PM when I was taken to theatre. By this time the nerves had kicked in. Mrs. Smith and a young guy called Andrew who was assisting, met me in the side room where the anaesthetic would be administered and the two of them kept me chatting jovially which I knew was an attempt to keep my mind occupied and so I just relaxed into it. I felt the needle spike into my hand and the cannula was attached. This was closely followed by the cooling sensation of the drugs filling my veins and before I knew it, I was waking up in a binder, job done.

I don't actually recall waking up. I just became aware that I was back in my room with Martin. I was hooked up to a morphine drip which allowed me to self-administer pain relief at controlled intervals, so despite not feeling any pain at all, I was acutely aware that I couldn't move.

It was as if my core had been removed and I had lost the ability to sit up on my own.

Thankfully, I was propped up on the bed.

'Is it ok Baby?' I asked Martin hesitantly.

'It looks amazing' he said reassuringly. 'Mr. Ahmad came to show me the photos'

I looked down and pulled up my gown but my tummy was covered in a white binder, obscuring the view of the body. I pulled the gown back down and gave in to resting.

Mr Ahmad visited later that night and said the operation had gone well. I'd been under the knife for more than five hours! Mr. Ahmad was so meticulous with his stitching that his operating time was much higher than other surgeons had quoted for the same procedure. I asked Mr. Ahmad if I could see the photos - he gave me his word he would email them to me when he got home. He kept his promise and I when I opened the email attachment just before midnight, I couldn't believe it was me.

The tummy was flat and there was nothing hanging. It was miraculous.

He also sent me a picture of the 4lb slab of skin that had been removed. It looked like two butterfly wings and I decided to post it on Instagram. The response was mixed, with several people commenting that it was inappropriate and one lady - who loves to take the moral high ground - saying it was not right to post bleeding flesh on Instagram and that I shouldn't be sharing these elements of my journey. To my mind, I was just sharing my journey warts and all, in the way I always had. The reality of a tummy tuck is that a huge piece of skin is removed. I hadn't realised that until I'd done the research and it seemed lots of other people hadn't appreciated that it was the case, either. Alongside those who disagreed, there were a huge number of supporters and one lady who made me giggle when she said she was eating butterfly chicken when she'd looked at the photo. Probably no butterfly chicken for her for at least a few days, then!

That night, I remained hooked to morphine and a permanent flow of oxygen. My blood pressure and heart rate dropped several times and I tried to drink as much water as I could to keep myself hydrated. In the middle of the night I needed to use the loo. I was not up for using a bed pan, so I called the nurses and asked for assistance with getting up. They helped me to adjust the bed and get myself into a position where I was sitting with my legs dangling at the side of the bed. It felt like my body was ten times heavier than it actually was as I tried to stand up. I became aware that I couldn't get into an upright position. My tummy had been pulled so tightly, I was bent over at a 45-degree angle and I suddenly panicked that I would never be able to straighten. I didn't feel any pain, thanks to the morphine and remnants of the anaesthetic, but I struggled to walk and getting down to the toilet felt like I was trying to sit on the floor. It was a lot lower down than it had seemed earlier that day. I was exhausted when I made it back to my bed, but proud that I had done it.

151

I was determined that my recovery would be flawless and speedy. I would do anything I could to help that along. The next morning, after a morphine-fuelled night of broken sleep, I got up again, this time unaided, to use the loo. I felt an odd burning sensation at the front on my hip. It was weird, but I just put this down to the stitches. As the morning progressed, each time I got up, I would feel this pain. I tried to take my mind off it by changing into my own night dress. While changing I caught a glimpse of a huge swathe of purple bruising spilling out of the top of the binder that was wrapped tightly around me. I was also aware that the binder was covered in pink stains which I guessed must have been the liquid used during liposuction mixed with my blood. It made me wince a little and I quickly pulled on my night dress. As I sat in the chair next to the bed, still hooked to the morphine, I noticed how swollen my legs were. They looked enormous, as did my breasts and if I didn't know better, I'd have thought I'd had implants. I asked the nurse about the swelling and she said that this was completely normal and not helped by the tightness of the binder around the torso. She said to drink plenty of water and keep positive. Simple, right?

Later that morning Ruth and H came to visit and we chatted for a good hour, laughing and joking though I tried to refrain from laughing because it hurt! The girls lifted my spirits immensely. I was enjoying the company and the distraction until the nurses came in and said they needed to fit a compression garment. Ruth and H went out of the room and I struggled to my feet. As one of the nurses pulled the garment tight to fasten one side with the other, I screamed. A searing pain was shooting down my leg and the skin was burning as if there was an iron pressed against the skin. The sister looked at me puzzled and I explained the pain to her. Each time the nurse pulled the garment to fasten the next button, the pain would repeat its punishing stabs. I had tears rolling down my face and the Sister suggested that I needed to see the Surgeon.

When I finally got back into the bed, I felt relieved that the pain had eased, but also worried as to what was causing it. H and Ruth returned and they'd heard the commotion despite being in the corridor. They had Neil Marsh and Saskia who I'd met a few weeks earlier at Neil's training unit with them. Neil and Saskia lived very close to the hospital and had offered to visit. Whilst it was lovely to see them and I was hugely appreciative that they had made the effort to come and see me, my mind kept wandering off to the cause of the pain. After an hour or so, everybody left and I tried to get up. Once again, the pain shot down my leg and the burning sensation returned. Coupled with this was a horrendous pain in my back from walking in the bent over angle. Walking a few steps felt like running a 5k and I was regretting the decision to have the surgery immediately and immensely.

Martin and the children arrived later that day. It was a pure joy to see their smiling faces. They were fussing around me and had brought me amazing handmade cards. I quietly discussed with Martin that I was worried about my leg whilst the children played air hostesses with the bedside trolley table. Mr. Ahmad arrived and I explained the pain I was feeling. He said he believed that one of the internal stitches may have trapped a nerve in my leg and that it might take six months to right itself. I was in a fog of confusion and didn't challenge this at that point, but overnight, as each time I stood up the burning hell returned, I knew I couldn't live with it.

Something would need to be done.

The next day I should have been going home, but instead I told the nurse that the pain needed to be seen to. She asked Mrs. Smith to come and see me to assess if she could prescribe pain relief to help. She suggested a walking frame to relieve the pressure off my back and legs, as well as regular doses of diazepam. I said I didn't want to be taking such strong pain relief for months so a physio replaced the walking frame with crutches, as they would serve me better and be more realistic to use in the real world. I, on the other hand, had no intention of using crutches, clinging onto the hope that my leg might right itself.

When Mr. Ahmad returned, I explained that I couldn't continue being in this state, because the pain was acute and my job meant I needed mobility for travelling. He clearly felt terrible about the situation, although it wasn't my intention to make him feel like that and several minutes after leaving the room, he returned and said that he was taking me to theatre and he would release the stitch under local anaesthetic. I was instantly relieved, followed by a whiff of anxiousness, because he had mentioned the word 'local'. That meant I would be awake.

'It's not going to hurt, is it?' I inquired hesitantly.

'You'll feel the initial injection, but it will be numb after that' he assured me calmly.

I was wheeled to the theatre in a chair by THE Mrs. Smith. It seemed odd to me that she had been the one to collect me from my room, rather than a Porter and I asked her why she was there, given I was only having a local anaesthetic.

'I just want to make sure you are ok' she said caringly.

This time I was taken directly into the Theatre Room and it immediately conjured up memories of my C-section procedures. There was one operating table in a vast room which was peppered with bleeping machines, large screens and people. There were people everywhere, which made me very nervous.

'Why is it so busy?' I asked, addressing my question to nobody in particular. This was just another red flag that was raised in my head.

'We are in the presence of a star' said a familiar voice behind me who I recognised to be Andrew.

'It's great to see a patient after the event' said another nurse, 'it's just a shame you need another procedure'

Andrew helped me onto the table and I suddenly felt extremely embarrassed that I wasn't wearing any underwear. He was far too handsome to be seeing me in this predicament.

'We'll need to take your compression off' he said gently, but firmly.

As the nurses unhooked the compression garment it occurred to me I would see my tummy for the first time since the operation. As I looked down at the flesh that was pulled tight over my abdomen the emotion took hold of me.

I couldn't believe my eyes.

There was no overhang and my hip bones were no longer covered in rolls of fat. I was also shocked to see the extent of the scar across my lower tummy which looked like a giant shark bite. I was so overcome I started to cry and the team smiled as they realised that they were tears of joy.

Moments later, I was dragged back from the serenity of the flat-side into the stark reality of the Operating Room. I could hear pop music playing in the Theatre and while part of me thought that it was totally inappropriate, another part of me was grateful for the distraction. I was discombobulated to say the least! I was covered in a weird puffy blanket which was filled with hot air and I immediately felt warm. Too warm.

'This is to regulate your body temperature' said a nurse with big, brown, calm eyes and a green skull cap.

'I am sure it is, but it feels totally weird' I wanted to say, but stayed quiet.

A screen made from green sheeting was erected over my chest so I couldn't see my tummy and I was surprised to suddenly see Mr. Ahmad's face popping over the top of it. He was wearing a surgical cap and gown and was his usual jovial self which in most circumstances I loved him for, but in my current state, was less enamoured.

'Will this be like a C-section where there isn't any pain, but it feels like you are doing the washing up in my tummy?' I asked. I already knew the answer, but I just wanted somebody to say that it wasn't going to be painful.

'Don't worry' said Andrew reassuringly. 'You are in safe hands'.

I noted that he hadn't actually answered my question.

Mrs. Smith and another nurse stood either side of me and each held one of my hands.

I suddenly felt a huge internal surge of panic.

Why on earth would they need to hold my hand?

Or were they trying to hold me down?

What was going to happen?

'Squeeze my hand if you need to' the nurse said.

I shot her a panicked glance.

I wanted to shout 'Right, come on now, tell me why I need hand-holders? You are keeping something from me' but again I kept quiet, not wanting to appear rude.

I saw the cruel spike of the local injection above the screen as it was primed with the anaesthetic. I didn't mind injections so this didn't bother me too much but I asked myself why the needle needed to be quite so long.

'I'm going to put the local in now Angela' said Mr. Ahmad in his usual hypnotic tone. I wish you were a Hypnotist so I wouldn't have to face the next fifteen minutes awake, I thought.

I was jolted out of my day-dream by a searing pain savaging my leg like a shark attack. It was just a needle and yet it felt like a 10-inch jagged blade slowly dragging its way through the muscle of my thigh.

I let out a noise that I don't recall ever making before. It wasn't a scream, it was more of a long, whining siren noise which even as I was making it, made me embarrassed.

'I can feel it' I whimpered as I caught my breath, squeezing the nurse's hand within an inch of its life.

'That's the worst bit over, Mr. Ahmad has administered the local and now it will take effect' said Mrs. Smith comfortingly.

The next step was for Mr. Ahmad to locate the stitch. He explained that he would press down onto the incision before the local took hold. As he applied pressure I felt the familiar sensation of the iron being held against my leg.

'It's burning' I screamed at the top of my lungs.

'We've found the spot' said Mr. Ahmad.

I wanted to jump up and smack him on the nose!

I lay there feeling exhausted and fearing the next step. I winced when Mr. Ahmad stated he was about to cut me open again.

'Try to stay calm and breathe' said the nurse who was holding my hand. Or rather the nurse whose hand had been deprived of blood circulation due to my squeezing.

'Mr. Ahmad is an expert' confirmed another.

'I really don't need you to acknowledge his credibility' I uttered in my head, frustrated. I was bound by my Nan's rule of thumb, if you don't have anything nice to say, say nothing.

The next five minutes were the most painful of my life. As the knife made contact with my skin, the torturous pain commenced and was punishingly unrelenting for the whole duration. Once again, unfamiliar sounds escaped my throat, generated deep within my core.

I was begging them to stop.

I was asking how long it would take.

I was pleading with them to take the pain away.

I felt totally out of control.

The noises fell silent as my body and mind submitted to the pain. I began to sob and could feel the warm tears rolling down my cheeks as my heart continued to pound at an alarming rate in my chest.

Mrs. Smith was telling me over and over how brave I was and she was encouraging me to talk about Finley and Coral.

'Shut the f*ck up!' I wanted to scream at her.

But being ridiculously British even in this most stressful situation, I endeavoured to answer the countless questions she was firing at me, politely!

It seemed to take forever to reach its conclusion and when it finally did, Mr. Ahmad looked apologetic and somewhat shaken. I was struggling to meet his gaze as I wasn't feeling at my most forgiving. I was nearly sure my bottom lip was protruding like that of a six-year-old girl.

'You said it wouldn't hurt' I uttered grudgingly.

'Mr. Ahmad needed to make a decision: either stop, meaning you would be in the pain for weeks and months, or continue and release the stitch' said Mrs. Smith.

'That sounded pretty horrendous' said Andrew. 'Well done, Brave Lady'

Mrs. Smith stayed with me in the Recovery Room. I remember telling her that I felt stressed and I wanted to see Martin. She wheeled my bed along the corridor and into the lift. I was shocked to see my ashen face in the large mirror. I became aware that I was still crying and couldn't seem to stop, even though the pain had departed. I was grateful to Mrs. Smith for staying with me throughout.

On reflection, I concluded that the team probably knew that the operation would be painful from the outset and they didn't tell me because I would have been fearful and stressed before it even began.

That night I recorded a vlog about the operation and it has become one of my most watched vlogs. I guess human beings like to see people battle with adversity and come out the other side, stronger.

Chapter Eighteen

After three nights in hospital I was ready to come home, even though I was a bit apprehensive about travelling in the car for an hour. I still couldn't stand upright and was walking as if incontinence had been a prevailing side effect of the surgery! The crutches helped because at least they provided an indication that I was temporarily disabled in some way and I was also glad to have them because I was still experiencing the burning sensation in my hip, which Mr. Ahmad assured me would pass in a few weeks. My leg was also completely numb down the side of my quad which again I was guaranteed wouldn't be permanent.

One of the horrendous side effects of a tummy tuck is swelling, or 'swell hell' as it is lovingly referred to by those who have suffered through it. The operation is particularly invasive and when the skin is peeled back from the abdominal wall, the lymphatic system is significantly disturbed. It can take up to twelve months for this to return to normal. Add to this the aggressive nature of the muscle repair and the liposuction which, if you have ever seen it demonstrated, is not dissimilar to being stabbed repeatedly, so it is no wonder that swelling occurs. I resembled a barrel around my torso and my legs were so ridiculously swollen I couldn't wear the chino trousers which had been very loose before the operation. Instead, I had to wear tracksuit bottoms and a hoodie. There is lots of advice about how to mitigate swelling including wearing compression garments, drinking lots of water and eating pineapple, all of which I tried.

I walked the short distance from the wheelchair to the car door, wriggled into the car and sat exhausted in the front seat. Coral was immensely excited to tell me that she and Martin had been out to purchase a hospital style bed side trolley so that I would have everything I need close at hand. This was so sweet and summed up Coral's thoughtful demeanour perfectly. Finley was quiet and obviously concerned. He has his own little ways of showing he cares and I was touched during my recovery when each day after school he

158

would sit with me on the bed for half an hour before going off to play.

On the way home from hospital we stopped at Costa and though I felt very self-conscious hobbling in, it was lovely to feel a sense of normality. Having not eaten properly for three days, I treated myself to a hot chocolate with cream and we sat as a family chatting about how I would be looked after at home.

That day, Caoimhe (pronounced Queeva) had joined the Admin Team to replace Bev who had left to set up her own page as a Personal Trainer. Caoimhe had lost a lot of weight and had been a huge influencer on the page - she was the perfect choice. She lived in Ireland and I was pleased that she would be joining us on the 'BGJTL Admins On tour' trip to Ireland we'd planned in 7 weeks. Most of the admin crew would be flying over to meet with Bob and Caoimhe at Bob's house in Lahinch and I had my sights set on this as a reason to put my all into the recovery.

The first few days at home were hard work. I spent most of the time propped up against a pillow mountain in bed and was reliant on Martin and the children to do everything for me. I was an emotional wreck and would burst into tears for no reason. I would do no more than 300 steps in a day and this would feel like running a marathon. My back was giving me grief every time I tried to stand up, protesting vehemently at the fact I couldn't fully straighten due to the tightness of the skin stretched across my tummy. It can take up to two weeks for the skin to stretch enough so a patient can stand tall again and in the meantime the pressure on the lower back is immense.

My heart rate was soaring and I was in fat burning mode for large portions of the day despite the fact I was barely moving. My recovering body was a fat burning machine and my mind was a pit of emotional mush. You burn a large number of calories when you are in recovery and I continued to eat carbohydrates (oats and dates) to make sure my body was getting what it needed.

I wasn't allowed to shower until day 10 – annoying, but somewhat welcome, too, as I definitely didn't have the energy for it. I was meant to wear both the compression garment and the binder 23 hours per day for six weeks. The compression garment resembled something Nora Batty might wear: a highly unattractive, flesh-coloured garment which fastened with hook & eye fasteners and a zip at one side and came up to the just under the breasts. The binder was a highly elasticated swathe of material which wrapped tightly around my middle and fastened with Velcro. French Lingerie it was not!

It took me until day 5 to work up the courage to remove my binder. This was mainly because I was too frightened to look at what lay beneath. When I did take it off, I felt incredibly unstable; it was as if somebody had removed my back bone.

Walking to the mirror was daunting and I was initially shocked when I glanced at myself. I was still covered in dressings and bruises and the side view looked horrendous. My torso was thick and swollen and I had bruising all over my sides which was purple and angry. The front view was better and I loved how my pants lay flat across my hips and pubic bone. I also noticed that most of the dressing was covered by the white material of my pants which meant I wouldn't be able to see the scar in a bikini. I took photos at both angles and then when I was back in my garment, I compared them to my before photos. Even with the swelling, the front view showed a huge improvement, but I couldn't help but focus on my huge legs. I posted the front view on Instagram and laughed at how silly I looked in my white underwear with matching white compression socks. I'd been asked to wear the socks for at least 2 weeks because I'd gone from being so active to inactive. It prevents pulmonary embolism.

Whilst I was warned about the risks of general anaesthetic such as the potential to not wake up, there isn't a warning about how it and the narcotic drugs can impact post-operative recovery. I liken it to the feeling of being on anti-depressants. I felt like I was in a fog, vacant one moment and emotionally unstable the next. It was a difficult few days.

Equally there is no warning about how little you feel allowed to moan because you have elected to have the operation.

I felt the weight of the latter like a millstone. I felt I had to present a positive outlook because I'd chosen to put myself through this ordeal. In reality I was in a state of shock. The gorgeous flat tummy I was expecting was in essence, a swollen Santa-like stomach covered with a shark bite incision. My beautiful toned legs were now 6 inches bigger than before I'd gone in and covered in cellulite. My fit body was now struggling to walk to the bathroom and my positive mind-set had been overtaken by Miss. Meddler who was intent on making me feel totally inadequate, useless and fat again. My pre-operation jeans had a four-inch gap between the button and button hole and I couldn't fit into anything but tracksuit bottoms. This was exacerbated by comparing myself to others. One of the ladies who I was following in a surgery group on Facebook had had the same operation the day after me. I was flabbergasted that just three days after her operation she was out shopping for clothes and yet I couldn't even make it downstairs without feeling lightheaded. My logical mind knew that comparison is the thief of joy, but I appeared to be in a rut and wasn't utilising with the logical part of my brain at all.

I was honest in my daily vlogs and social media posts about how I was feeling and tried hard to find the positives. One of these was that I was continuing to eat clean and stay focussed, not succumbing to chocolate or junk food which could have been so easy. I was jolted out of my misery by a lady who had posted in the group. She essentially stated that there were people in much worse situations than me and she was fed up of hearing me saying how hard it was to have an operation I had elected to have. She said that she was experiencing real issues in terms of caring for an Aunt who was dying and that I should get a grip. This was wrapped in some pretty cruel words but I understood what she was getting at and was inclined to agree at one level. The thing about situations like the one I was in, is it didn't matter what other people were going through, the playing field wasn't level and having somebody in a worse position didn't make it any easier to endure my current situation. The fact that I had voluntarily chosen to have the procedure didn't make it easier either.

I was aware that members of the group were having their say on this girl's post and the vast majority were stating that whilst they were sorry to hear about her situation, she was out of order in her approach. I tried to think about how she must be feeling and show compassion by simply saying 'I am sorry you are going through such a tough time and I am sorry you feel this way about me'. The Admin Crew established that she had left the group and we deleted her post. As usual in these situations, people post follow up comments to show support which is lovely, but not helpful as it then keeps the episode alive for longer than we would want.

I decided to reflect on what the original Poster had said and agreed that I needed to get a grip. And so, I did. I thanked her the next day in my vlog and I set about finding strategies to help me recover. The first of these was to measure my legs and track each day how the swelling was reducing. I set myself mini goals for improving my step count, just by 100 each day and after the first week I went for a short walk. It took me nearly half an hour to walk 500 metres, shuffling along step by step, metre by metre, but I did it and it felt like a little triumph. I built on this day after day and some days I was more successful than others in terms of distance travelled. I was still unable to stand upright two weeks after the operation and Mr. Ahmad assured me that this was a good thing. The swelling in my legs was subsiding and each morning when I removed my binder, I'd catch a glimpse of my tummy and see what the future had in store.

Tummy tuck recovery is long and the final results do not show themselves until months after the operation. Patience is required; I kept telling myself it would amazing. Taking photos helped a lot, especially when I compared them with my 'before' photos and the lovely comments generated by my followers gave me a daily boost of motivation and positivity. What astounded me during this period of time was the amazing support I received from people I didn't know or hardly knew. Every day I was receiving messages, cards, flowers and gifts from people I hadn't met before. Encouraging and touching, I felt so grateful to have such wonderful people in my Tribe.

The Venus awards were around the corner and as a Finalist, I was asked by the judges to attend a breakfast meeting in Reading. I couldn't get to it because I was still taking strong drugs and was unable to drive and so I dialled in via teleconference. The other two finalists were at the meeting in person and it felt a bit strange being on the end of the phone line. We each gave an account of why we had been nominated. The other two ladies had been chosen finalists based on the work they did for their businesses and obviously my story was very different to that. I suddenly felt a bit silly when the two judges and two finalists said they weren't too keen on the dress code which was 'full length and fabulous'. I was thrilled about the opportunity to wear a long, glamorous dress and felt like the odd one out. That said, the meeting went well and the next step in the process was to produce a report outlining what we planned to do in the future. This took some thought, because BGJTL wasn't a business and thus I didn't have a business plan.

The pain in my hip just ceased one day, which came as a huge relief. I could finally move around more! Getting back into the car and out to work brought a sense of purpose once again. I was able to fit into some of my clothes and four weeks down the line I had more energy and my confidence was back and growing. I'd gained a few pounds whilst being inactive but was proud that this hadn't been more, because I'd controlled what I'd eaten so carefully.

On the night of the Venus Awards I was nervous, feeling the weight of expectations driven from so many of those 'You will win!' comments. What if I didn't? What if I'd be letting everyone down? The clouds gathered above me. I shook myself out of the thought. I drove to the hotel in Reading and saw Donna and Bev, Emma and Jim and a lady called Mickie who I hadn't met before. She was in the group and had written to me to say she would like to help me celebrate the evening. The five of them were enjoying a few drinks and I chatted with them for a while before returning to my room to get ready. I had bought a stunning red dress and though I needed to wear Spanx to minimise the swelling, I felt like a film star when I pulled it on. I swept my hair into an elegant 'up do' and I did my usual smoky eye evening look. I took the obligatory selfies and loaded them to my various pages and was delighted to see that 1300 wonderful people had given me a 'thumbs up' on Instagram.

I sauntered down to the event reception feeling fabulous in my dress, but wishing it wasn't an awards ceremony so as to remove the mounting pressure I felt. The first person I'd seen was one of the judges for my category and she'd given me a fleeting and apologetic look. It immediately told me I hadn't won. She and I chatted and talked about how exciting the process had been and the more was

163

said, the greater a sense I got that they had chosen somebody else. My ability to accurately read body language and visual cues is sometimes very unhelpful and on this occasion, I was not thankful for it.

Martin had arrived and tapped me on the shoulder. I spun around and instantly felt better that he was here. He looked gorgeous in his navy tuxedo.

'You're beautiful', he said.

I leaned in to hug him.

'I didn't win', I whispered in his ear. But it was her, little hurt and confused nine-year-old me who uttered the words from under the gathering clouds, blocking out the sun.

'How do you know?' he inquired, clearly surprised.

'I've just seen it written on the face of the judge', I responded, trusting my intuition.

'You don't know that for sure. Smile and enjoy yourself', said Martin encouragingly.

After I'd had photographs with the fellow finalists, Martin and I went in search of our friends and we took our seats at the table.

According to the programme, the Inspirational Woman was the last award of the night. It was an enjoyable wait from an entertainment perspective, with lots of amazing women winning awards, but it was an agonising wait from a personal perspective as I felt the mounting pressure to win, knowing that I most likely hadn't. I recognise that this pressure was largely created by myself, but the thought of posting that I didn't bring home the prize, was a hard one to contemplate. When it came to my moment, Martin and Donna held my hands and I waited patiently. As soon as another name was read out I felt the sense of failure and hard as I tried to fight it, I allowed it to consume me as I struggled to paint on the smile. I was back in 1987 with her once more, standing awkwardly in a green leotard, not feeling like I belonged, not feeling good enough. I was greeted with the usual commiserations and 'You're our winner' comments, which I appreciated greatly, but they did little to numb the feeling of having let people down.

When I went to bed that night, I told Martin how I felt and actually had a little cry. I explained that I was more disappointed in

164

my reaction to not winning than the not winning and that I was never satisfied with my lot. He did as he always does and helped me to see things from a different perspective and then he kissed the disappointment away. As I waited for sleep to take hold I realised that the feeling of failure hadn't sent me into a tailspin of binge eating and I was thankful for that.

The next morning when I woke up, I lay in Martin's arms and said:

'I am an inspiration to myself and that's all that matters. An award doesn't define who I am or make me any less of a person. It's amazing that I was thought of as an inspiration to be nominated in the first place'

And it occurred to me in that moment how far I had come.

I have wobbles, and as quickly as they come, I process them, learn from them and move on. I haven't turned to bingeing because I have finally recognised that this adds no value to me and I've made a very deliberate, conscious decision to cease this behaviour and learn new ways to control my emotional triggers. I no longer let my old habits and their root causes consume or define me. Instead I choose to emulate the behaviours of the successful people I admire. Rob from Trinity Transformations taught me that it is a good idea to think like an athlete. I say, 'I am an athlete' to myself every day. When I am faced with a decision I think:

'What would an athlete do? Would an athlete choose the cream bun or a green smoothie?'

It makes the answer really easy when you think about it this way and I truly believe that what we think, we become.

I have stumbled into unchartered territory and managed to conquer the challenges each time with a fierce determination and willingness to learn from my mistakes. I have a level of self-belief that, whilst not completely unshakable, is strong enough to allow me to brush off criticism, fear, failure and shame much more quickly rather than allowing it to stick to me like tar.

I am growing into myself, becoming happy in my skin while being open to receiving whatever the Universe has in store for me and while I still see the clouds that have sometimes shadowed my existence, my life is full of sunny days.

I am strong.
I am learning.
I am different.
I am resilient.
I am fallible.
I am happy.
I am relentless.
I am consistent.
I am motivated.
I am enough.

Part Three

The Lean Girl's Way

All you need is the plan, the road map, and the courage to press on to your destination.
Earl Nightingale

Lean Journey Continues...

July 2017 was the month I celebrated 18 months of being on a Lean Journey and the monumental achievement of living without binge eating, secret eating or allowing feelings of shame to override my senses. It was a liberating and freeing sensation and although my resolve would go on to be tested very soon after this milestone, I could, for now, feel proud of how far I had travelled. As each month of my journey had passed, I moved closer towards my vision, learning to love my shape while helping others to love themselves. I think it is very easy to say, after losing weight, that how you feel about yourself is more about how you think than how you look and while I agree it might be easier to say that while wearing a wearing a size 10, I honestly believe this is the case.

No matter what size, shape, hair colour, intelligence level, career, wealth or other attributes we have, if we don't believe we are enough, we will never be enough, either in our mind's eye or in our hearts. I have proven that even after major weight loss and a tummy tuck, there are days when my inner critic, Miss. Meddler, is able to de-rail me. I have to work hard to silence her and learn to love what I see in the mirror. It's a deliberate practice, and I know that I must exercise my mind as often, and with as much rigour as I exercise my body.

When I reflect on my Lean Journey, I can identify a number of tools and techniques that have combined to deliver the success and I would like to share these in this book to give others the opportunity to devise a formula that will work for them.

It must be said that the clean eating approach – or rather lifestyle - coupled with exercise, have played a huge role in getting me to where I am today. Had I chosen a 'diet' I would probably have been back to square one before the first week had ended. Clean eating has never felt like a diet for me because it allows me to eat an abundance of great food and I have never felt like I was in a fail/succeed scenario.

If I was to give anybody guidance on the best approach to use in conjunction with these tools and techniques it would be to...

1. **Eat a healthy, nutrient-rich diet.**
2. **Eat within a calorie limit which is aligned with your goals.**
3. **Exercise four to five times a week and find a pursuit you love.**

It is worth noting that eating healthily doesn't mean you have to be a slave to the spinach leaf, although I am now wedded to spinach and eat its green goodness daily. Clean eating yields the opportunity to eat an array of delicious food including burgers, pizzas, sweet potato fries, puddings, lasagna, roasts etc. It's all about how it is prepared and what ingredients are used. I eat pizza most weeks but the base is made from courgettes and almond flour rather than salt and fat-laden dough. You don't need to miss out - you just need to think differently.

I shall continue to use these techniques and will apply them rigorously during the next phase of my journey. As I write this, I am thinking about my training plan for a 10k I have signed up for in November 2017 in order to raise money for the NSPCC. Running 10k always felt like an impossible task when I was a big girl. Now I know I will do it and I will give it my all.

I should make it clear that the tools and techniques I outline in this book are not scientifically proven, I'm not an expert, a psychologist or a health coach. I am simply a woman who is finally getting to grips with her demons and found tips, tricks and formulas that have helped me along the way, which I am now happy to share with others. I hope that they provide you with as much success as they have brought to me.

Above all else
ALWAYS
Keep the Faith
and tell yourself
I CAN and I AM

Tackling the fear of failure

If you are anything like me, you will have tried and subsequently failed at a new diet regime umpteen times. You attack it with gusto, eat everything in sight on a Sunday evening so you are fired up and ready to survive on four slices of pepper and a crispbread by Monday. The initial enthusiasm is wavering by Tuesday morning and that evening you find yourself delving mouth first into the nearest cheesecake which, incidentally, you have to drive to a supermarket for because you've cleared the fridge and cupboards of all things 'fattening' in a bid to stick to the diet.

We've all been there. I used to like to refer to this as 'giving up' rather than 'failing', because it somehow made me feel better. What I have established through bitter experience is that giving up can lead to a fear of failure and this often manifests as an unwillingness to start something over or start something new. None of us like to feel like we suck and so avoidance is often the lesser of two evils.

I speak to dozens of people each week who are waiting to start their own lean journey but haven't quite found the oomph required yet. I often ask them 'What are you waiting for?' and the response is generally 'The motivation.' People who have not been overweight can often misinterpret this procrastination as laziness. This is rarely the reality and it usually transpires that there have been many failed attempts at losing weight or getting fit previously and it's the fear of failure that is holding back the start. Fear of failure dilutes the motivation to commence and makes pushing through the early stages of the Change Curve more difficult.

The 'Change Curve' is a difficult beast to deal with but deal with it we must if we are to be successful. I first learnt about the Change Curve in a work capacity and understanding it has proven invaluable. It was developed by a Swiss psychiatrist Elisabeth Kubler-Ross in 1969 and was originally intended to articulate the emotions experienced by terminally ill patients prior to death or by people who have lost a loved one. It has later been recognised as a model to help people understand the stages of personal transition in a change scenario. It outlines that people move through a number of emotional states such as:

Shock
Denial
Anger
Fear
Depression
Understanding
Acceptance
Moving on

I have worked as a Change Agent for many years and when implementing large scale transformational change in businesses, I often have to contend with colleagues who are going through the emotional states of the Change Curve. This has, on more than one occasion, resulted in me being shouted at, sworn at and cried upon. It has caused colleagues to take sick leave or disengage, wishing they were anywhere but within 500 yards of me and my 'stupid ideas'. Fast forward a few months down the line and I am told, by the same people, that the new way of working is the best thing that ever happened to them. They made it to the other side and the grass is indeed greener - yay!

In my personal experience of weight loss, I was much more likely to submit to failure when I was experiencing the initial tranche of emotions felt on the curve. Let me share some examples of how I might react whilst trying to adapt to the latest fad diet.

Shock

'Oh my god! 4 slices of pepper & a crispbread for a whole day! That's not enough to sustain an ant! I can't do this diet.'

171

Denial

'I really don't need to lose this weight. I am fine as I am. I have great hair. Who cares if I am fat? I don't. I can't do this diet.'

Anger

'Why can't I just be slim like Jess?! She eats cream cakes every lunch time and is a size 8. Why do I put on weight every time I smell a cake? It's just not fair! I can't do this diet.'

Fear

'What if I can't do it? What if it's too hard and I am not cut out for it? I've told everybody at work I am doing it, what will they think of me if I give up? I can't do this diet.'

Depression

'I might as well just eat cake, I am destined to be fat because I just can't exist on 4 slices of pepper and a crispbread, it's impossible. Eating a cake will make me feel better. I can't do this diet.'

And that's where I'd end up, deep in the Depression stage of the curve, not even dreaming of progressing to Understanding, Acceptance and Moving on.

These internal exchanges may sound familiar to you. They were certainly familiar to me and were very much associated with a closed, 'I can't' mind-set coupled with self-deprecation. They were powerful enough to throw me out of kilter on many occasions before I recognised them for what they are and developed ways to move through the stages quickly by establishing a 'growth mind-set'. Carol Dweck, a Professor of Psychology at Stanford University is known for her work on mind-set. Her research shows that those with a growth mind-set see effort as a path to mastery, challenges as an

172

opportunity for development and feedback as a learning opportunity. Through her work I recognised that I could cultivate this mind-set and use it to help me succeed.

Here's the good news: moving through the Change Curve isn't insurmountable. Have you ever moved the furniture around in your home or changed the colour of the décor? For the first few days it feels like your head is on backwards because the room just doesn't feel or look right anymore. It might be that you have changed cars and the indicator paddle is on the opposite side to that of your previous car. How many times do you curse because you activate the windscreen wipers instead of the indicator? A week later you don't even notice anymore because it's become the new normal, you have accepted the new layout and the new colour, and have re-trained yourself to choose the correct paddle. What's more, you prefer the new way. That's the feeling when you reach the final emotional state of the Change Curve. That's reaching the greener grass.

The trick to ploughing your way through begins with understanding the steps. It helps me to think about - and write down in advance - what I might be saying to myself at each stage. What could the tripwires be? This might seem like a laborious task, but putting some effort in at the 'mobilisation stage' of something new can help to disarm the mines that stand between me and success. I use this approach in a work setting. Before starting any new project, I meet with the team and walk through the 'what could go wrong' or 'what's the worst that can happen' scenarios. It always feels like such a bore at the time, but when something goes wrong, it's been pre-empted and has a suggested remedy already; it means the project isn't derailed and we can get back to steady state quickly.

By way of an example, if I was starting out on the Body Coach plan, after the initial read through of the material I might think:

Shock

'Oh my goodness, this feels so different. I can't do it.'

173

'I can't eat all of this spinach. 200g in one meal!!! I can't do it.'
'The cooking takes too long, I'll be chained to the kitchen. I can't do it.'
'I won't be able to exercise for 20 whole minutes! ARGHHHHHH!!! I can't do it.'

In this example I have already created a whole heap of reasons why 'I can't' before I've been eaten a single spinach leaf or put on active wear. This could quite easily allow me to slip back into my comfort zone and avoid the potential to fail.

However, if I think about what my reactions might be in advance of them happening, I can devise strategies that will cut the negativity off at the knees. I call this the **'FT'** or **Failure Tackle**. I approach the FT like a world class football player trying to win back the ball.

Shock FT

'Wow this is different, it will be great to do something I haven't done before. I can do this.'
'So much spinach, it's going to be soooo good for me. I can do this.'
'The cooking will give me the opportunity to switch off from work, listen to music and chat to the children. I can do this.'
'I get to rest after every 30 seconds of exercise. I can keep going for 30 seconds so it's going to be fine. I can do this.'

Reframing the way I think about each emotional trigger by preparing in advance and then steadfastly addressing it when it happens in a very deliberate, positive way gets me quickly through the unstable territory and rapidly into the acceptance phase.

Sometimes preparing FTs can't be done in advance, because the change isn't planned. I might have forgotten to pick up my prepared nutritious lunch from the fridge this morning and I'm suddenly faced with the requirement to source lunch from the high street. In this

174

scenario, challenged with an abundance of choice and a feeling of stupidity for being forgetful, it can be easy to be overwhelmed and find myself saying:

'There won't be anything appropriate so I might as well have a burger and chips.'

In these instances, when I find myself in the spiral of succumbing to the emotional trigger, I have created a technique I call **STARS:-**

Step back from the emotion.
Take a deep breath.
Acknowledge what I am feeling.
Reframe the thought.
Say it out loud.

Step back from the emotion

In the past, when I experienced an emotional trigger, I allowed it to consume me, which could send me quickly spiralling into the depths of self-pity and excuse making. Nowadays, as soon as I recognise this is happening, I take a step back. I like to make it a physical step and I acknowledge I am doing it whilst I do it.

E.g. As I step backwards I say to myself (or out loud)

'I've identified it's happening, and I am stepping back so I can breathe.'

This physical and mental interruption stops the spiral in its tracks and provides a solid foundation to build on.

Take a deep breath

When I am experiencing the stress emotions, I find my heart-rate quickens and my breathing becomes shallow. By deliberately taking a slow deep breath in for the count of four and out for the count of four I can gain control of my thoughts and my composure which allows me to move to the next stage of the STARS process.

Acknowledge what I am feeling

I believe it's hugely important to face into feelings, however negative, painful or disruptive they may be, to move swiftly out of them. I find it useful to think about what I am feeling and understand it rather than letting it wash over and consume me. The act of acknowledging what I am feeling helps me to focus and stay in control. Note that I am not denying having emotions – it's the acknowledgement part that is key here.

In the forgotten lunch scenario, I could be feeling anger at my stupidity and feel that to make myself feel better about my self-criticism I should eat some junk food.

Often the feelings are accompanied by thoughts presented by my inner critic – Miss. Meddler - such as:

'God, I am so stupid, I'll never stick to this plan because I can't even remember my lunch. I'll just have a burger and be done with it.'

Acknowledging what she is saying is important and I have learned to respect that she is trying to help me. It's just not the kind of help I need. I physically tell her I am going to seek an alternative approach and this helps to keep the emotional reactions in perspective and provides the headspace for me to move on to the next stage. It is worth noting that I will have these conversations with Miss. Meddler silently, so I don't appear to have lost my marbles ☺

Reframe the thought

Once I've acknowledged the feelings and know exactly what I am dealing with I can move on to the fun bit.

The first thing I like to do is to reframe the original problem to solve by replacing negative language with positive.

Taking the example I have already used:

176

'God, I am so stupid, I'll never stick to this plan because I can't remember my lunch'

I would reframe this as,

'So, I've been forgetful, it's no big deal. I can find a lunch that is on plan and actually it will be a good learning experience for the days when I can't bring my lunch with me.'

Once I am thinking about the problem in a positive way, the next step is to find a solution.

Originally, I had decided,

'I'll just have a burger and be done with it.'

To focus on a more positive solution I would ask myself:
What is the best possible outcome from the situation?
What can I learn from it?
How can I personally feel good about the solution?

The reframed solution might look like this:

'If I choose a burger I'll blow my calorie deficit and I know from experience that I'll be fed up with myself afterwards.
I'd prepared chicken breast, spinach leaves, tomato and mozzarella. If I go to the supermarket I'll be able to find all of those ingredients and recreate it. I can do this.'

Say it out loud

Once the positive has been established, I like to say it out loud, or if I am surrounded by people, I'll shout it in my head. This reinforces the positive language and eliminates or at least dilutes the negatives.

177

'I forgot my lunch but it's no big deal because I can purchase a nutritious lunch from the supermarket, I don't need a burger. I can do this'

This process might seem daunting initially, but once you have practiced it a few times (and pushed yourself through the change curve) it happens very quickly and becomes habitual. I have found Failure Tackles (FTs) and STARS invaluable for helping me shift my thought processes into a more positive space and to push through the change curve quickly. They instantly move me into the growth mind-set space.

Previously, failure to lose weight and/or sustain weight loss was partly due to the methods I had chosen; but mostly due to the fact I would position it in my mind as something different to my norm that would totally revolutionise my weight in a ridiculously short timeframe. In other words, I'd set myself up to fail because my anticipated outcomes were not achievable. 'This time it will be different, I'll start on Monday and by next week I'll have lost 10lbs' I'd tell myself.

I would 'climb on the wagon' with rigour and a determination to succeed. I would set an expectation or requirement which was measurable and therefore had a pass/fail outcome. The issue with this of course, is that if the method is unsustainable then frequently it leads to the inevitable 'falling off the wagon' or 'failure'. Earlier in this chapter I wrote about failure and how it can manifest as an unwillingness to start something over or start something new. I believe this is the reason that periods of weight loss can often be followed by periods of weight gain, above and beyond the pre-diet starting weight. It can take a long period of time to gain the courage and motivation to try again. The fear of failure can be too great a deterrent.

Finding a sustainable method for weight loss and moving through the change curve to adapt to it is the first step. My method involved eating clean foods, lifting weights and cardio sessions. The positive impact of this was instant and whilst I had a period of time pushing through the change curve to adapt to new ways of working, it felt different from the start. I was never hungry, never restricted or

178

deprived and this - together with the endorphins regular exercise provided - became a successful formula.

On this occasion, there was also a shift in mind-set; a different way of thinking about my situation and relationship with food. I decided that I was not going to think about what I consumed as a 'diet' or something that could go right or wrong. I wasn't going to 'get on a wagon'. I wasn't going to set an expectation of losing x many stones or not eating chocolate. This wasn't something I could fall off or fail at. This was a new mind-set. This was a new lifestyle, not a project with a start and an end. This shift in thinking has been a significant contributor to my success.

Every day involves a series of transactions or processes that we carry out. I started to look at meals as transactions. Whenever an individual carries out a transaction, there are a number of decisions that can be made. We often make these without thinking, our brain works through a decision tree and decides on an outcome. I have trained myself to make these decisions more consciously with regard to food.

My choices are influenced by how well the food or drink I am considering will nourish my body. I have learnt that if I nourish my body appropriately, I will feel good on the inside and look great on the outside. These outcomes are the prize and the prize is something worth winning again and again. Rather than being an expectation or specific requirement, it's more of a guiding principle that can be followed to a greater or lesser extent as I move through life. With this in mind, it makes decision making straightforward.

A chicken, spinach & avocado salad will always nourish my body better than a pizza and the awareness of it helps me to make the choice. That said, if I choose to take the pizza, I do so knowing it isn't going to nourish my body as well as the salad, but equally knowing that it's ok to do so. It's an informed decision and one that I make rarely because the goal of providing nutritious food for my body, and the ultimate prize, is important to me. The critical thing is that because eating pizza is a definite choice, I don't feel the sense of failure or 'falling off the wagon' that I would have done had I climbed on a wagon in the first place. This then means that I don't then spiral into a week of eating pizza, and ice cream and, and,

179

and… Interestingly, in 18 months I have only eaten the unhealthy, fat- and carb-laden style pizza once and it made me feel awful, keeping me awake for much of the night. I swapped that type of pizza for a nutritious version of it, consisting of a base made from shredded courgette and almond flour. I have a video of the recipe on my you tube channel.

Setting myself up for success has involved removing the ability to fail and instead being led by the guiding principle which can be consistently followed. If one day I don't nourish my body as well as I could have, the principle still stands. I haven't passed or failed, I've simply made a series of choices.

In essence, it comes down to how we think about things. We can choose how we respond to situations, decisions and actions and we in the end label ourselves with either positive or negative attributes. By taking informed decisions, owning them, being mindful in the moment and then moving on we can escape the pass/fail mentality and just 'be'. Let's leave the wagons in the eighteenth century where they belong.

Above all else
ALWAYS
Keep the Faith
and tell yourself
I CAN and I AM

Creating capacity in your day

If I was given a pound for every time I have used the phrase 'I'm too busy to exercise' before I got my act together, I'd have been able to take a dream holiday every year.

If I was given a pound for every time I have read the words 'I am too busy to get lean' or words to that effect in the hundreds of messages I receive each month, I'd have a fabulous collection of Louboutin heels.

The cold, hard fact is this: We are never too busy, we are simply making excuses.

The dictionary explanation of the word *excuse* reads like this:

1.   Seek to lessen the blame attaching to a fault or offence; try to justify.

2.   Release (someone) from a duty or requirement.

This is precisely what I was doing day after day for years when I was telling myself and others that the reason I didn't exercise was because I was busy. The truth was I wasn't exercising because I felt fat, unfit, terrified of looking like a fool and if I was to hold the self-reflection mirror very closely, I'd probably say a little bit lazy too. But even all of these things are excuses in the end.

In January 2016, when I embarked on the clean eating and exercise mission, I was and still am busy - there is no denying it. I have a full-time job which means I often work 12 hours' days. I stay away from home 1-2 nights per week. I have a husband, two young children, a large house and garden. The thought of fitting in 4-5 hours of exercise and preparing clean meals was a daunting one. Daunting, but not impossible; because whilst I was busy, I was not *too* busy. It was simply a matter of creating the time.

In my role as a Management Consultant, I spend my life helping clients create capacity to do more with the same resources. I decided to apply the same principle to my own time and look for opportunities to eliminate, relocate or simplify tasks to free up precious minutes which could be repurposed for exercise.

To find these opportunities I needed to log and evaluate my current ways of working which I did using a tool I use at work called WILO (Week in the Life of).

Essentially a WILO is created by logging how I spend my time in 15 minute segments all day, every day, for a week. To make it easier to analyse I used some categories to log my time against as follows:

Working	Reading	Chores
Commuting	Shopping	Sleeping
Driving	Cooking	Personal Care
Using Internet	Eating	Exercise
Watching TV	Family Time	Doing Nothing
Calling/Texting	Socialising	Other

Every fifteen minutes I would mark down which activities I'd done during that segment of time and whilst this was a laborious task, it provided lots of insights as to where I was wasting time. It also presented lots of opportunities for how I could combine tasks and create the capacity in my week that I needed for exercise.

Let me share some examples:

Weekly Shop
The weekly food shop would take approx. 2 hours of my time every weekend. This was broken down into:

Other time (checking cupboards, fridge and freezer for what was required) - 10 minutes.
Driving time – 40 minutes.
Shopping time – 60 minutes.
Packing away time – 10 minutes.

By switching to online shopping and investing some time up front creating a 'favourites list' I not only saved the driving time, but also 40 minutes of the shopping time because the online shop would only take 20 minutes. I also bought a small note board and put this up in

182

the kitchen so that the whole family could write down what was required from the weekly shop, adding items to the list as they ran out.

I often travel on trains and by using the supermarket app on my smart phone, I could use the dead time commuting to do the shopping which created even more capacity.

Watching TV

I spent at least an hour each evening watching TV, more at the weekends, and on reflection I realised that this wasn't adding any value to me. Being an Empath, I would often go to bed stressed because I watched a crime drama or a hard-hitting documentary and this would mean I would take longer to go to sleep. I decided to eliminate TV completely from my routine Sunday to Friday, meaning I only watched TV on Saturday evenings. This created oodles of time in my week and I have found that I rarely watch programmes on Saturdays now, too.

Driving/Reading/Calling

The study showed me that I didn't spend any time reading books during my typical week and yet there were lots of books I wanted to read. I spent lots of time driving each week, often for hours at a time. Driving is the ultimate waste of time. I decided that I could repurpose some of this dead time to exercise my mind and rather than read books, I could listen to books instead. I downloaded the Audible app and purchased books in audio format instead of written. This allowed me to listen to books in a matter of days that it may have taken me months to read in a traditional way. 'The Power of Vulnerability' by Brene Brown is a particular favourite. Brene is a goddess in my book.

I also used my driving time to make calls to family and friends. This dual-purpose use of time gave me back precious minutes in the evenings and on weekends.

Cooking

I spent approx. 20-30 minutes each evening preparing and cooking dinner. This would make me feel stressed because after a

183

long day at work it's the last thing I wanted to be doing. The Body Coach suggested 'prepping like a boss' which meant preparing meals for the week on one day. I repurposed the time I saved from not going to the supermarket to cook meals for the week. Thanks to this, I spent no longer than 5-10 minutes each evening heating pre-prepared meals. It also stopped me from reaching for the takeaway menus when I couldn't be bothered cooking from scratch.

Doing Nothing

This accounted for large chunks of time, particularly on weekend mornings when I would wake up early, but stay in bed for a couple of hours, napping. I recognised this time could be used much more effectively and instead of staying in bed, I could get up and fit in an exercise session before the day had really started. I also acknowledged I could use some of this time to meditate or practice affirmations which would contribute to my wellbeing. And occasionally, I would allow myself to just do nothing other than lie down with a face mask on and be still, because now and then, I think that's allowed.

Being a working mummy, time with the children is even more important due to it being limited. I try to involve the children during the time I spend exercising and cooking. My children love to chop vegetables and measure out ingredients for me and we can spend time together while I get the prep done. This is teaching them good habits, too.

They both enjoy HIIT routines and will often join in with mine or be my round timer and blow a whistle when 30 seconds has passed.

Scrutinising time in 15-minute segments throughout the week using the WILO tool is an excellent way to find the hours required to exercise.

Once you have the whole week documented follow the steps outlined below: -

Total up the minutes spent against each category. Be honest with yourself!

Look for the numbers that stand out.

Work through each category asking yourself if you are happy with the amounts of time you spend on it.

Take out the things you absolutely cannot change such as 'fixed working hours'.

Identify the things you must do, but could find an alternative quicker way to do it, e.g. online shopping or outsourcing the ironing (if it's an affordable option).

Look for the things you do that you could do without such as watching TV or lying in bed in the mornings.

Think about how tasks could be combined e.g. listening to audiobooks whilst driving.

Note down the time you believe you can save from doing the things outlined above.

Repurpose that time to do the exercise, food prep or whatever else it is you needed to create capacity for.

This is about being creative in finding ways to give you the time you need within a busy working week. If you had to pay a pound to the government for every minute you wasted, you would think very differently about how you spent it!

Ultimately, I know that if I want something badly enough, I can create the time and for me, nourishing and exercising my body provides such magnificent payback that it is worth the investment.

Above all else
ALWAYS
Keep the Faith
and tell yourself
I CAN and I AM

Treating yourself with kindness

'I really need your help. I am 35 years old and feel like a fat, frumpy waste of space. I sit and eat all day long because I am at home with my toddler and a baby. I look in the mirror and feel disgusted at myself because I still look like I'm pregnant but my daughter is 11 months old. My husband doesn't touch me and I don't blame him because I look a mess. I try to diet and then end up giving in and eating chocolate and biscuits. I am so fed up and just hate myself. What can I do?'

This is one of the hundreds of messages I receive from women who have reached the end of their tether, but seem immobilised to do anything about it. I recognise the language they use, the anxiety and the self-hatred because I have been there, said it and done it. What is shocking to me is hearing other people describe themselves in this way. The words seem to jump off the page and tug at my heartstrings and I just want to find these people and give them a big hug.

Imagine this scenario another way. Imagine that a lady posted a picture of herself on Instagram and I responded with a comment as follows:

'Look at you, mid-thirties and you look like a fat, frumpy waste of space. It's no wonder because all you do is stuff your face all day. You still look like you're pregnant, for heaven's sake. I bet your husband can't bear to look at you, let alone touch you. You are a mess and I hate you for it!'

I can envisage the furious responses that would ensue and I would be labelled as a heartless troll within minutes - and rightly so. If most of us deem it totally unacceptable to treat another human being in this way, why do we seem to give ourselves permission to speak to ourselves like this? When I thought about it from this perspective, I suddenly had an 'ah ha' moment and knew I needed to do something differently.

This is the process I went through to start being kind to myself:

186

Step One
Recognise the inner voice

I hadn't ever focussed on the way I spoke to myself before. It just happened. I was used to the constant patter of thoughts in my head and I hadn't recognised how negative or damaging these were. I spent a week or so tuning in to these thoughts and whenever I did that consciously I would write them down in my journal.

'You'll make a mess of that presentation'

'God, you look fat in that dress'

'Your ankles are enormous'

'He thinks you are an idiot'

'Look at the fat on your underarms, it's all puckered and gross'

'She is staring at you because you are fat'

'You're such a rubbish mum'

'You are not good enough to manage this project'

I don't know what made me write them down initially, but I am pleased I did because I was faced with a plethora of self-criticism which shocked me to the core. I couldn't believe I was being so mean to myself. What was interesting to observe is that the negative self-talk was actually attacking many areas of my life, not just the weight.

ACTION
Listen to your inner voice for a week.
Note down what you hear when you hear it.

Step Two
Make friends with your inner voice

I have learnt not to argue with my inner voice. What is it they say? Never feed the troll. However, I respect that she is part of me, and is, in her own way trying to help me, however ineffective that may be. I decided to give her a name and, with tongue firmly in cheek, I called her Miss. Meddler as she does like to constantly meddle in my affairs. She will always be there and I know she will always be the voice of negativity, but I now have ways to minimise the interactions I have with her which I will cover later in the chapter. The key thing is, I always thank her for her contribution and acknowledge her presence. Also, like I do with most unhelpful feedback, I file it in the 'not required' tray.

ACTION
Give your inner voice a name.
Respect his/her opinion.
Thank him/her for the contribution.
Let it go.

Step Three
Develop the positives

One of the greatest tools I have found to dilute the negative impact of the inner voice is to use positive affirmation. These are positive and specific statements that allow me to reframe or diminish self-critical thoughts. When I first read about positive affirmations I thought it was bonkers, but I was desperate to change and decided to give it a go.

To start the process, I used the things I had written down in my journal and applied the reframing technique outlined in earlier. I reframed the negatives presented by Miss. Meddler and imagined what my 'ideal state' would be.

For example:

'Your ankles are enormous' would become 'I have beautiful, slender ankles'

'He thinks you're an idiot' would become 'My colleagues think I am credible and professional'

Some of these things weren't strictly true at the time. I didn't have beautiful, slender ankles, for example, but the premise of affirmation is largely about visualising the things you would like and learning to love yourself.

When I'd practiced the art of writing affirmations in a simple form, based on what I'd heard myself saying, I progressed to thinking about how to write more specific ones. I wanted to address some of the more fundamental limiting beliefs I held about myself and boost my self-esteem. Ultimately, I wanted to invest more time in being kind to myself.

Within a month of starting my lean journey, I came up with a list of five affirmations and tried to keep them short, in the present tense and relevant to me: -

I enjoy exercising regularly and eating healthily to give me the body I deserve and desire.

I am credible in my work and I add value to my clients and colleagues by applying my talents and skills effectively.

I feel beautiful and confident in my skin and I choose to feel good about myself every day.

I no longer need to hold on to the events of the past. I release the feelings of shame and embrace new beginnings.

I am worthy of love, joy and abundance and I welcome these with open arms.

These five affirmations are my staples.

I also add to them for specific situations. If I am trying to win new business at work I will write an affirmation to help:

I am attracting new business and my clients can easily see the value I will add.

As I have spent my life deleting and ripping up photos, before one is taken I will say to myself:

I am beautiful and my beauty will show on the photograph.

I even use 'in the moment' affirmations, like when I am trying to find a parking space at the train station:

I will easily find a parking space and be on time for the train.

ACTION
Develop simple positive statements to reframe your negative self-talk.
Think of 5-7 meaningful staple affirmations which address your key limiting beliefs and/or the things that jumped out when you wrote down the ramblings of your inner voice.

Step Four
Repeat, repeat, repeat

Write down your affirmations.

I have mine written in a fancy journal and I also have a copy of them in my purse and in the notes section of my mobile phone. I don't need to look at my staple affirmations anymore because I know them by heart, but despite this, I still read them off the paper occasionally.

Some people choose to say affirmations out loud. I never have. I simply repeat them in my head when I wake up, when I am on the train, when I am running, when I am cooking and before I go to sleep - anytime I have a spare moment, really. I have repeated the same staple affirmations religiously for 18 months and I won't drop them - they are now part of my routine.

The more I say it, the more my unconscious mind hears it, the more I believe it and it appears to be the route to happiness. I used to think happiness was driven from others. Now I understand it comes from within and I can honestly say that investing time in these practices is making me feel happy.

Don't knock it until you've tried it ☺

ACTION
Write your affirmations down in several places.
Repeat them several times per day.

190

Your staple affirmations are part of your daily routine, don't miss them out.
Don't be afraid to develop new ones for specific events.

Step Five
Be a Self-Love Ninja

Ninjutsu is a life-long pursuit which takes a lifetime to master and requires oodles of patience. Being kind to yourself is much the same. It takes practice, dedication, enthusiasm and ninja-like persistence. I came up with the term 'Self-Love Ninja' because it made me feel I had an inner ally to help me in my quest to silence Miss. Meddler. Ninja's use weapons which look like stars and so the STARS technique I introduced earlier is the ultimate Self-Love Ninja weapon.

I must admit, I got a bit despondent after a week of practicing affirmations and nothing changing. I think I was expecting some major epiphany to occur which would suddenly diminish all thoughts of binge eating, shame and self-doubt from my mind. It didn't happen like that. It was a slow, gradual process and over time, I noticed I wasn't hearing the negative droning of Miss. Meddler as often as before. When I looked in the mirror the 'you look fat' was replaced with 'you look great in that dress' and this was before I had lost all of the weight. The persistent repetition of the affirmations started to pay off. Not only did it manifest in more positive, kinder self-talk, it also manifested in positive things happening, too. I was winning more work, receiving great feedback, gaining qualifications and smashing my weight loss goals. My 'I can't' approach was replaced with a 'course I can' and I felt like I was winning.

Being a Self-Love Ninja and practicing affirmations regularly has changed the way I think and approach things and helped me create a growth mind-set. It doesn't mean I don't get phased or daunted by new situations. It means I approach them from the point of view of:

'Ok, I can do this, I'll break it down into bite-size chunks, ask for help, treat it as a learning opportunity and enjoy it'

Another benefit of being a Self-Love Ninja is that when Miss. Meddler strikes - which she still does on occasions, especially if I am tired or stressed - I am skilled in self-defence. I have the tools, the knowledge and the mind-set to deal with her and silence her quickly.

When I hear her say *'you feel fat, you know you feel fat'*, I prime my Self-Love Ninja powers and repeat:

'I feel beautiful and confident in my skin and I choose to feel good about myself every day'

'Thank you, Miss. Meddler, but I feel just fabulous'

ACTION

Be relentless, persistent and deliberate in your affirmation practice.

Use your positive powers often and effectively.

Be prepared for the occasional onslaught.

Be a Self-Love Ninja.

The famous Buddha quote 'we are what we think' is incredibly relevant. I have faith that this is true and I ensure as many of my thoughts as possible are filled with reference to me being absolutely fabulous. I would encourage you to think the same way about you because it really does help to change the way you behave.

Above all else
ALWAYS
Keep the Faith
and tell yourself
I CAN and I AM

Developing a winning strategy

There are many Writers out there much more qualified than me to write about strategy and goal setting, but I want to share the things I have learnt, and the reality of making it happen. Goal setting involves the development of a roadmap which is meant to motivate and steer a person towards a defined outcome or destination.

I have always been a goal setter, but in all honesty, that just because I have always set goals doesn't mean I have always smashed them, particularly in a weight loss context. During the 18 months of my lean journey I believe I have come to understand the reason for this.

In the past, I would set myself huge, all encompassing, immense goals that would be as doable as trying to fit a whole watermelon in my mouth. It always had to be grand, end state goals and as I expressed in an earlier chapter, they were always measurable - that's the consultant in me.

An example of this would be 'I need to lose a stone in two weeks' or 'I need to lose 8 stones in six months'. Pure watermelon territory.

CREATING A VISION

The first change I needed to make to my personal goal setting approach was the requirement to start with a vision. All good strategists begin with this in a business capacity and I thought it would be a good idea to do the same for my personal journey.

What does creating a **VISION** actually mean?

A vision statement sets out a desired future position or, to put it simply, I asked myself:

'What is it I want to achieve?'

In this instance, I didn't want the vision to include metrics, I wanted it to be holistic, heartfelt and enduring.

I landed on:

193

'I will create a healthy, fit and toned body and a positive mind to be proud of.'

This encapsulated all of the aspects I wanted to work on and gave me something to aim for.

FIND YOUR WHY

With the vision defined, the next step was to develop the 'WHY'.
The 'WHY' question was one I often disregarded in the past. If I did think about it, I would let Miss. Meddler answer it, generally in this way:
'Because I am fat and disgusting'
Respecting the premise of 'what you think you become,' listening to Miss. Meddler was never going to be a good idea. I needed to be much kinder to myself and find a WHY that was valuable and with a big enough hook to keep me gunning for it.
Realising this, I approached it from a positive place and tried to think beyond the size and shape of my body and make the reason so compelling I couldn't escape from it. There is an old saying that 'he who has a why can endure any how'.
I was lucky enough to figure out very early in my journey 'why' I was doing this. Why it was important. Why I wanted it so badly. The most important thing in my life is my children and by including them in my reason to achieve the vision I couldn't have made it more compelling. My 'why' developed like this: -

When I achieve the vision, I will: -

Be a strong role model for children, showing them that healthy eating, exercise, positivity and self-love are the key components of a happy life.

Reach my 40th birthday and be the better, stronger version of myself and genuinely feel that this is the case.

194

Create the healthy habits that will allow me to lead a long, and abundantly happy life.

Walk in to room full of strangers and feel truly confident without acting.

DEVELOP STRATEGIC OBJECTIVES

The next step was to define the objectives. These were the long-term strategic areas which would help me achieve my vision to create a healthy toned body and a positive mind-set. Essentially these are the key activities I would need to perform to accomplish the vision: -

Reduce the size of my body by following a sustainable fat-loss plan.

Improve my fitness and the tone of my body through exercise.

Invest time in developing mind-set tools and techniques to improve positivity and wellbeing.

SET SHORT-TERM GOALS

With the objectives set, I then needed to break them down into shorter-term goals that would allow me to achieve the objective. The shorter-term goals are more specific and include timescales.
Some examples are set out below: -

Follow the Body Coach plan in 30-day segments, applying 100% effort.

Exercise for at least 30 minutes five times per week.

Walk 10,000 steps per day.

Develop a set of positive affirmations for daily use.

Get at least 7 hours of sleep per night.

DEFINE THE PRACTICAL STEPS

The goals are then broken down into tactical steps or bite-size chunks which make them easier to digest and to achieve (remember how I mentioned this before?). Some of these steps may seem very basic, but breaking them down in this way really helped me to focus and to see that the vision was totally attainable by taking small steps forward every single day.

Goal – Follow the Body Coach plan in 30-day segments, applying 100% effort.

Tactical Steps
Write down the meal plan for the week ahead.
Prepare meals in advance for the week ahead.
Eat 3 meals and 2 snacks each day.
Drink 3 litres of water each day.

Goal – Get at least seven hours sleep per night.

Tactical Steps
Switch off all devices by 2200.
Be in bed by 2230.
Use lavender oil on pillow to induce sleep.
Practice deep breathing before going to sleep.

MEASURE PROGRESS

The final step was to think about measuring progress. I didn't want to make this about arbitrary measures like stones or kg lost and so I measured my progress in this way:

Monthly
Monthly photograph comparison looking for changes in size, shape, tone and size of smile.
Waist, hip, chest, shoulder, thigh and arm measurements.
Improvement in fitness (measured through Personal Bests).
Total steps for the month (using fitness tracker).

Weekly
Number of A1 plan days out of 7.
Number of times trained out of 5.
Number of days practicing affirmations.
Number of days sleeping for more 7 hours or more (using fitness tracker).
Number of days achieving 10,000 steps (using fitness tracker).

I wrote each aspect of the strategic plan in a journal and referred to it regularly. Noting things down and ticking them off really does help to keep the vision alive and maintain concentration on objectives and goals. Tracking progress via the measures helps you to be realistic about your progress. For example, if you have low scores for the weekly measures, it shouldn't come as a surprise when you don't see an improvement in the photographs and body measurements. It stops you from pretending you are following your plan.

Key elements of your Strategic Plan

Create your vision – What do you want to achieve?
Find your 'why' – What's the compelling need?
Develop your strategic objectives – Long-term areas to deliver the vision.
Set the short-term goals – Steps to achieve the objective.
Define tactical steps – Activities to deliver the goals.
Measure progress – Weekly and monthly metrics.

Like all of the tools in this part of the book, this might feel time-consuming - but we do it for our businesses, functions and teams in a work capacity, so why shouldn't we as individuals be just as important?

We deserve this level of thought, planning and investment because this is our life plan. Putting the effort in reaps rewards. A good strategy prevents us from losing sight of our aims. It helps us visualise our progress and when the inner voice strikes or you feel the need to eat a huge cream cake it's a good document to refer to and remind you what you are trying to achieve, why you are doing it and how you are progressing towards it. The cream cake never seems so appealing after that.

Above all else
ALWAYS
Keep the Faith
and tell yourself
I CAN and I AM

Consistent motivation & deliberate practice

'Do or Do Not. There is no Try' Yoda
When you are attempting to drive significant changes to your lifestyle, motivation plays a key role. There is no doubt about it.

In my view, committing wholeheartedly to a lean journey 100% of the time is much easier than giving 99%.

99% can take up lots of time without producing results.

I have walked this journey beside many friends who have put in the same effort as I have for 6 days of the week and on the 7th day they have taken a 'day off'. Over a month this erodes the calorie deficit created over the 6-day period and impacts results. Over a year it means despite putting in oodles of effort, they are no further forward.

A day off each week may be a great strategy if you are already at your goal. In fact, there have been many occasions when I have been criticised for not taking days off because 'even Joe Wick's does'. Joe Wicks has an amazing body, though. He's already at the destination. 6 good days and one-off plan day is a good way to sustain weight in a very balanced way. But when you are on the journey, lack of progress can be soul destroying.

Think about it a different way. Imagine climbing a mountain and for every 5,000 steps you take up the mountain, you must take 500 steps down again. At first, this may not be a big deal. The further into the climb you get, the harder going backwards becomes because the effort to climb becomes greater. This is going to de-motivate you and before you know it, you are eating the Kendal Mint Cake from your rucksack because it's just too hard.

I told myself I was making a choice to eat clean; nobody was forcing me to do it and I wasn't being deprived. I was making a choice to transform my body and 100% effort and commitment would get me to the destination quicker. 99% effort lends itself to pitfalls, treat days can quite easily turn into treat weeks and the

199

calorie deficit created by exercise is soon replaced with treat calories. 100% is easier, because there are fewer decisions to make. This approach has helped me achieve the vision I set out to accomplish.

Consistent Motivation

I firmly believe that consistency is one of the key ingredients required on a healthy eating/exercise journey.

I would further refine this as needing to be consistently motivated.

It's not an easy thing to achieve.

But I categorically and deliberately state that it is something we 'achieve'.

Consistent motivation isn't something you wake up with. You have to practice being in the mind-set. In my view, it is linked to the compelling need driving you to change; your 'why'. If the 'why' is strong & well defined, the motivation is easier to find. So, put in the work to make your 'why' count for you.

Interruption

When people say, 'I wish I had your motivation', my response is always to say, 'you have, I am no different to you.' I believe we all have the ability to motivate ourselves and the aptitude to apply it consistently, but we often *choose* not to.

Motivation, as I see it, is a mental state that guides us and inspires our actions. It creates a desire or a need within us to reach a goal. What I've learnt from my failed attempts at weight loss and/or maintenance in the past, and from listening to others, is that we are truly skilled at arguing with our motivational state. We are experts at turning off our motivation or dumbing it down in line with how we feel or what we think. This interrupts the consistency and the inevitable 'falling off the wagon' occurs, often immediately followed by feelings of frustration and guilt and the action of 'giving up', both covered in a previous chapter. Let me repeat this: let's leave the wagons in the eighteenth century where they belong.

Beliefs

When we believe that we can't do something, our mind interprets that as a negative and we are soon fighting a losing battle. Understanding that a closed 'I can't' mind-set shapes the outcomes I achieve allowed me to retrain my thought processes to start thinking 'I can'. I made a conscious effort to reframe my thoughts using the Failure Tackle technique.

This mind-set shift has played a key role in establishing the levels of motivation required to eat clean and train five times a week. By thinking positively and having confidence in my ability to reach my objectives and goals, I have changed my beliefs about my own capability, overcoming the fear of failure, starting with gusto and demonstrating to myself that I am able to follow and stick to a plan.

Snowball effect

Long-term, consistent motivation is enabled if you can build up momentum in the early days. Once you've started, staying in motion and picking up speed becomes a lot easier. I have found that through using the power of a positive mind-set, a snowball effect occurs. The more I think positively, the more motivated I become. The more motivated I become, the more able I am to reach my goals and of course this makes me feel successful. I have identified that my many failed attempts at losing and maintaining weight in the past have been because I haven't established positive thinking strongly enough and often dumbed down the motivation. In fact, at times I would tell myself I *wasn't* motivated - which is of course the very opposite of what I needed to be. My inner voice would listen to that, give me a pat on the back and tell me to eat a cake!

There are times now when I don't want to exercise and I've realised this doesn't mean I lack motivation. I have a choice and I weigh up the pros and cons of that choice. Being consistent doesn't require perfection, but becoming consistent does mean I have to acknowledge the ability to make a choice without resorting to feelings of failure or guilt. By accepting this, the motivation levels remain intact. The practice of positive thought, proactive decision making & an 'I can' approach are the key drivers of consistent motivation.

A friend and colleague of mine, Wojciech Busz, is training for an IRONMAN (triathlon consisting of a 2.4-mile swim, 112-mile cycle ride and 26.2 mile run) and writing about it on ironconsultant.com. He puts in many hours of training during the week and sees food as fuel. I asked him to articulate how he stays motivated:

If you want to learn how to maintain a high level of motivation, you have got to start with getting to know yourself a little bit. What makes you tick? Are you a goal-orientated person? Or maybe you'd rather cherish the journey / the process without having a destination at the end of it? Why do you do what you do?

I was rather a chubby kid – not super-overweight, just one that would enjoy a few more sweets now and then. Around the age of 13 I grew taller and the chubbiness was left behind – but make no mistake, the little sugar-lover is still very much a part of me and would be delighted with the immediate gratification of e.g. a donut-fiesta, which the grown-up in me would later regret.

That's one key bit of information to learn about yourself – make an effort to understand what shaped you as a person, what events or people influenced your current self, as in the moments of weakness, these aspects will most likely surface with immense power.

The second key part is the question from the very beginning – what makes you tick? I used to go to the gym 4-6 times per week, lifting heavier and heavier weights, bulking up on proteins and becoming increasingly more muscular. I've got the luck of having a rather mesomorph frame, hence the gym results would become visible within a short period of time, providing me with motivation to go further. Having said that, I never lasted more than 6-8 months at the gym, gradually starting to find excuses like 'it's already too late today' or 'it's raining and the gym is sooo faraway' etc. – anything would work, really. My internal sugar-lover was over the moon – I'd stay in, munch on some Ben & Jerry's Caramel Chew Chew and watch an episode of Sons of Anarchy (thug life all the way here). Even though I have a mesomorph physique, I'd end up putting on weight, getting appalled at that fact and starting to go to the gym again. And the cycle would continue.

What I didn't understand back then was the fact that I don't necessarily enjoy the process on its own – I need to have something that I am striving for in a form of a SMART goal. Gym-going is fine, you get chiseled, fit and strong – but I would subconsciously ask myself the question 'so what?' and wouldn't be able to find the answer. What, am I going to be a bodybuilder now and take part in competitions? What's the purpose of what I am doing? Just being 'fit' didn't cut it for me.

So, when my wife started doing some running, I joined her and almost immediately signed up for a half-marathon in Reading. My wife ended up signing up as well and we had four months to get in a half-marathon shape. We got an app with plans set out for the next 12 weeks and off we went. It was so easy to stay focused! Suddenly, the excuses vanished – they got replaced by 'if I don't do this training, it will be detrimental to my progress and I might not achieve my goal of finishing a half-marathon'. Regardless of weather or time of the day, the training for that day was to be done. Period. I finally understood that this is the way motivation works for me.

20 months, 6 half-marathons, 2 marathons, 1 sprint triathlon, 2 Olympic triathlons and 1 half-IRONMAN later, I am keeping strong on my journey to becoming an IRONMAN by the end of 2018 (if health permits) – all because of that revelation that I need a goal to work towards. Even though I work 10-12+ hours' days, I still do 1-2+ hours of training during the work week and 6-8 hours during the weekend. I don't have thoughts like 'I'm not doing training today, can't be bothered', because becoming an IRONMAN requires that training of me and that's enough to keep me going. Of course, I have those days when I'm going 'this will be absolutely terrible, I so do not want to do this' – but I know these might come and am ready for them. When they come, I smile at them, put my running shoes on and outpace the excuses.

Bottom line #1: find out what makes you tick and use that knowledge to your benefit.

Bottom line #2: of course, I train almost only because my internal sugar-lover wants his donuts! And he gets them sometimes, God bless carb-loading pre-endurance events.

Bottom line #3: if you don't overindulge on carbs, even a roll with sunflower seeds will taste like heaven.

Bottom line #4: give yourself time. Be patient. It will be hard. You know it will be. So, when it becomes tough, just embrace it. You were ready for it.

Deliberate Practice

When my children were toddlers, I would watch them slotting wooden bricks into the shape sorter. Both would repeatedly do this until they had perfected the process. It wasn't ever simple repetition, it always appeared to require a lot of effort. Even when they had learned to do it correctly, they kept practicing it with a look of satisfaction. Scientists believe that expert-level performance is primarily the result of expert-level practice, not due to innate talent. So, whether it be a toddler or a violinist, deliberately practicing something we want to excel at must be the key.

I noticed this very early on in my journey and made a conscious effort to implement it. If I wanted to be consistently motivated and achieve success on my journey, I needed to do more than eat the right foods and lift weights. I needed to deliberately practice positive thinking, affirmations and mind-set tricks to ensure I excel on my journey to lean.

I set up deliberate practice rituals which I carry out daily/weekly - even now, 18 months on. I have added to this list as I progressed and it now includes:

Looking at my 'before' photos every day.
Posting side-by-side photos weekly.
Prepping food in advance.
Repeating my staple affirmations throughout the day.
Being mindful during my training sessions.
Repeating my mantra 'I can & I am'.
Noticing when my inner voice is in self-sabotage mode and acting on it.
Trying on an item of my 'before' clothing each week.
Reading through my vision, objectives and goals each night.
Tracking progress against my measures each week.

Visualising myself achieving my next goal.
Being a Self-Love Ninja.

As I outlined earlier, I believe we are not born with the motivation to succeed. It's about how consistently and deliberately we work to improve our performance.

Deliberate practice is not always fun; but once it's incorporated into your life, it becomes a routine and yet continues to be incredibly powerful. If I drop any of my deliberate practices I immediately notice the difference in my performance, motivation levels & the will to succeed.

Above all else
ALWAYS
Keep the Faith
and tell yourself
I CAN and I AM

Hold yourself accountable

I have read so many posts that go along the lines of:
'The plan I'm following doesn't work. I stuck to it for 3 months. I put the effort in. I exercised five times a week and I stuck to the food 90% of the time. It's a waste of money. I might as well have stuck with slim-fast shakes.'

The *90%* part of this post sticks out like a very sore thumb. If a person sticks to a food plan for 90% of the time, they are going to get a 90% result, which is a long way from a WOW result. What is interesting about this type of post is that the person writing it blames the plan, produces lots of justifications as to why the plan didn't work and fails to see the massive flaw in their approach.

I must sound like I am on the moral high ground here, so apologies in advance.

The thing is, I recognise this behaviour because I have been there. I have sat in the Slimming World sessions, and with a whiter than white expression, I have categorically refused any acceptance that the 2lb gain had anything to do with me.

'I stuck to the plan all week' I'd insist.

Conveniently disregarding the fish & chips I had after the last weigh in, the half pizza I'd eaten on Saturday night and the chocolate binge I'd had on Wednesday. Nobody knew about those things and therefore it was like they hadn't happened.

It was easy to deny the reality, blame others and accept little responsibility for my actions but in the end, the only person who was impacted was me. It was MY goal that went un-achieved and MY body that wasn't getting any smaller. I could place the blame wherever I wanted but the reality wouldn't change. I believe this behaviour of 'blaming others' comes from the same closed mind-set as the 'I can't' mentality I touched on earlier.

To move beyond this, it's important to focus on a growth mind-set. Accountability is absolutely something that can be learnt - it can be developed like a muscle. People who take responsibility for their actions look for solutions to problems and refrain from blaming others. Not only does this approach gain respect and build trust with others - I believe it builds trust in ourselves and increases our self-worth. Lying to yourself and knowingly blaming others for your own mistakes is never going to be a playground for the Self-Love Ninja and therefore contributes to self-sabotage. There is no such thing as blame when you own your actions.

My thoughts on how to be accountable:

Step One
Know what I am accountable for

This is linked to the Winning Strategy Plan we built earlier. I know that my vision/objectives and goals are the elements I need to focus on. This is what I am accountable for. With these clearly defined, it is easy to know when I am achieving them. The important bit is remaining true to myself and honest about my performance against them. If it's lacking, I need to hold a mirror up to myself, understand why and plan to put it right. I must have the humility to admit when I've made a mistake or not given it my all. Underperformance is recoverable and can easily be rectified with the right attitude and behaviours. I focus on my role in the situation and what I can do differently.

Step Two
Sharing my intentions

From the outset, I have found sharing my journey through social media very useful. In the early days, it worked very well with my known need for approval and over time has actually allowed me to dilute this need.

If I am going on holiday, I will share my holiday plan in advance and then will post regularly during my leave to prove I am sticking to the plan. I am sure nobody checks or even cares, but it keeps me focused and means I don't return 10lbs heavier.

If I am having a motivation wobble, I will post my food pictures throughout the day to make sure I stay on plan.

I will post my progress pictures every 30 days to show how I have altered in the month and knowing that I do this keeps me accountable to the goals.

If I set myself a challenge - like running 100k over 8 weeks - I will announce it and post updates regularly, sharing my fitness tracker stats to show I am putting the work in.

It's the same principle as having your quarterly performance review or appraisal at work. Sharing my intentions and my performance against them helps me to remain consistent in the pursuit of my vision.

Step Three
Owning the stumbles

It is not enough to be honest and humble when it comes to accountability. If I mess up, stumble or eat a cake when I didn't intend to, I OWN IT!

I don't blame the busy day, my lack of sleep, a tough meeting or rough commute. I accept that I made the choice to eat and drink things that weren't part of the plan and draw a line under it. I don't complain or whine. I don't feel guilty. I don't throw in the towel and have another cake. I don't blame others. I take my pride out of the equation, admit my stumble to myself and others and move on. It's as simple as that.

When you are personally accountable for your own journey and your own success, you take ownership of the situations you find yourself in. You see things through and you manage what happens, both positive and negative. You don't point the finger of blame, instead you strive to solve the issue and find ways to make sure it isn't repeated. Over time you build new skills and find better ways to deal with situations as they arise and you move consistently forward towards your goals.

When you make excuses, you are doing yourself a disservice and you deserve more than that. Plus, nobody cares, excuses fall on deaf ears because it ultimately doesn't matter to anybody else that you ate three chocolate bars.

Being accountable is always the best option. Accountability rocks and it helps you to be a Self-Love Ninja which is the best job in the world ☺

Above all else
ALWAYS
Keep the Faith
and tell yourself
I CAN and I AM

Surround yourself with people who 'get it'

I recently visited Ireland with the BGJTL admin crew and we spent the weekend laughing, exercising and eating healthy foods. We were in bed before midnight both days. Two years ago, I would have thought this sounded boring; a girl's weekend would have meant starting on the cocktails at 2PM and continuing in that vein until 2am when the night would finish with a fat-laden burger and chips.

There was a moment of clarity for me during the Ireland weekend. We'd completed a long cliff top walk and had a heathy dinner at a gastro pub. When we arrived back at the house Donna had checked her step count and announced that she had done over 23k steps. This was the most she had ever done during one day. We congratulated her and then Ruth advised she could get to 25k if she walked around the house. I then watched Donna as she paced around the lounge determined to reach that goal. This vividly demonstrated how like-minded people inspire like-minded people and it's infectious.

On the occasions when I am feeling lazy and not up for a workout, I dip into the BGJTL page and there is always a post that encourages me to get up and get it done. Seeing Nat Rudley from the Admin Crew start virtual running encouraged me to do the same. Ruth Warner and her amazing daily step counts made me want to hit at least 10k a day. There is motivation and inspiration at every turn if you surround yourself with people who have the same vision and goals.

What's also very positive is that like-minded people know how to respond to an 'I'm having a bad day' post. If I said I wasn't feeling it today and was craving chocolate, a non-leanie friend would likely say:

'Have a chocolate bar, it will do you good'.

Whereas my Leanie support network would say:

'Go for a run, you'll feel better for it, and have a chocolate protein shake afterwards to curb those pangs'

Leanies understand that munching on chocolate would only satisfy my immediate needs and be detrimental to my longer-term goals. Leanies naturally grasp the concept of 'delayed gratification' and we remind each other that giving in to providers of instant gratification is not the lifestyle we have chosen

I rarely share my progress with my non-leanie friends these days, and if I do, the response is minimal. This used to worry me and I have seen members of the Leanie community post to say, 'My friends don't even mention my weight-loss'. Often the response to these posts is that the friends are jealous, but I don't think that is the case. I think it is more likely that true friend's just love us for who we are, and not what we look like and therefore they don't 'see' the change.

What I love about being part of a like-minded community is that it allows me to feel safe being myself. I have found that I can be truly honest and open about what I think and feel and this has helped me work through my issues without being judged. In some instances, this has aided others in the same way, too. The encouragement and support is invaluable and there is always something to learn from others. For me personally, it's important that like-minded people share the same values rather than just the same interests. This makes the connections stronger to me.

My top tips for finding like-minded people

Join a social media community

There are so many groups out there providing support and inspiration for some myriad activities/lifestyles. You will quickly sense whether the group feels right for you just by reading the most recent posts. If they aren't in line with your beliefs – don't waste your time.

Find & follow 3 celebrities who inspire you

I can draw inspiration from celebrities who are following a path to health and well-being. I recognise they lead a different life to me and I ensure to take that into account. Equally I recognise that they are human beings facing into the same struggles as the rest of us in terms of inner voices, motivation and being consistent. I love following Joe Wicks because of his boundless energy, zest for life and the nuggets of inspiration he shares. I am energised by Holly Willoughby and how she balances working with being a mummy and looking fabulous. And my third choice is Oprah Winfrey who has had a difficult relationship with food in the past – she is the prime example that if you are persistent, you can get there.

Find 10 people who make you want to get up and smash it

These people are the non-celebs who are trying to be the best version of themselves every day. They are the positive lights that I am attracted to like a moth to a flame and those I go in search of if my own light is dimming. I'll flick into Instagram and see what they are up to and draw inspiration from them. Fiona will have posted a video saying she'd been for a 6k run in the same week she's had chemo. Nat will have earned another virtual medal. Theresa will be showing that at nearly 60 years old she can enter a bikini competition and hold her own. Sarah will be showing that you can battle cancer in a very positive, inspiring way. James will have posted a thought provoking write-up about nutrition. And then there's a handful of people who I don't know and they don't know me, but I follow them and love their vibe. These people make me want to get up, find my Self-Love Ninja and kiss ass! And I love them for it.

Post and let people find you

I have come to know so many amazing people through posting my updates and attracting followers. Their posts and comments help me to strive to be the best version of me and I am thankful for their support.

'By surrounding yourself with people who are positive, caring, intelligent, loving and open-minded, you create a

personal environment that is conducive to your emotional and personal growth.

By surrounding yourself with the opposite, you create a personal environment that is conducive to the opposite. Choose accordingly.' Dr. Steve Maraboli.

Dealing with Negativity

One of the downsides of changing my lifestyle is that other people can become uncomfortable with it. Often this is because I am holding a mirror up to them and allowing them to see their own insecurities. Sometimes, if it's a friend or loved one, it may be that they miss the activities that we used to engage in together.

The critical thing to remember - and something that I have learned the hard way - is that it has absolutely nothing to do with you.

When I got attacked by the trolls, I used to want to curl up in a ball and fade away. It hurt my heart.

I realised over time that it was often the things I was most insecure about, that, when attacked, would sting.

Generally, this was 'what will people think when they read what the troll has written'.

Over time, through deliberate and consistent practice of the growth mind-set tools, such as affirmation, I have become far more resilient to the comments of the trolls. I see their feedback as an opinion based on the way they feel I should act/look/dress etc. I then think about whether I am happy with the way I act/look/dress. If I am content with the way I am behaving and I am being true to myself, then their opinion doesn't matter to me and therefore is useless. If I feel there is something to be learnt from the feedback, I will reflect on it and think about how I could change my behaviour. The solitary nugget of learning might be amidst a tyranny of abuse, but if it is there, I will find it.

The following steps have helped me get to this place whenever I receive negativity:

Ask myself 'Is this what I think about myself?'
I do this through a very honest lens.

213

I have had feedback that I am exploiting women. I am totally comfortable that this is not part of my make-up and therefore accept it as criticism, but disregard it as not true.

I have had feedback that I take endless selfies in order to feel good. I would agree that that is the case, it's a big part of my Self-Love Ninja strategy. I therefore accept that this is part of me, don't take it as criticism (despite it being intended as such) and feel comfortable with who I am.

Ask myself 'which parts of the feedback sting and why?'

To do this effectively I keep in mind that feedback is an opinion, not a reality. However, understanding which parts hurt the most is useful because it allows me to highlight my insecurities and limiting beliefs. The comments that can hurt the most are those directed at my 'sour spots'. Those are the things that Miss. Meddler likes to focus on.

Ask myself 'Am I going to do anything differently?'

I may decide, having identified that the feedback has highlighted a personal insecurity that I want to do some reframing or develop specific affirmations to help me build positivity around the insecurity. I may decide that I will change nothing as a result of the feedback because I don't share the opinion or there is nothing valuable to learn from it

Forgive and forget

Part of this step for me is to thank the person for the feedback, to come from a place of compassion and let it go. I then decide to forgive the person for what they have said. Most times this is purely a conversation I have internally rather than with the troll.

I have found the steps to be hugely helpful in building resilience, taking away the emotional reaction and moving on quickly.

Let me give you an example. Here is an extract from a comment posted by a troll following an upload of a video I'd asked a popular PT to film for the BGJTL group. This was posted on my YouTube Channel.

riend? How can you describe this guy as a friend on ?? You are so full of shit. All you have done is seen how is becoming and thought you'd jump on his band wagon . with Joe Wicks, Sustain and Trinity. Earning money on the back of others peoples hard work. I suppose you ignore the fact he's normal and swears like a trooper if it makes you look good and earns you lots of dosh. You are nothing but fame hungry. Bit of advice, get the doc to do your tits while he is doing your tummy tuck, spaniels ears aren't a good look in a bikini.

Is this what I think about myself?

No. I have built relationships with several fitness experts to help me lose weight and to provide support to the BGJTL community. I have not made any money and have turned down affiliation agreements. I am not looking to be famous and up to this point I thought I had good boobs.

Which part of the feedback stings and why?

You may have identified it… 'Up to this point I thought I had good boobs'. She's attacked my body image and now I am doubting myself. Body image has always been my sour spot.

It stings.

But hang on.

I've always been proud of my boobs, even when I was bigger and they have actually improved with exercise. So why is it stinging? Because I have worked so hard to improve my body and this criticism feels mean. But I don't share the opinion.

Am I going to do anything differently?

I will develop an affirmation to reinforce the positive view I have of my boobs and eliminate her negative jibe.

Forgive and forget

On this occasion, I chose not to acknowledge her comment at all. I didn't see the value in doing so. I simply blocked her, forgave her and moved on wearing my favourite Pepperberry dress which shows of the shape of my boobs in all their glory.

The only way to avoid criticism is to stay confined to your shell but how stifling is that? I love the quote by John Shedd, 'Ships in harbor are safe, but that's not what ships were built for' as it summarises the point.

The moral of the negativity story is to when somebody goes low, we need to go high and stay there and my good friend Emma Farmer reminds me of this often.

Another aspect to be mindful of is how to deal with the people who care about you, but don't fully understand your new approach. I have friends and relatives who believe I am being deprived if I don't eat cake and they are genuinely concerned for my well-being. It's as if in their eyes cake contains a drug that I can't live without. I remind myself that these people are coming from a place of love and not dissimilar to my treatment of Miss. Meddler, I need to respect them for that. But, also like with Miss. Meddler, I need strategies to deal with it.

Top tips

Bake a 'clean' cake at home and take it along to a friend's so you can control the macros (Clean Eating Alice has fab banana loaf).

Suggest alternative meeting places such as a park for a walk or a spa rather than the pub or restaurant.

Just be honest, explain how important your lifestyle is to you and how happy it makes you.

Above all else
ALWAYS
Keep the Faith
and tell yourself
I CAN and I AM

Grab your pom-poms and cheer

I always wanted to be a cheerleader when I was a girl. They didn't have them at my school and I am nearly sure, if they had, I wouldn't have volunteered due to my size (as per my school play story from Part One). I watched them on television with envy. They were so energetic, had great outfits and always gave their all, encouraging the players, recognising their effort and celebrating with them after the final whistle.

These days I take the essence of being a cheerleader and I give myself the job, embracing every single second of it. Imaginary pom-poms shaking with pride as I thrash out my display of high kicks and splits. I am my very own cheerleader and I make sure I am kept busy!

The thing I love the most about cheerleaders is that they are not just there to celebrate the result. They are there right from the start, ready and willing to celebrate the small victories, and provide encouragement all the way through the game. When the game isn't going well for their team, they don't give up – quite the contrary, they increase their volume and commitment! Their energy and enthusiasm helps remind players how far they have come and this gives them the boost to keep bringing it.

On my journey, I have recognised the requirement to acknowledge the successes, however big or small. In doing so it's critical I don't lose sight of how far I have come. Sometimes, when progress is slow, it's easy to get disheartened and by looking back at the magnificent amount of progress I have achieved, I find a renewed energy to carry on. It's a sizeable part of my Deliberate Practice that I described in a previous chapter.

The other key element for me personally is how being my own cheerleader has helped me to gently move away from the need for approval and external validation. It has also allowed me to deal with criticism more effectively.

217

I believed that the only way to feel good about myself was to have somebody else tell me I was attractive, funny, good at my job etc. I would rely on others to provide the love and support I needed and to pick me up when I stumbled. Through self-encouragement, self-belief and celebrating my achievements, I have slowly let go of the years of learnt behaviour and created new habits centred on loving myself. This doesn't mean that I am blind to the areas of improvement, but actually embrace my flaws and approach the journey with love. This has given me the confidence and esteem to achieve great things, be content with my own validation and to view the praise from others as the icing on the cake rather than the vital ingredient. This has been immensely liberating and feels like the first ray of sunshine on your face when you step off the plane on your summer holiday.

Like all the other tools I have shared, it takes effort to make it happen. Just as the cheerleader does for the players, being our own cheerleader means doing three things for ourselves:

Encourage and believe in yourself.
Give yourself a pat on the back for how far you have come.
Celebrate the victories when they happen.

Doing this whilst wearing a short skirt, pig tails in your hair and sneakers and waving pom-poms is entirely optional.

Encourage and believe in yourself

By now you may have recognised my mantra 'I can and I am'.

I say this to myself at least twenty times per day (sometimes whilst waving the imaginary pom-poms). A lady recently questioned why I say, 'I am' rather than 'I will'. The quick answer is that 'I will' states intention whereas 'I am' states action now. Being my own cheerleader means finding the drive and motivation to do what I need to do through self-encouragement and by nudging myself to improve. Sometimes, when I am halfway through a workout and Miss. Meddler is telling me to stop at 6 reps instead of 12, I imagine myself dressed as a cheerleader willing myself on and chanting 'I can and I am' in a fabulous American accent. If you are rolling your eyes at this point, you have never tried it. It works and it works wonders. My inner cheerleader puts Miss. Meddler back in her place every time.

Believing I can achieve what I set out to achieve is key and reminding myself of this often helps to cement it. I cheer myself on with the rigour and excitement I would display if I were cheering on my children in the school race at sports day or Mo Farrah in the Olympics. I deserve that level of support and my cheerleader knows it and provides it.

Give yourself a pat on the back for how far you have come

When you are on a journey, however long it's been, it's good to look back at how far you've come. If I am running a 5k and I have 3k to go, I'll cheer myself on by saying:

'You've already done 2k! That's 2000 metres, that's 2/5 of the journey smashed.'

I'll apply this same principle to the rest of my journey. By constantly telling myself I am proud of myself and what I've done, I provide myself with the recognition and drive to keep going.

I will give myself a pat on the back for all manner of things, including:

For staying on plan for a whole week when I wasn't feeling it.
For recognising I've made a mistake and learning from it.
For losing over 8 stones.
For not bingeing for 18 months.
For being kind to myself.
For not eating a cake at a work's meeting.

Some of these things are small and some of them are monumental and they all make up part of my journey and represent how far I have come. On that basis, the pom-poms come out and I do a little shimmy.

Celebrate the victories when they happen

There are so many things to celebrate on a lean journey and I am pleased to say that many of these things are not focused on the

219

weight showing on the scales. It feels phenomenal when you lift a personal best weight or you fit into a dress that wouldn't zip up. Initially I felt embarrassed shouting about these things on social media, thinking that it made me look like a big head, but I came to realise that being cheerful about my accomplishments was important for me because it kept me optimistic and gave me the drive to forge ahead.

Examples of things I celebrate are:

Dropping a dress size.
Moving down a notch on my belt.
Saying no dessert.
Walking 10k steps or more on a working day.
Achieving a PB.
Eating a new food.
Getting an email saying I have helped somebody get started.
Doing a workout when I didn't want to.
Fastening a seat belt on the plane without any issue.
Running upstairs without getting out of breath.
Zipping up my knee-high boots.
Sitting in the bath and not touching the sides.

In the days of Slimming World and Weight Watchers I would celebrate losing a few pounds by having fish and chips. If I'd lost a few pounds, I'd commiserate myself by eating fish and chips. These days, I don't use food to celebrate or commiserate. But I do reward myself and have found several ways to do this:

Taking a candle-lit bath filled with lovely bath oil.
Having my nails done.
Buying some new workout leggings.
Booking a day at a spa.
Doing a home face mask.
Putting coconut oil on my hair and relaxing for ten minutes.
Going for a walk.

Meditating.
Online shopping.
Having a sports massage.
Watching a movie with Martin or the children (or both.)
Buying a new set of pom-poms ☺.

Being your own cheerleader and giving yourself praise for a job well done or at least for a step in the right direction helps you to take giant leaps towards feeling truly worthy. If you are not the type to share your successes with your virtual friends, work colleagues or family and family, then write about them in a journal. Sharing our successes through written or spoken word is powerful.
Start waving those pom-poms with pride ☺

Above all else
ALWAYS
Keep the Faith
and tell yourself
I CAN and I AM

Be the best you, you can be

In August 2015 I'd visited Lanzarote for a holiday and worn a size 20 swim dress. In August 2016 I returned, having lost lots of weight, and wore a bikini. I got ready in the hotel room and posted pictures of my bikini body on Instagram. I felt amazing. I walked to the pool and lay on the sun lounger feeling slim and confident. And then suddenly I spotted a lady with a figure to die for. She was no taller than 5', she was wearing a triangle bikini. She had slender shoulders, a small chest, tiny waist and a pert bum. She was no older than 30. I began to feel self-conscious and wished I looked as good as she did. The 'wonder' feeling I'd felt in the hotel room moments before was melting away as I compared my body with hers. I have done this many times in the past and it is utterly bonkers.

It's fine to admire, be inspired by and draw motivation from others, but it is not reasonable to compare yourself to others. It has taken me a good few months after that episode to learn this. I am 5'6 inches tall. I have broad shoulders, DD breasts and a large ribcage. I have very slim hips and slim legs. I cannot possibly ever look like a petite lady with small breasts and narrow shoulders and I will never be able to wear a triangle bikini without looking ridiculous. It's akin to comparing an apple with a banana and insisting that one day they could look the same. It's never going to happen.

We are surrounded by perfection everywhere we look. The magazine pages have now been joined by thousands of images on social media sites and even your best friend has access to great camera lenses, lighting and the myriad filters available. Nothing is real anymore, it's all highlighted, enriched and edited. This is one of the reasons I often record my vlog wearing no make-up and with bed hair. It's real. I want people to see that there's no such thing as perfection. It's all about progress and striving to improve ourselves for ourselves and not to look like 'Erin' or 'Joanna' on Instagram.

If you get sucked into wanting somebody else's legs, abs, boobs, hair or whatever, you are on a direct train to Miserable-ville. It's not going to make you happy. If someone can run 5k quicker than you can run 3k, that doesn't mean you are not doing a great job. If we do insist on looking like or performing like others, we will always be at risk of feeling like we are not enough and that is the rocky foundation of self-hate and misery.

The only person to compare yourself to is *you*. How you were yesterday, last week, last year and beyond. The mission is to be the best version of you and this should be all-encompassing. It needs to be more than how we look or what dress size we wear. It needs to include how we feel, what we've learnt, how we behave, how we perform, how we live. And it also needs to be kept in perspective. If you can run 5k in 30 minutes and one day it takes you 31 minutes but you gave your best, that's ok. You still ran 5k. Being the best version of you doesn't mean you must be stronger, faster, fitter and smaller every day. It means you have to bring it, own it, live and breathe every day in your most wholehearted way, and the reality is that could include a day under the duvet if that makes you happy and if it's what you need – as long as you're truly ok with that choice and won't regret it later.

If you have lost a lot of weight the other element you'll need to deal with is coming to terms with what you ACTUALLY look like. As a big girl I spent a lifetime denying my size. It was easy to convince myself that I was a lot smaller than I was. Oddly as the tables turned and I became smaller, it was easy to convince myself I am bigger. I often have to have to remind myself that I am wearing size 10 jeans so cannot possibly be fat when Miss. Meddler is trying to convince me otherwise. I have realised that it takes a while to come to terms with the changes to my body. The wake-up call is often a photo taken by somebody else. This was true for the big girl as well as the lean girl. The camera never lies.

You hold the key to your own happiness. Nobody can give it to you. Nobody can make you feel it. You create it and by focussing on improving and loving yourself, you can have it.

Tips for being the best you, you can be:

Daily
Admire one thing about you that has nothing to do with looks.
Admire one thing about your looks.
Admire somebody else and tell them what you love about them.
Write down three things that you are grateful for.

Weekly
Take a photo and compare with a previous image.
Write down five things you are proud of achieving.
Write down one thing you have learnt this week.
Write down three things you have done for others.
Put on your favourite song, dance the whole way through and tell yourself you are amazing.

As often as possible
Carry out a Random Act of Kindness (RAoK)
Examples:-
Send a card/email saying thank you.
Pay for a coffee for the person behind you in Costa.
Leave £10 in a book borrowed from the library.
Bake a cake for an elderly neighbour.
Take a food donation to the food bank.
Tell a stranger how lovely they look in that top/shirt.
Cut next door's grass.
Drop £10 into a homeless person's hat.

Doing this type of thing will make you feel on top of the world. Honestly.

Above all else
ALWAYS
Keep the Faith
and tell yourself
I CAN and I AM

Being a social butterfly

The life of a Leanie does not mean that you have to spend your evenings and weekends locked indoors eating spinach and reading books on body composition. I lead a full life and cultivate many social engagements, parties, events, meals with family, friends and clients and holidays. None of this has stopped because I started to follow a certain way of eating and drinking. It's just been a case of thinking differently.

If I am going for a lunch or dinner with a client, I will look at the menu on the restaurant website and find a dish that suits my clean eating approach. If there isn't a suitable dish, I will phone ahead and order something specific so when I arrive with my client, the restaurant is prepped and I don't need to have the conversation with a waiter/waitress. Often, even the salads on restaurant menus can be laced with dressings which add lots of calories. I find that the menu contains all of the components I want to eat spread over several different dishes. I therefore know that they venue can cater for my needs and ask them to pull together something like chicken breast with avocado and greens. I've never had a negative reaction from the staff.

Similarly, if I am staying in hotels for work, I will look for one that has a fridge in the room so I can store food or I will ask the hotel to store it for me. I will inquire if I can talk with the chef. Chefs love to accommodate special requests and if the menu is overly fussy or the room service options are particularly unhealthy, I will ask for salmon, poached egg and greens or chicken with avocado and green salad and they are always happy to help.

When dining with family and friends, I will again check the menu in advance and decide what I will be eating. This means I am clear in my mind before I step foot in the restaurant and I don't even look at the menu and instead spend the time chatting. Martin and I went for a meal recently and we'd not been to the chosen restaurant for a while. I chose steak with vegetables and had a dessert of cheesecake which is rare for me. We talked about the last time we'd visited the

225

restaurant with friends in our pre-lean days and we'd had three courses, bread, wine, champagne, dessert, wine, liquor coffee and truffles and we then had cheese and biscuits with liquors when we arrived home. The difference was insane. And yet was the experience different? The answer to that is no apart from the horrible bloated feeling of course from the mountains of food.

Socialising is about making connections, chatting, laughing and having fun. I have found that I don't need copious amounts of alcohol and obscene amounts of food to feel great. Previously, my focus has always been on what I will eat and drink and now I've consciously shifted that to be more aligned with what I will learn about the person I am with. I find I am much more 'present' as a result.

Cooking for people at home is my favourite. I make lots of yummy dishes from various clean eating cookery books such as Joe Wick's Lean in 15 and Clean Eating Alice. If we are having a BBQ, I'll ask the local butcher to produce chicken breast sausage - which are totally delicious and less expensive than the chicken sausage available in shops. I'll make homemade turkey burgers, vegetable kebabs, sweet potato fries and roasted pineapple. This food tastes amazing. It feels over-indulgent, but it isn't. It's a pure win-win.

If I am going for dinner at someone's home, I will speak to them in advance and find out what's cooking. If it's not appropriate, then I'll take something along with me. I don't feel bad about doing this. I am loving myself and nourishing my body. When I explain how important my nutrition is my friends understand and I always say for me the important thing is seeing the person and spending quality time with them.

Christmas is another interesting time. The rule book states that the number of calories consumed on Christmas day should equate to that consumed in a week, or at least that was what I knew to be normal. Why is that? Why is Christmas Day the day when it's deemed ok to eat half a Terry's chocolate orange for breakfast and consume so much at lunchtime you look seven months pregnant all afternoon. And even this doesn't stop you from eating roast ham, cheese and biscuits, trifle and a Toblerone (or was that just me?). From today's perspective, Christmas is about enjoying time with my family, building Lego with Finley, playing schools with Coral, and marvelling at the fact I am wearing a dress size 10. It's also about having a nice, yummy meal together, but it's not the main attraction of the day - it's merely an addition.

Eating in this way is simple and enjoyable. I put my knife and fork down regularly and engage in conversation, listening and being mindful. I seem to get so much more from social engagements than I did when I was engrossed in the food and how much of it I could eat. I don't worry about tracking calories or macros when eating out. I aim to choose the sorts of foods I eat at home and just relish the thought of not having to clear up afterwards. Now that I am nearing my destination of a healthy, happy lean body, I will have dessert now and then, but I don't have this regularly, because I simply don't need it.

If you can make eating out and socialising about building relationships and having fun rather than about calorie-laden foods and drinks, you will see it through a new lens and enjoy it for what it actually is. Rewrite the rulebook your way.

Above all else
ALWAYS
Keep the Faith
and tell yourself
I CAN and I AM

Size really doesn't matter

I have never been one for fashion items, particularly when I was bigger. I knew what suited my shape and I was a master of disguising my size through clever dressing. I seemed to obsess over the details and would waste time every evening switching handbags, watches, and jewellery to ensure everything matched my shoes and dress. I even refused to wear a fitness tracker because it didn't look very nice – or at least that was what I told myself. I bought a ridiculous amount of shoes and reflecting on this I can say that it's largely because I knew what size shoes I needed and finding them to fit was always much easier than finding clothing. Oddly, having lost so much weight, many of my shoes are now too big. Yikes!

I reached a point where I stopped going to stores because the changing room scenario caused too much angst. I am sure many of you have been there. I'd wrestle my way into a top that was too tight, kidding myself I was smaller. My size could fluctuate in a matter of weeks so I never knew what size I was. I would stand looking into the mirror with tears brimming as I observed the rolls of fat, magnified by the stark lighting, and wondering why it didn't look like this on the plastic model. By the end of the ordeal I'd be hot, bothered and feeling ashamed that I'd gained weight once again. To save myself some heartache, I would shop online and recreate the scene in my bedroom which was still miserable - but at least nobody would notice. I'd then spend a lot of time returning items via the Post Office because I'd ordered a size too small.

Fast forward to Lean life and I can honestly say shopping still creates challenges. I thought it would be much easier to dress a smaller body, but that isn't the case. What I have noticed is that I get less stressed about the details. I hardly ever change my handbag and I wear my fitness tracker all day every day, whether it matches of not. The thought of missing out on the step count is too much to bear (said with tongue in cheek – or maybe not?).

I have learnt that I still don't do fashion very well. I have experimented with various looks and have concluded that well-cut, classic clothes are much more suitable for me than trends. I am a size bigger on the top half of my body, with broad shoulders and big boobs, so I have to take this into account, too. I have been shopping with a stylist and this really helped me to understand what suits me and what doesn't. I would recommend this approach to anyone and there are plenty of personal shoppers on hand in department stores who can help. Taking pictures and then comparing them also aids in the process. I look at my body in various outfits and note which styles compliment my figure. Does a v neck work better than a high neck for example?

My top tips for shopping are as follows:

Don't Focus on Dress Size

I would get so hung up on the size of the clothing as I got smaller. The reality is: it doesn't matter.

I have clothes ranging from size 8 to size 14 in my wardrobe and they all fit me. It depends on the shape, cut and the shop sizing and it doesn't mean anything. Regardless what number is on the label, my body remains the same on any given day, so I can't use clothing size as an indicator. The critical thing is how it looks and how you feel in it. Often a dress size bigger than I think I should wear will hang a lot better and make me look slimmer than slightly squeezing into the smaller size.

Use a Dress Maker

I always buy dresses to fit my top half properly, because there is nothing worse than having squashed boobs. This means the dresses are then too big on the hips and waist, so I take them to my dress maker who charges less than £10 to take them in. My biceps sometimes mean dress sleeves are too tight so I have the sleeves removed – a tip taken from Shelley Baker, BGJTL admin. I also love my legs and often have dresses for work or otherwise shortened to sit just above the knee because this makes me feel sexier. I seldom wear dresses that are much shorter than this unless I am wearing opaque tights. I have good legs but always believe less is more in terms of exposing flesh, something I learned from my Grandmother.

During my weight loss journey, I used a dress maker to take in my clothes. This was cheaper than buying new ones because I only spent a month wearing one size at some points.

Apply Caution when the Sales are on

I've always been a sucker for the sales and have wasted so much money on clothes that have never seen the light of day. I now apply three rules:

1. **Purchase timeless, classic pieces only.**
   Coats, blazers, tailoring, jeans, shift dresses, knits. Not fashion trends.

2. **Only buy it if it fits**
   I no longer buy anything that I will 'slim into'.

3. **Get a second opinion**
   I'll always ask my husband what he thinks before buying something, he is very honest which I appreciate.

Take Photos at all Angles

I think mirrors have a way of fooling us. For some reason I always prefer mirror selfies more than photos taken by others. I think this is because a mirror shows the image I am used to seeing every day. When purchasing new clothes, I've found it useful to have full length photos taken at several angles and then I can truly appreciate the fit of an ensemble and how it makes me look, especially from behind which is difficult to see in a mirror. If it doesn't fit properly, I don't buy it because ill-fitting clothes lead to me fidgeting, which draws more attention to the issue.

Do a Wardrobe Edit

Whether you have changed size or not, chances are you will have things in the wardrobe you haven't worn for ages or at all, that don't suit you or that don't fit. Clearing out the clutter and really thinking about the things that are truly your style will allow you to see the gaps in your current wardrobe and therefore identify what needs to be bought. It also practically means there is more physical space on the rail and your clothes don't get creased.

Create piles for charity and for selling. There was such high demand for a clothes selling site in the BGJTL group that we created a spin-off site on Facebook and I sell my clothes there. I also use eBay. I tend to find that it's the high end high street brands that sell best second hand. If I paid less than £40 for something originally then I would donate this to charity. If items are imperfect I wouldn't attempt to sell them either.

Invest in Great Underwear

I spent my life wearing Spanx, sometimes two pairs at the same time for extra suction, and now, even with a tucked tummy there will be occasions when I will wear them depending on the type of outfit I choose. They provide a really smooth foundation. I have a little trick of wearing my cute panties underneath and then if I am expecting a night of passion I can whip off the Spanx in the bathroom and have my lovely underwear on under the dress for my husband to discover ☺

A good bra is equally important, particularly for the larger chest. Have a fitting and make sure you are wearing the right size and style for the outfit you are rocking. For a high neck dress, I will choose a full cup bra to avoid four boob syndrome; a v neck dress calls for a push up balcony style. Finding a decent strapless bra is also a godsend and proves very versatile. If I am wearing white, I now opt for a flesh coloured bra, it's not the most attractive underwear, but it means it can't be seen through the white material and is much more aesthetically pleasing

Remove Labels from Shoes
This is just a little pet hate of mine so worth a mention.

Other Quick Tips

If you have a larger chest, buy shirts with a hidden placket to stop the gape. Marks and Spencer do a great range or you can have one added by a dress maker.

Wear a light vest top under a v neck dress if it's cut too low.

Purchase a 'bobble off' to remove bobbling from fine knits.

Try a *Booband* which prevents your chest from jiggling when running (Godsend).

Carry safety pins in your handbag for emergencies.

Clean your leather jacket/skirt with baby wipes.

Be cautious of horizontal stripes if you are top heavy.

Check voucher code sites for discounts before buying online.

Get to know your shape and what suits you.
Buy the best quality you can afford.
You are worth it ☺

Above all else
ALWAYS
Keep the Faith
and tell yourself
I CAN and I AM

A girl (and boy) with a plan, can

I work hard and therefore whenever I take time off, we tend to go somewhere on holiday. Holidays in the past have always resulted in weight gain as I have already articulated earlier in this book, and often the weight gain has been significant.

I now view holiday time totally differently. It's no longer about consuming copious amounts of food and drink. Instead I frame it in my mind as:

Precious time with my family.
An opportunity to be more active without any time pressures.
A chance to show off the body I've worked hard for.

Even as I type the last one I can't believe I am saying that. After years of not wanting to expose my flesh it feels alien to look forward to it! I have certainly reached the greener grass of the change curve on that score.

For the last 18 months I have made the clear decision to plan my holiday in terms of exercise, food and treats. Being deliberate about this means I have prepared in advance and I'm less likely to be tempted to overeat or lie on the sunbed all day. I have found long walks with my husband whilst the children spend the morning at kids' club to be very relaxing. We talk so much more than we would if we were to lay in the sun all morning and I feel much more energetic as a result.

I don't do rest days on holiday. I believe that rest days are crucial in general and I take one or two per week, but on holiday I take the opportunity to exercise daily because I enjoy it and it affords me a few additional treats without weight gain.

I choose not to have alcohol and instead focus on drinking at least three litres of water daily which is very easy to do in the heat. I have a *Chilly's* bottle which I take on walks and to the sun lounger and it keeps the water ice-cold for hours. In the evenings I take a small squeezy bottle of sugar free squash in my handbag and add it to water. I avoid fruit juices which are sugar-laden and tend not to drink fizzy drinks as they make me feel bloated. I will have the odd slim-line tonic water now and then, though.

I always write my plan down, post it on my social media pages and report back against it every day. I'll post photos of my meals; fitness tracker outputs and treats and this assists me in staying accountable to the plan. I am sure some people think this is extreme (as described in Part Two), but it very much helps me and when I post my outfit and bikini selfies, I am feeling fabulous. It also means when I return from holiday, I have not gained weight.

We tend not to take all-inclusive holidays anymore. I found that we never actually had all four of us sitting at the table as a family because there was always somebody at the buffet. It is also very easy to overeat because there is an abundance of food on offer throughout the day. We'll book bed and breakfast occasionally, but often we do self-catering and eat out a lot, particularly when we are in Costa Teguise, Lanzarote which is our favourite holiday spot. The restaurants tend to have a copy of the menu on show outside and so on our morning walks we will browse the offer and find out if they have a suitable option. We recently found an amazing restaurant called *Mi Piace* which makes the most amazing goat's cheese salad and fabulous children's meals too.

I am taking a holiday shortly and create a plan a month ahead of time which looks like this:

Day	AM Work	Breakfast	Lunch	PM Work	Dinner
Sun	20 min HIIT	Low Carb	Low Carb	Arms/Abs	Carb Meal
Mon	3k Run	Low Carb	Low Carb		Carb Meal
Tues	20 min HIIT	Low Carb	Low Carb	Legs/Abs	Treat Meal
Wed	5k Run	Low Carb	Low Carb		Carb Meal
Thurs	20 min HIIT	Low Carb	Low Carb	Shoulders/Abs	Carb Meal
Fri	3k run	Low Carb	Low Carb		Treat Meal
Sat	20 min HIIT	Low Carb	Low Carb	Back/Chest/Abs	Carb Meal & Dessert
Sun	4k run	Low Carb	Low Carb		Carb Meal
Mon	20 min HIIT	Low Carb	Low Carb	Circuits	Carb Meal

My Holiday Principles
Exercise every day.
Aim to walk 15k steps daily.
2 low carb and one carb meal each day.
Enjoy two ice-cream treats during the holiday.
Have one dessert per week.
Have two treat meals during the stay.
Drink 3-4 litres of water daily.
Avoid alcohol.

I stick to two lower carbs meals and one carb meal each day. I tend to have the carb meal in the evening although will mix this up if I feel like it.

For breakfast I tend to make up reduced carb oatmeal before we leave for holiday. I'll incorporate the dry ingredients like chia seeds, flaxseed, protein powder, maca powder and oats together in a container and carry this in my luggage. I'll add almond milk when I arrive and soak overnight. I'll top this off with berries. This makes a great breakfast after a HIIT and doesn't leave me bloated - always a winner. If I am staying in a hotel which has a breakfast buffet I'll opt for an omelette with salad or veggies and some cheese. This combination of healthy fat and protein keeps me fuller for longer and helps me say no to the crepes, croissants and pastries. Toasted rye bread spread with nut butter and banana is another good option and it doesn't leave me bloated which is always a winner. Training before breakfast motivates me to eat clean and helps me remember how hard I have to work to burn off the number of calories in a pancake. A large croissant for example, contains 400 calories and I will burn approx. 220 during a 20-minute hard HIIT. You do the math.

Lunch tends to be chicken or tuna with salad and some avocado which is as easy to make in the villa as it is to source on a trip out. There are so many colourful vegetables and fruits on holiday - I can be truly spoilt for choice. The children love tortilla pizza (made using flour tortilla), so if we are having lunch at the villa they make up their own toppings, I'll bake them for ten minutes in the oven and have a slice of Coral's creation. Mixing flour and Greek yoghurt in equal parts also creates a fabulous pizza dough and it's a little more authentic without being fat laden.

Dinner is always a meal out. I choose wisely from a palette of grilled chicken, salads or steaks and have these with a baked potato or a wrap to incorporate some carbs. I'll opt for melon with Parma ham as a starter or share a starter with Martin if it's something more calorific like nachos. On a nine-day holiday I will factor in two treat-meals. This might be a creamy pasta dish from our favourite Italian or a paella and I am a lover of sizzling garlic prawns so like to choose these as a starter.

I'll plan one dessert and two ice-creams from my favourite ice-cream shop (Antiu Xixona in Costa Teguise, Lanzarote). I enjoy these treats so much more than I did when I ate whatever I wanted whenever I wanted it. I look forward to them and have them free of guilt.

Snacks don't tend to be consumed on holiday. I never feel the need to snack in the sunshine so save the calories for the main meals. If I do snack it will be a Nairn's Dark Chocolate Chip Oat Biscuit, which I buy for the children, or a rice cake. Gone are the days when I would polish off a family sized packet of crisps at the pool side.

The step count is a target. Some days I will do well over 15k and other days under this so I average it across the holiday. I tend to spend the morning being active, going for a long walk and then laze around the pool in the afternoon. To keep my step-count high, I will get up from the sun lounger every 20 minutes and take a walk around the pool.

This type of planning allows me to remain consistent and feel fabulous for the whole holiday. It means my travel clothes still fit, I don't return home with a Carb- baby and I don't have the slog of trying to get back on track when I get home, which to my mind, is the most difficult part.

The way I live is exactly that, a way of living. I don't need to alter it to have fun, it's purely a different way of thinking.

Above all else
ALWAYS
Keep the Faith
and tell yourself
I CAN and I AM

Decisions, decisions, decisions

How we choose to behave is down to us.

What we choose to eat is down to us.

Whether we exercise or not is down to us.

Whether we wear a size 10 or a size 20 is down to us.

We have the power and ability to make decisions that shape our lives. It has taken me too many years to realise this. Our own happiness is totally achievable if we choose to be happy.

If we feel that we will have a terrible holiday if we can't eat ice-cream every day then we have made the decision that unless we eat ice-cream it's going to be pants. The reality is we can have a perfectly wonderful holiday without eating a drop of ice-cream. It all comes down to how we decide to think about it.

This is one of the more recent tools I have adopted and like anything it takes practice. We are faced with choices and decision making all day every day and we often make them without any thinking at all. The upshot of this is usually perfectly fine and has no detrimental effects whatsoever, e.g. which shade of nail polish to run with or whether to choose vanilla or strawberry protein powder.

But there are some decisions that stand in the way of us moving towards our vision and it's these that deserve our undivided care and attention. When faced with these decisions it's important to be definitive because our minds dislike uncertainty. I also avoid caveats, if, buts or maybes. I make the intent clear and precise. And it works.

There is a world of difference between:

'I really want to run, but it seems really hard. Maybe I will try it and see if I can do it'

And

'I am going to run 5k' PERIOD

I often don't make it to 10,000 steps on work days unless I decide in the morning it is going to happen. If I make the decision with rigour and purpose then my day usually goes like this.

March on spot whilst brushing my teeth.
Go for a quick walk when I arrive at the client site.
Offer to get the coffees so I can walk.
Walk around when I am taking calls.
Go for a walk at lunchtime.
Go for a walk when I get home from work.
March on the spot when I get home until I reach the number.

If I don't make the decision I might do some of those things listed above, but not with the clear intention of hitting the 10,000. I can decide how I feel about food. If I decide that by eating clean I am depriving myself of a life worth living then that is what I am going to think and I will be resentful and grumpy most of the time. If I decide that by eating clean I am nourishing my body and feeling fabulous then I reach a totally different outcome.

I see this approach being a key part of sustaining this lifestyle going forward, together with the ongoing practice of the tools and techniques outlines. If I feel myself slipping it's often because I am not applying the rigour to the practices and I get a grip of myself and put them all firmly back. I make the decision to succeed.

'No external victory is ever going to satiate the self-esteem monster. It's a hungry f*ucker. You don't need it, you need to slay it. To feel better, it's a waste of time trying to change my external world. I have to work on the inside not the outside. It's about

changing my perspective and attitude- not just about achieving more.' Nigel Marsh

This is a journey and it continues beyond the vision we have created because as we reach our goals, we set new ones. As we achieve greater things, we set the bar higher. It's about progress and being the best version of ourselves.

We can live the life we want to live if we choose to.

It all comes down to want we decide to do.

You can draw inspiration and gain support from others, but ultimately…

You have to bring it.
You have to want it.
You have to put the effort in.
You have to lose the word 'Can't'.
You have to be honest with yourself.
You have to love yourself.

For the first time in your life, make it all about YOU.

When you wake up in the morning and the first voice you hear is Miss. Meddler telling you to roll over and stay warm, greet her with a very loud 'Today I choose happiness and it's going to be a fabulous day'.

Be accountable, own your journey, believe in your ability and you will achieve beyond the highest expectations.

You truly deserve it.

Above all else
ALWAYS
Keep the Faith
and tell yourself
I CAN and I AM
And know that **YOU ARE ENOUGH**

Part Four

An Unexpected Epilogue

One day you'll make peace with your dreams, and the chaos in your heart will settle flat, and maybe for the first time in your life, life will smile right back at you and welcome you home.
R.M. Drake

When I sat to write this book in 2017 and wrote what I believed at the time to be the very last sentence, I could never have predicted that I would be adding this new ending. This new 'to be continued'. They say that life is what happens to you while you are busy making other plans and boy oh boy, how true that is. So Dear Reader, let me share with you the chapter I didn't expect to write.

My day started like any other, with a session in my garage gym followed by a healthy breakfast and a skip in my step. I had a big meeting in London that day and so I chose my outfit carefully and off I went happily on my way.

There were no signs of things to come.

No sense of foreboding.

It was a beautiful, if rare, Indian Summer's day without a cloud in the sky.

A country girl at heart, London and I aren't natural bedfellows. I can never quite step to the city's often disengaged rhythm, but over the years I've learnt to navigate it best I can. I was meeting with a client in Central London and so jumped on a tube to get there. The train was particularly busy that day, full of people with places to go and things to see, so I stood at the door's entrance and held on tightly to the sunshiney yellow bar along with a few other passengers. My mind started to wander to my meeting. I ran through a mental 'to do' list and looked forward to seeing my clients again. We had a huge challenge ahead of us that day with a 5pm deadline to meet.

The tannoy announced our arrival at Leicester Square, with reminders to 'mind the gap' for those who alighted. The doors slid open ready for the choreographed dance of people leaving and joining the train to begin, for new people with new plans and new places to go, to fill the carriage. At the next station, I too join in the merry dance and make my way to the fresh air of Covent Garden outside. Feeling ready for the day ahead, I saunter towards my

242

client's building. It starts to pick with rain just as I get to the doors and I smile at my impeccable timing.

I find the room in which we will all be spending the day and after pleasantries and a quick catch up, it is time to get down to business.

'Right then Everybody. We have until 5. Let's do this!' I say with a smile.

After a couple of hours of analysis and planning, we break for coffee and as we do so, my phone rings. I am often contacted by unfamiliar numbers and so I do not question who the Caller might be. It's usually a new client and I am always happy to take their calls. I say hello with a smile and move away slightly from the table full of relaxed chatter and the clinking of china cups full of coffee.

There is a momentary pause at the other end of the line and so I prepare myself to hear the usual robotic parler about my recently having been in an accident and ready myself to disconnect the nuisance call.

'Hello?' I say again.

And then, a voice.

A voice from the Dead.

A voice from the Dead saying my name.

A voice I had erased from my ears and from my life a long time ago. I had buried the voice and the man attached and yet here he was speaking to me. He was speaking to me on a telephone in a room in a City, surrounded by chatter and the clinking of china. He had somehow found me and was speaking to me, violating my space and my life again and I find myself unable to respond to his violation once more. Bound by painful silence once again, I begin to shake.

I might have muttered something unconsciously to myself, I do not remember. Maybe I was muttering something to her. To 9-year-old me. Telling her to hold on tight. It was him. The man who stole my childhood and replaced it with a lifetime of shame and confusion. I want to throw the phone to the floor and smash it into a thousand pieces but I know that I cannot make a scene and so instead I grip it as tightly as if I have my hand at his throat. I am barely breathing. He is on the other end of the line, who knows where? He could be in another country or at the other side of the door, it doesn't matter. He might as well be standing over me, close enough to touch me, invading my space again. And the worst thing is that I become aware that I can taste him. I can actually taste him in my mouth again and I am paralysed by fear. I am surrounded by people but feel utterly alone and exposed.

I suddenly hear a child crying. I know that it is only me who hears her. 'You promised! You promised that we'd never hear from him again. You said we were safe!' I want to reach back and hold her. I want someone to hold me. My breath quickens. My heartbeat pounds in my ears just like it would back then. Right back when.

Every cell in my body begins its decent into trauma. I manage to pull the phone away from my ear, disconnect the call and excuse myself from the room for a moment.

I walk outside and into the rain. I lean against the wall of the building away from the busy entrance. I am shaking. I think I might faint or vomit, or both. As the rain falls upon me, I try and make sense of what's just happened. I am trying to scramble to find a cord for the parachute while I hurtle towards the ground. I close my eyes tightly and attempt to regulate my breath.

The rain continues to fall upon me. The clouds gather overhead. There is no sign of the sun. It is long gone. He's back, I thought. He's back and I can feel him. I am overwhelmed by the urge to do the only thing that I know will take away this pain and rising panic and that is to binge. It is all I can think about while I spin out of control.

I am suddenly distracted by a man's voice calling my name from the entrance of the building, 'There you are!' he says. It is one of the team with whom I'm working.

I click immediately into Automatic Pilot. Activate smile. Keep moving.

Inside I am a mess. Inside, I am nine years of age again and terrified to my very core.

We walk inside together. I can't remember what we spoke about but I nodded and smiled and managed to get myself back into the room.

I spend the rest of the day feeling like I am under water and I barely remember much of it now, looking back. We manage to meet our deadline and I keep up the act of Automatic Pilot Angela until I bid the last of the Team goodbye. It was on the train home that I allowed all the feelings that had been kicking at my door, smashing all the windows and demanding they be let in, to hit me. How had he found me? Did he know where I lived? I shuddered.

I barely remember getting home. That night, for the first time in a long time, the horrific dreams of my childhood come back to haunt me. They would haunt me for some time to come.

The next fortnight is a living hell. My waking hours are a constant battle with myself. I do not hear from him again, but I do not need to. The damage has been done. I am constantly fighting the overwhelming impulse and urge to binge and become withdrawn as I try and cope. I attempt to be as normal as possible, fixing on my smile and getting on with things but it is like dragging myself injured, through mud. I am there, but not there. I am never present, and am barely managing to keep on the mask. I become emotional and short tempered. I sit outside shops willing myself to go in and buy food whilst also urging myself not to. I am in a constant, cruel tug of war and it is almost unbearable.

After two whole weeks of torment and pain, the battle becomes too much and the day before I am due to return to the hospital for a corrective procedure on my tummy, I find myself standing with my heart beating in my ears, at a counter that is selling cakes. I order. I pay. I leave, clutching on to the box as if holding on to the side of a life raft. I sit in my car, shaking, devastated, and I start to eat the contents of the box. One after another. I cannot taste them. Still I fill my mouth, swallowing hard.

'Make it go away' says Nine-year-old me 'Keep eating. Keep going. I can still feel it. I can still feel the pain Angela. Make it go away!'

I keep swallowing. Not tasting. Eating. I do not care who sees me. I am filling a hole that is not hunger. My pulse racing. My head spinning. I am lost in the grip of something greater than me. The storm continues to close in and I swallow. Again. And Again. And again. I swallow but nothing fills me.

I have lost track of time. I have been too busy spiralling into a vortex I thought had finished with me a while ago.

The box is empty and I am immediately full of regret.

I close my eyes. Slowly, my breathing and pulse stop racing.

I look around me.

I am alone.

And, I am alone.

A familiar sensation washes over me. It's been a while, but I know it well. Shame. I feel ashamed. After 20 months of winning against the Demons that have chased me through my life, they have caught up with me once more. I sit there with my head spinning, feeling sick. How could I let this happen? After all I'd learnt? How could I give in? After all my hard work, I was back here. At Rock Bottom, frightened and confused.

And thank goodness I was, because little did I know it at the time, but this incident was about to save me.

Sitting in the car after the binge, I knew I had to do something to try and redirect myself from the road back to my former Hell, back to the wicked merry go round of binge eating. With the Demons looking at me over my shoulder, waiting for me to unravel, I knew that I had to lift the lid on the secret in order to quieten them. I couldn't keep this to myself like I had done in the past and so I decided to tell the person I trusted most in the world, Martin. I had never done this before and burst into tears as the words fell from my mouth that night. He was, of course, amazing and gentle and kind and once I'd told him, I felt immediately better. I wasn't alone. It wasn't a secret. I wasn't a hostage.

A few days later, I felt strong enough to share the 'blip' as I'd chosen to refer to it, with the members of the page. I explained about the phone call, without going into details, and shared how bingeing had become my coping mechanism for anything related to feelings of guilt, shame or rejection over the years. The phone call, I explained, had been a trigger. It was not an easy admission to make. I went on to talk about the binge incident and that I'd told Martin this time, in order to combat the secrecy that had kept me as its hostage in the past. I shared that I had immediately felt better for having done so and that I was able to forgive myself as a result, congratulating myself for at least remaining focussed on exercise throughout.

I smile when I think back at this now because not even I would understand the true implications of what I had written. This 'blip' would not be a solitary incident and the binges would continue for ten days. It was a tough battle but it would lead me, thank Heavens, to the decision to try and truly understand the nature of my bingeing once and for all, by seeking professional help. When I met a wonderful Clinical Psychologist called Sally, I realised that most of my life had been spent in a room where I had become accustomed to the dark but could not truly see. Where all the things I thought I knew, had a far more complex explanation than the one I had written for myself.

After a few sessions with Sally, who has years of experience in Childhood Trauma and Eating Disorders, she diagnosed me with PTSD, Bulimia and Binge Eating Disorder. Suddenly the darkened room in which I had been living, was flooded by light. It was the beginning of my meeting my true self for the first time. Of my being able to step out of the shadows and into the sun. To begin to understand and in understanding, to forgive and accept and love myself. I had carried the burden of shame with me for most of my being. I had lived a lifetime normalising a dreadful secret, believing that I deserved it.

I did not.

I could stand in my new light and know that I did not deserve what had happened to me. It is not the sum of who I am. Through therapy, I have felt safe enough to unlock many other fragments of memories long buried. Memories so dark and painful that they took away the light even before the horrors of abuse at 9 years of age, when I was 6. Six little years, even younger than my beautiful, innocent daughter Coral is now. When I was at the big house with the long gravel drive and Bill the Millionaire would take me to the sickly pink bathroom, and abuse me. In stepping out of the darkness and meeting myself, accepting myself, I can let go of the shame and self-loathing that such unspeakable acts burdened me with for over 34 years.

My therapy with Sally is ongoing, as is my understanding of all that has happened and all that I am. I have learned so much but still have more to learn. I am grateful for the deliberate practices which have become the foundation of my existence and have undoubtedly supported me through this challenging stage of my journey. Unbeknownst to me, I had battled eating disorders throughout my life and had somehow managed to keep them under control for 20 months without professional help. I feel encouraged that while the disorders will always be a reality in my life, by understanding the triggers, I can continue to build on successful coping mechanisms to keep them at bay. I am still not immune to the detrimental effects of criticism however and continue to battle the Trolls who will remind me of this fact, but I do have a strong sense of who I am and who I am not when they come a'calling.

Neither am I without my old frenemy, Self-Doubt. In reading the final draft of this book, I found myself questioning myself and it. Even though I have strived to be open and to tell my story as it is, warts and all, without exaggeration or, I hope, self-pity, I found myself doing the Trolls' job for them - picking away at events, criticising the details. Judging. Did I sound like a victim there? Or when that happened? Because I have never felt victimised and have certainly never seen myself as a victim. Who did I think I was, writing a book?! There were plenty of people who'd been through worse than me, had achieved more than I and hadn't done so.

And on and on my Self Doubt rattled. This time however, I had a few things to say to Miss. Meddler.

I understand that being the Me that I was always meant to be means that I no longer have to be bound by caveats or make excuses for who I am. I had kept so much hidden for so long. The box was crammed full of darkness and pain until a devastating phone call one day, blew off the lid. I am learning to place that lid back on loosely, knowing that the illuminated contents of the box no longer burden me or my future. I am a Survivor who is healing, not a victim who is defined by her past. It is like coming up for air and I finally feel free.

The truth is that I have written this book for me and for anyone else who has also struggled along life's path. I do not have all the answers but I do have a sincere intention to help anyone who finds that my journey resonates with them in some way, however big or small. I will leave you with a fitting quote by Stephanie Bennet-Henry that so perfectly captures all I have learnt.

'It's a journey in itself to come to the point where you can say, I am enough, without needing to add something to the end of that. I am enough...but I would be more than enough if I was thinner, stronger, prettier, taller. I am enough...but I would be better if I were richer...No. I AM ENOUGH.'

And so, I give you my story, nervously but willingly, and I hope that it will be your invitation to believe in better things and to know to the core of your being, that you too, are ENOUGH.

Your vibe attracts your tribe

The BGJTL followers

Make a conscious effort to surround yourself with positive, nourishing and uplifting people. People who believe in you, encourage you to go after your dreams and applaud your victories.
Jack Canfield

Angela was someone I admired from the side lines. I was quietly inspired by her determination, screenshotting her workouts to try for myself and following her journey with amazement. I never imagined that this woman would become someone I could, hand on heart, call my friend. When Angela put out her post for admins, I jumped at the chance and put in a plea for her to consider me. Our friendship grew under the umbrella of the page and more importantly the admin chat, a place I turn to for support more often than asking those I see face to face. Angela has helped me in more ways than one, and more ways than she will ever understand. Meeting her in real life was a nerve wracking prospect, but one that I relished and I needn't have been so worried! She immediately put me at my ease, smiling like I was the only person in the room and what a smile! This is a woman who always has time for those around her, noticing if we're off grid or not ourselves. **Natalie Rudley @runruddersrun79**

Angela posted about her journey in a Facebook group and I was always in awe of her dedication and motivation. When BGJTL was born, I joined because she's a real woman just like me. She had a lot of weight to lose and she smashed her weight loss journey and did it in style. Her posts and her photos gave me inspiration and hope that I could stop the cycle of yoyo dieting and bingeing. From the outset, I loved the positivity and what Angela offered on her page. I realised there are a lot of like-minded people having the struggles I have but they want to get lean and healthy and need support. Angela messaged me and asked me to be a member of the admin team and I was so excited and honoured really as I knew she was creating something special. What I love about Angela is she constantly provides support to others, even when she gets trolled and people say hurtful things, she won't lower herself to their level and she handles everything with dignity and grace. She gives straight talking advice in a lovely supportive friendly way. **'Hannybobs' Hannah O'Brien @hannybobs55**

In a group of over 30k people, Angela stood out straight away and I felt a real connection to her. When she set up BGJTL I was happy to follow and later when Angela asked me to be admin, I felt 10ft tall which at 5ft 2, is no mean feat. Since those early days our relationship has flourished both as part of the admin team and on a personal level. We have shared confidences and have built a relationship made up of trust and mutual interests that will last a lifetime. There is no one I would rather go shopping with. I hope that this is only the start of Angela's journey and friendship that will last a lifetime full of crazy, happy memories. Wishing her all the very best. **Donna Moorhouse @donna5703**

Having been part of the BGJTL community since the beginning, I can say without doubt that Angela has influenced me to be the best version of myself. Her positive mind-set and encouraging words have helped thousands of people. She is passionate about helping others and has committed so much of her time to building this wonderful community. She has a beautiful, caring and giving soul and I am so thankful that I found her. **Emma Farmer @Emma_farmer14**

For years my weight moved up and down as I jumped from one diet to the next. This had a major psychological effect on me and I was desperate to lose the weight. I came across Angela on Twitter. I realised there was someone else out there who had gone through much the same as I had but had gained the courage to change. She had seen an amazing transformation in her health and physique using the Body Coach plan. Her tweets were inspirational, encouraging and thought provoking, and she proved to me that I did not have to be a super human woman to get fit and healthy again. I signed up to The Body Coach and started tweeting about my journey expecting no one to be interested but Angela always responded with encouragement and further inspiration. She had guided me through the initial weeks and I was in awe of her, especially when she announced that she was running a one-day seminar on her story so far. This was exactly what

I needed but the tickets sold out almost immediately and I was left to carry on being inspired through Twitter. Then one day, completely out of the blue, Angela offered a complimentary ticket as her special 'act of kindness'. I was blown away. Angela truly is an individual I am proud to call a friend. **Amanda Dodwell @mandi_64**

BGJTL has been a life changing experience for me. If anyone had ever said that I would be part of a group of 22k 'virtual friends' that I spoke to every day, let alone become an admin in the group and become 'real life' friends with such an awesome group of women I would never have believed them. Way before I was an admin I knew how special Angela and the page was. To have created and maintained such an inspirational and supportive place, kept it safe and true to itself, and to have opened herself up so much to share her story and help others shows how special she is.

Angela is the anchor that holds us all together and has built a diverse, feisty, caring, passionate team of admins that I am so proud to be part of. Meeting Angela and the team in person has given me a whole new group of friends - we all have each other's back- and they are the first and last people I 'speak' to on most days!

Thanks Angela. You rock **Kathy Allison-Henry @Kathy_allison**

I was shocked when Angela said I was the reason she started fundraising and honestly, I was blown away! I had no idea, and felt/feel so incredibly flattered! Especially as she has raised thousands of pounds for the wonderful Macmillan Cancer Support.

She has been someone I've long admired from afar & always felt some kind of affinity for. Her sunny outlook, determination, focus, motivation, consistency, authenticity & warmth were some of the qualities I was drawn to. The whole day was riveting & the time flew past. If you didn't feel inspired beforehand, I defy you not to be after listening to her talk. Plus, she looks gorgeous in the flesh! I was not disappointed!

I am flattered & more than humbled, but the credit lies entirely with her. It was a brilliant seminar, inspiring & wonderful, and whilst it was a tiring day, I wouldn't have changed a single thing. I think it was fate that made me suddenly decide to go and I'm thrilled that I did. **Sarah Frost @the_real_sarah_frost**

Angela's lean journey and the many other incredible transformations I see daily on BGJTL are phenomenal. I have been inspired to take up running again and the support I get is incredible. Not only have I transformed physically, but also mentally. BGJTL has been instrumental in my journey and is my daily 'go to' for inspiration, pick me ups and to share my ongoing journey. Forever grateful. **Shelley Louise Brady @shelleyBrady21**

Angela was always extremely positive inspirational and very motivated which is what drew me to her. She has such a lovely way of making you feel so special. I loved following her journey and seeing her amazing results. When Angela set up BGJTL, I was one of the first to join and not even Angela could have foreseen how the group would grow. People soon realised this was one special lady. Her page is nothing but respectful, motivational, positive and most of all Inspirational which sum up who she is.

The biggest life changer for me is the friendship we have made during our journey. We often message each other and just talk together. She has always been supportive not just with the weight loss and exercise but on a personal level too she always says I need to be kinder to myself. She is a busy lady with so much to do but never fails to be there for me. We have never met and some may wonder how I can be such good friend, but as Angela herself has said we just are. I don't think she will ever know just how much her words mean to me. **Janice Schofield @schofjan**

I stumbled across Angela and the BGJTL Facebook page when I started the 90 Day SSS plan. I was in awe of this amazing woman and what she had achieved in such a short space of time after endless years of yo-yo dieting. I jumped at the chance of attending the seminar in February 2017, dying to meet Angela and the admin crew. It was like going to meet a bunch of celebs, seriously I was nervous and excited at the same time.

They were all amazing and made me feel loved and proud to be part of an amazing group. I offered to help if Angela was ever on the lookout for more to join her and the admin crew.

A lot happened in the next few months for me and while I battled against breast cancer, Angela was there in the background giving me encouragement and support.

When Angela messaged me to ask if I would I like to join them, I was unbelievably proud and over the moon. Joining the admin couldn't have come at a better time for me, it's a place where I feel at home. I consider them all part of my family and I know they will be friends for life. We all fit together so perfectly. Angela is an amazing woman, who I am proud to say is my friend and I will always be there for her no matter what. **Fiona Maunder @fitnessfi**

It's always a pleasure to work with people who are determined, strong willed and happy to sit outside of their comfort zones. Angela is one such person.

We first met in September 15 and got down to some serious training right from the off.

Kettlebells, rower, Bulgarian bags and suspension trainers were amongst the tools we used to work on Angela's strength and fitness. I helped guide her through the initial stages of The Body Coach. We have also shot several workout videos together which have proven to be very popular on her YouTube channel. I feel proud to have been a part of the incredible journey she has been on. **Del Wilson @Kettlebelldel**

To me it's positivity that sums up BGJTL, its fun, supportive solidarity. Like an extended family, but not the ones you wish you weren't related to. BGJTL has an ace admin team and an inspiring founder. **Natalie Jenkinson**

People come and go throughout your life and I believe that people enter it at times when you need them. This is never truer then when I found Angela and the BGJTL group. Supporting people is what I have always done but I have never given myself the time that I deserve. Angela and her ethos were what I needed to put me on the path to commitment, discovery and acceptance. I can honestly say that because of the support from Angela her amazing team and everyone on the BG JTL site that I have never been happier and more content. Thank you, Angela. **Kathy Harris @kafharris**

In the summer of 2016 I came across Angela through social media and was instantly inspired. We connected and she came to take part in some sessions with our fitness family at my gym. She continued to inspire me in 2017 and gave me the confidence to Vlog every day about a running journey and challenge I was undertaking all year. As a result, Angela asked me to talk at her seminar as she was inspired by the challenge and we soon realised early on how we share the passion of inspiring others and paying forward what we have gained through our fitness journeys. Visiting Angela in hospital during her recovery from her operation our friendship has continued with our support for each other continuing from afar and in person. **Neil Marsh @coach_marshy**

I have nothing but praise and admiration for Angela. By opening herself up to others and sharing not only her current journey but also the motivation that got her started, is to me unbelievably brave. Her unrelenting attitude is not only inspiring but also infectious, she clearly wears her heart on her sleeve and will go out of her way to help anyone. Through resilience and perseverance, she has come out of a dark place and is now willing to guide others. I am proud of what she has achieved so far and look forward to supporting with her in the next chapter. **James Walker @sustain_nutri**

Angela and I have met in person several times. When I spend time with her I feel better about myself. We talk about common goals and she makes me want to do better. I leave feeling inspired. **Wendy O'Beirne @notestoselfjournal**

It takes a new level of bravery to share where a life of yo-yo dieting has taken Angela both physically and mentally. She opens herself up to an array of opinions, but in doing so Angela has shown us what is possible through mind-set shift, hard work and pure determination. Being part of her journey and finding fellow kindred spirits in the BGJTL family has lit a fire in me which has allowed me to embark on my very own voyage of discovery. **Cath Marks**

The fact that Angela takes the time to reply to comments is such a motivator. She is clearly a lovely genuine person who is non-judgemental and basically gets it because she has made the journey and made it work in the life of a busy working mum. I am so appreciative of the support of BGJTL in helping me on my journey. **Emma Upton @emmaupton19**

Angela has been a great inspiration, I love following her journey, she has achieved so much. I'd like to say I love her workout journal so much so I'll be on the 3rd very soon. **Clare Louise Ball @clarelouiseball**

BGJTL is about empowerment. Every woman or man who joins the page is lifted up, supported and respected. It's a truly safe place to share your own journey at your own pace and not feel as though you are competing against anyone. Angela's honesty and accountability has given so many people motivation, companionship and inspiration. What a gift. **Julie Smith**

BGJTL came into my life when I needed to know that I wasn't alone. I was welcomed into the biggest family ever. **Paula Lackie**

I joined BGJTL in the first couple of days. I had not long been on my own journey and found Angela's very inspiring. The atmosphere on the page was incredible. It was a very proud moment when I joined the admin crew. I am truly honoured to call Foxy Coxy a friend and feel like the team are my chosen family. I wouldn't be where I am today on my journey without the support and encouragement from this safe and motivating environment. Thank you, Angela, for everything. **H Cater @hbaby76**

When I found the page it was as if I'd been searching for this all my life. I've always tried to live a healthy and active life, but never had the support I needed and wanted. I found that in this group and it means a great deal to me to have the support and virtual friendship of such a large group of like-minded people. **Tamsin Blake**

Where would I be without BGJTL? - I shudder to think. It keeps me on track, makes me smile and boosts my confidence. **Sasha Warr @sashawarr**

How I found Angela's Instagram account is now lost to time. I do however remember at one point finding a post of hers detailing her journey and I commented on it, explaining my own journey was similar. The next day this woman who was followed by tens of thousands and followed 197 now followed me, I was 198! From then on, I've watched her post unflattering comparisons, painfully honest accounts of her struggle, liking each other's content back and forth and reminding me every day that we are both on a marathon, not a sprint. Or a HIIT. Thank you, Angela. **Ron Kane @ron.kane**

I feel safe. I feel encouraged. I feel normal. I feel empowered and all because one special lady was brave enough to share her journey, with no frills.

The rest of the team are also amazing it shows there is courage love and positivity all around us, thanks. **Heidi Lyon**

BGJTL is the safe place you go to when you don't trust in yourself. The place you can read others' comments, NSVs, support, ideas, tips or join in yourself. The place that makes you stop giving up when you've lost your mojo, when you realise people are feeling or have felt the way you are feeling, but if you pick yourself up success is just around the corner. A helping hand and I wouldn't be without it. **Jan Frecklington**

Angela is my companion on my journey that didn't let me down.

The group is my daily inspiration, with a multitude of members at different stages.

It's my haven, my peace, where no one ever tires of transformation pictures, where no question is unanswered, where no one is left behind.

Angela doesn't fully realise what she has created through her own journey, she accidentally created this positive ever giving group.

I'm very proud to be a part of this is in some small way
#longliveBGJTL **Doreen Calder Lundie @dotlun**

Watching Angela on her lean journey has been a real pleasure. She is of course inspirational, but her clarity about what she is doing and why, and her positivity is reflected in the group. Every single person in the group is positive, complimentary and supportive. It wouldn't be that way without this clear leadership. She has inspired thousands of people to keep on their lean journey. Even on days when she has found her journey tough, her message is still positive and inspiring. **Angela Ireland @irelandangela**

A BGJTL Poem...
Angela is the heart & soul of a Big Girl's Journey to Lean,
She looks out for us all, along with her fab admin team.
Her journey's inspired & helped us to be,
The version of ourselves we'd most like to see.
She's there with a "whoop" or a cheer to help us celebrate,
When we've had an NSV, or done something great.
Or if we're struggling, & have fallen off track,
Her words of wisdom help us get back.
We're safe to discuss our feelings & thoughts,
Without fear of judgement or nasty retorts.
She's created a group that means so much to so many,
I'm proud to be part of the BGJTL family!
Julia Hemingway

I can always rely on the beautiful BGJLT family to support me and lift my mood. I love reading all the posts. I have been told I am inspirational but Angela and her family always inspire me to go that extra mile and be the best person I can be. **Theresa Lovelace @fromfittofitter**

I love the phrase 'you can always tell who the strong women are. They are the ones building each other up instead of tearing each other down'. BGJTL is the epitome of that for me. A very rare environment where there's nothing but encouragement, nothing but support. A few giggles along the way, a few tears, but people open up and share in ways they can't anywhere else. Because they're safe in the knowledge that all those around them are going to build them up, not tear them down. I have been dieting for years with no success. The difference this time has been BGJTL. Thank you from the bottom of my heart! **Jo Gordon @Jogordon**

BGJTL has helped me know that just being me is enough! I am human and sometimes mess up but that's OK. Just reset and start again. **Sindy Cross**

BGJTL is like a massive hug on a rubbish day. It's full of positivity, has amazing inspirational members and is a safe place to ask for help and encouragement or a kick up the arse. Or, to silently watch the inspiration until that moment you're ready to take the bull by the horns and smash it!! Love it here. **Debbie Hartin @debs_just_f_do_it**

To sum up this awesome group the support, the amazing Angela and her Admin have given, has been BGJTL - BLOOMING BRILLIANT, GUIDING, JUST INCREDIBLY INSPIRING, TRUSTING, LIFTING and LOVELY! **Karen Hornby**

It's a safe space to celebrate life's hurdles and podiums with others who have been there or want to be there, sometimes just to hold you up...it's like the best bra ever! **Sinead Osgood @lols4**

Angela, you meant the beginning of my healthy journey to a place I can finally accept and love myself. It was because of you and your amazing transformation and testimonial that I signed up to the SSS plan. This group is a blessing. It has been what drives me forward when I want to give up... what cheers me up when I'm down... what fuels my determination. **Angela Cardoso**

BGJTL gave me back something I had forgotten about even though I hadn't even realised it had gone....it gave me back. ....me. :) **Amanda Turner**

BGJTL inspires me daily, sometimes more than once daily. The people in it make you feel like you're part of a family, they have your back and they are cheering and willing you on. A lot of them have been through similar struggles to the ones you experience today and the inspiring stories you read show you that anything is possible...

Everyone has their demons but some people showing how they've overcome theirs or how they are powering on regardless is really inspiring. I love it. **Anna James**

Angela is an ordinary, hard-working wife and mother showing others including me if you really want to, you can lose weight and get fit. It takes hard work and dedication but it really is possible. Her vlogs help reinforce what many of us already know about the weight loss journey. I am sure Angela's book will be succinct and to the point, funny and insightful just like the author! **Jodi Sangster @jodisangster**

A positive, empowering place where there are like-minded people with encouraging attitudes that help me to be more content with the real me, without judgement. Also the group is full of fellow triathletes who I can ask for advice & share my accomplishments with. **Lois Muir**

BGJTL has literally changed my life! Angela's determination, honestly and can-do attitude continues to inspire me every day. The community has become part of my daily routine and motivates me through positive posts, non-judgmental advice, encouragement and support. So proud to be part of something special. **Victoria Maycock**

Angela is such a heart-warming lady who you feel like you've known for years. A lady who climbs that hill with every single one of us on our journey no matter how long it takes for us to reach the top. Our own Angel in disguise. **Denise Child**

Angela is the sort of friend who believes you can do anything you put your mind to, and she doesn't mind telling you so! Her honest sharing of the hurdles she has faced, and the strategies she has used to overcome them has been invaluable to so many. She's a work in progress, like many of us, and that makes her incredibly relatable. Angela, I love your attitude to change, bias for action, compassion and work ethic; you have helped so many people to change their lives for the better. You lead by example; you're a force of nature and I'm grateful to be part of your tribe. **Karen Saul @recoverin_perfectionist**

I love the fact that I can read & get involved in posts about so many different things, makeup, clothes choices and relationship advice as well as the fantastic support to help us keep on track. You know, the morning you wake up knowing you should do your training but think "naaa" then you have a sneaky & slightly addictive look at BGJTL & it makes you do it. I wouldn't be without my daily check in thank you Angela for being so kind, supportive & encouraging. **Joanne Swift @jo6014kbdtb**

About 2 years ago Angela scoffed at a book idea and laughed it off; planting the seed seems to have worked (luckily). I keep thinking about the word 'Inspirational' when I see what Angela has and continues to achieve, especially how she spurs others on. It's only through social media that we know each other but it's been great being on this journey with her. **Darren Savage @Da77rens**

Joining BGJTL, participating in posts, and seeing all the inspirational stories has added a completely new dimension to my life. Seeing Angela's journey gives me hope that one day I too can have a healthy body I can be proud of ... she leads by example, shares her struggles and keeps it real. On tough days, there are always many people to help lift one's spirits and provide the strength to move forwards, and on good days when someone shares an NSV there is a huge crowd cheering them on from the side lines... BGJTL gives me hope, inspires me to make better choices, reminds me to find happiness in small victories and that I am definitely not alone in my struggles. This group is amazing and I am so grateful to Angela for starting it and to all the admins who make it possible. **Leanne Peasnall**

I first met Angela through The Body Coach's Twitter account. I noticed a few comments she had tagged Joe into which made me become curious about her journey and weight loss and am I so glad I found her. Having struggled with weight myself my whole life I started watching her Vlogs on YouTube. Angela was so inspiring and positive it gave me the courage to enroll onto the Body Coach 90-day SSS plan and with Angela's encouragement and support I found I sailed through the first 30 days. If I was struggling I'd pop a little message on twitter and I knew Angela would be right there to cheer me along and help me believe I could have the same amazing results as her. Although I've never met Angela in person her friendship, positivity and courage shines through into my life and I often find myself telling people about Angela and how she has inspired me to believe I can be a better me. **Kerry Smith @Kez77kes**

Safe happy fun place with no egos. Can ask the group anything and get an honest answer. It motivates and supports people and that's driven by Angela's values **Angela Sumbler**

If you have never met Angela and are reading about her for the first time or have only ever followed her on Social Media, you'd never have guessed that the pictures you see today are the same person that I worked with only two years ago. Angela has always been a driving force and inspirational, even though she didn't show her demons, she always was a very successful business woman. From following Angela's transformation, I know that she started in the kitchen with the food, but watching her progress through to the training and the running she is doing has been amazing. A truly inspirational lady who #NeverMissesAMonday. Angela – You have done amazingly and look absolutely fantastic! **Adrian Moore @AdrianMoore58**

It was a photo from a family holiday that shocked me into action!

I had not realised how big I had become since having my first son. 11 years, 4 children and a whopping 6 stone had passed so fast I hadn't noticed.

In September 2011, I started tracking my calories and walking for 30mins every day and gradually I increased my speed and distance and was soon walking 5miles or more. The weight slowly came off, I got fitter, stronger and healthier and by 2016 I had reached my goal. It was around this time I stumbled upon Angela Cox on Facebook as I had been following The Body Coach. I was drawn to her smiley face and her story and had a look at her page. I joined BGJTL in April 2016. For someone like me, who has not followed a plan or diet, worked out alone and doesn't have any fitness friends locally, I was hooked from day one by the support, advice and friendship the group gave me. **Ruth Warner @ruth.warner**

The first time I met Angela was at the body coach 1 million Instagram party in May 2016. She was a week ahead of me on my journey and I'd watch her dedication and transformation on social media. When I got to meet her in real life it was like meeting a celebrity! She was so lovely! So smiley and genuinely interested to talk to me. She looked amazing in her stripy dress and was oozing confidence. I knew then she was a strong determined woman. I continued watching her journey and then met her again in Feb 2017 at her seminar. She was half the size she was from the previous year! She was so professional at the seminar and looked so comfortable

talking to a whole room of people, something I could never do. She asked me to join the admin team in June 2017 and the rest is history!
Emma Neal - @Miss.e.neal

Angela and the BGJTL community is just wow, wow and wow! She has inspired thousands to start and continue so many members' journeys that are both physical and mental. She brightens up people's lives with her personality and gorgeous smile. What I love about her is that she wears her heart on her sleeve and she pulls others in naturally to follow her and be inspired by her. I am so lucky to be able to call Angela a true friend. She has an absolute heart of gold and being there for her through the ups and downs, has helped us build an amazing relationship. We've enjoyed so many giggles on and off the page! She's an angel and I love her. Angela, you rock ❤
Suzy Watkins @Suzylwatkins

Angela first caught my eye at the beginning of her journey on another FB group. First it was with her friendly face and her gorgeous smile that also causes this cute crinkle on her nose. Then I was inspired by her motivation, hard work and kind spirit that made me instantly think... this lady was special!

When Angela decided to set up BGJTL I was on board in a flash, as I wanted to be part of what I knew would be something brilliant. Angela asked me to be admin I was so chuffed.

Later, I was ecstatic to be the person that Angela turned to for the cover artwork of 'Enough'. To trust me with such an important job was very touching. To meet Angela in person, well let's just say she is more charismatic, inspirational and above all, fabulous in person than her photos and post will ever show with a kind heart and gorgeous smile to boot. I feel blessed to have met Angela and to be able to call her my friend. Thank you for letting me be a part of your dream. **KT O'Shaughnessy @ilovekandi**

Forever Grateful

Gratitude unlocks the fullness of life. It turns what we have into enough, and more.
  Melody Beattie

To the catalysts, without whom none of this would have happened. Nicola Morris, who set me on the body coach journey. Del Wilson, my PT who helped me to fall in love with exercise by introducing me to the rowing machine. Sarah Manu Smith, a lady I have never met, who one Sunday morning sent me a message suggesting I set up my own Facebook group. And last, but not least, Angela Ireland who suggested I find a literary agent which led to me writing this book. I am forever thankful to all four of you.

To the BGJTL Admin Crew. So many special people who have given their time freely and provided invaluable help and support to so many, including me. In no particular order, Natalie Rudley, first admin, you have flourished during the time I've known you and your love of grammar, inflatable giraffes and running free is well noted & much loved; Kathy Allison Henry, you play a wonderful leadership role and I'm always grateful for your input and balance; Sarah McHugh, an inspiration, an old colleague and a friend for life; Shelley Baker, always giving, rarely taking; Emma Farmer, with your partner Jim, my cheerleaders and true friends; Gaelle Bryant, strong, determined woman, you amaze me; Emma Neal, you never fail to make me laugh and you have a heart of gold; Mary Worsley, quietly determined and always willing to help; Fiona Maunder, you are a true warrior of the highest order and a brave inspiration who kicked cancer's ass;

Hannah O'Brien (Hannybobs), Donna Moorhouse & Ruth Warner. Like sisters, always supporting, always there, laughing, loving and learning. The connection is special. I love you all. Goddesses.

Suzy & Pete Watkins, thank you for your ideas, talent, creativity, time and unrivalled support. I have always felt you right behind me every step of the way and your loyalty is hugely appreciated.

KT O'Shaughnessy – Talented Graphic Designer, the lady behind the book cover and the 'little girl within' sketch, you have no idea how amazing you are and I cannot tell you how much you mean to me. Your rendition of Love Shack in a steam room will always raise a smile.

To the BGJTL Admin crew past. Thank you for your time and effort into making the group what it is, for the laughs and for your unmitigated support throughout. Bev Thoragood, you provided so many magic moments due to your hilarious typos; Lizzie Austin who provided the best Talent Tuesday video ever; H Cater, thank you for creating the Early Morning Crew and the amazing seminar movie; Doreen Lundie, you are the only person I know who sends beautiful handwritten letters and I adore you; Emma Gourley, Brooke Madison, Gavin Andrews, Christina Bray, Caoimhe O'Connor, you are all amazing and I am thankful I had an opportunity to get to know you.

To my followers across all the channels. I've never experienced so much love from people I haven't met. I can't thank everybody personally but I send a collective swathe of gratitude to anybody who has ever championed what I am doing.

A little shout out to Amanda Dodwell, my greatest cheerleader and wind beneath my wings.

James Walker (Sustain Nutrition), Faye Louise (Tikiboo), Sarah Frost, Fiona Maunder, Janice Schofield, Joanne Mullen, Lettie Cwinrragh, Sasha Warr, Mickie Trolley, Lorraine Picton, Rachel Hill, Anne Hyde, Kathy Harris, Emy Rumble Mettle, Neil Marsh, Saskia Fairs, Lisa Mabon, Kerri Smith, Angela Sumbler, Denise Child, Nick Jeffery, Darren Savage, Anne Hyde, Ann Franklin, Neil

Wilson, Rob Tomlinson, Karen Saull, Ron Kane, Jo Gordon, Chris Boston, Adrian Moore, Lynsey O'Keefe and Wendy O'Beirne…you have all stepped into my journey and helped me at the times I needed it most, maybe without even knowing it but your random acts of kindness, time & well wishes are appreciated.

To Mark Palmer & Martin Gibson, champions who have always believed in me. You have supported me through highs and lows. Your faith, support and mentorship is always gratefully received.

To Batman Simon, thank you for your support and for always listening to my hair brained schemes.

To Buddha Bill for keeping me sane, sharing the same sense of humour and helping me out of a few deep holes.

To Wojciech Busz (Iron Consultant), your help, advice and time during the early stages of writing this book was invaluable and I thankful for you being part of it.

To the amazing Samantha Whitney and Shirley Jarvis, you always make me smile and I appreciate you both coming the house at ridiculous times of the day to help me look fabulous.

To Tariq Ahmad, your talent knows no bounds and the gracious way you perform your art is to be respected. Thank you.

To the Body Coach, the amazing Joe Wicks. You'll never know how much you have helped me to change my life, a true hero and I'm eternally thankful for you, your floppy hair and your amazing 90-day plan.

To Sally Savage. You have helped me more than you will ever know. Amazing, wise, thoughtful lady with a talent for helping me to blast open doors that have been forever bolted shut. That knowing look you have will forever make me smile out loud and roll my eyes in equal measure.

To the gorgeous Sally Hill. From the moment you entered my life it has been shining a little brighter. In you, I have found my twin and I cannot wait for our trips to the sunshine. You are a special kind of star, a force of nature and a total goddess.

To my bestie, Michele Faulkner, fellow Charlie's angel. Thank you for putting up with me being incognito throughout the writing of this book and for being there regardless. Nobody does an impression of an upside-down ladybird like you do and the memories we have shared will never be forgotten.

To my family & Martin's family, thank you for your love, support, encouragement & for so many joyful occasions.

To Kitty & Bobbin. Love you both dearly and always proud of you. Kitty you are quite a woman for one woman. Brave fighter.

To my parents who have been there for me through thick and thin, I appreciate everything you have done for me, your love, belief and support.

To my gorgeous husband Martin, my Mr. Brightside. And my beautiful children Finley & Coral. You give me the courage to fly. I am the luckiest girl in the world to have you. The sky is full of sunshine and rainbows whenever I'm under it with you. **Love you all 'one hundred plus a lion' now and always.**

When she transformed into a butterfly, the Caterpillars
spoke not of her beauty, but of her weirdness.
They wanted her to change back into what she always had been.
But she had wings
Dean Jackson